MW01138221

The Miracles of Awareness and Attention
2015 Frederick Dodson

Table of Contents

1

Modes of Attention

Contents of this Chapter:

The Four Modes of Attention

1. Focused Attention

In this state, awareness is narrowed to a single item. Attention and object remain separate(this happens by default if the object is not enjoyed). We admire professionals (lawyers, doctors, etc.) for their ability to focus in this way for extended periods of time "no matter how they feel". This ability to focus regardless of enjoyment, occurs through the will. It requires the most energy and while producing lots of worldly success (because many are not willing to focus on certain tasks too long), too much of it can create tension, strain and overwork. Many years in this mode can lead to "burn out", Ideally you use this mode neither too often nor too rarely. Using it too rarely will weaken your mental muscle. Using it too often will exhaust that mental muscle. Find your balance. You will be able to focus longer and without as much tiredness if you apply "Immersed Attention".

2. Immersed Attention

In this state, awareness is also narrowed to a single item but attention and the object are are merged (because the object is considered enjoyable). Attention is immersed within the object and there is no sense of resistance and very little sense of time, space or self. Very little effort or energy are required to maintain this state. We experience it when watching a movie or fascinating event, when falling in love, when reading good books, when in the flow of an activity and so forth. The state is usually triggered by external objects of interest, but it can be produced intentionally. To maintain high energy throughout life, spend at least some time every day engaged in activities that draw in your attention effortlessly. You can also try to produce that state deliberately with tasks that you would like to do but would normally not fascinate you to that extent. This state could also be called "Superfocused Attention".

3. Open Attention

In this state, awareness is not narrowed to a single item, it is open and free and likely to be aware of several things, sounds, smells, objects, people. If the mind tries to grasp all of these impressions at once it goes into overwhelm or gets tired. But if one relaxes, then all these impressions trigger a pleasant state of widened awareness and calm-mind. Diffused, non-rigid attention feels free and pleasant. But unless it becomes Total Awareness, it still expends energy because there is a separation between the observer, giving attention, and all that is observed. To no longer expend energy but at the same time become even more aware, one would have to allow for "total attention".

4. Total Attention

Here attention is open and likely to be aware of several things, sounds, smells, objects, people. But unlike "Open Attention" there is no separation between observer and object but rather Oneness with all things. The total diffusion of attention into all-that-is stops the chatter of the mind. One is aware of all sounds, smells, sights, objects and especially the empty spaces between them.

While some say that one mode of Attention is "better" than the other, in reality they all serve positive purposes and your Attention Training should include familiarity with all 4 Basic modes: 1. Focused-Separate 2. Focused-One 3. Open-Separate 4. Open-One.

2015 Reality Creation Coaching

Relief from Rigid Attention

I'd like to show you how subconsciously rigid and strained "normal" human Attention is and how to let go and transfer from a flat, chronically stressed, two-dimensional, tense experience of life, to a more mellow, empowered and aware experience of life.

As you read these words, please notice how – no matter who you are – your eyes are more strained than they need to be. As you continue reading these words, see if you can loosen that strain just a little. You can still read these lines, but don't need to narrow your eyes to do so. Relax that strain. Soften your eyes. Bad eyesight comes from artificial strain. Tightening your eyes, eyebrows or forehead is a waste of energy. These words won't run away, no need to grip them.

These words you are reading are on a computer/smartphone screen or in a book. They are the foreground of your Attention. And then there are things in the background of your Attention, behind the screen. The foreground is this article, the background might be furniture, walls and sounds. See if you can effortlessly be aware of both these words and also of the background…without needing to split Attention or gripping anything in particular. Release your rigid grip, release your narrow focus. Rather than an unwelcome distraction, the sounds and background can be included in your overall Awareness. You do not have to focus quite as rigidly and narrowly right now, you are not taking an exam at school. So breathe softly and calm-down. It's not like you have to "concentrate either on these words **or** on the background". That's narrow; that's rigid. It's not "this or that". If you know to open your Awareness a little, you may notice yourself become more calm.

Now while reading these lines, see if you can become aware of the empty space between your eyes and these letters. Read, but stay aware that there is empty space between the two. Also become aware of the empty space that surrounds your computer. You are broadening your Awareness from an unnecessarily rigid grip, to a more relaxed and inclusive mode. Now, if I were to provide a link to a website here, what would your Attention do? Would it rigidly worry about missing something and reactively follow the link, or would you remain in a calm space, simply include that piece of data (possibly for later), and keep on reading?

As you continue to read, become aware of the empty space between these lines. Are you getting confused and wondering whether you should still be focused on the empty spaces around your computer while at the same time focusing on the empty spaces between these lines? If so, you have just slipped back into rigid mode. You are not in school. You are not going to get a bad grade or be shot if you do not do this correctly. Chill out! For now, it's ok to just focus on the empty spaces between these lines. And if you like and can, you can also be aware of the empty spaces around the computer and between your eyes and the computer. But only if it's effortless. This is not another chore, not another exercise. Can you imagine that all of this can be just effortless? Just a soft opening of Awareness? Can you see how this little process here relates to every single problem you have had in life? How every problem you have ever had was created by rigid Attention?

And as you read, even become aware of the empty spaces between the letters themselves. You are habitually used to and conditioned to zoom in only on the letters. Have you ever taken note of the spaces between the letters? In childhood, they fear-condition you to "Pay Attention!" and "Concentrate!"...."Or else!". That's how Attention becomes rigid. As you read this, gently remain aware of the empty spaces around your body, the text you are reading, as well as the sounds you hear and the background of your computer.

As you read these lines, become aware of how rigid your Attention is throughout the day...how you rush through the day, always subconsciously tense and trying to focus on something – anything – just so you don't have to relax and feel the here-now. Our escape from the here-now takes the form of rigidly focusing on food or the internet, TV or work, because when we relax we actually have to feel what-is, and that's sometimes unpleasant at first. But if we never rest back and gain perspectives, these emotions cannot process. Our attempt to divert Attention only temporarily moves us away from our existential sense of un-wellness. Sooner or later, when we relax again, those same unprocessed issues resurface. No movie, no new love affair, no novelty, no new purchase, no internet browsing, no sex and no food will make them disappear. Only softening Attention will.

As you read these lines, again become aware of the space between your eyes and the computer, as well as the space around your body, the space around the computer and the other visually peripheral things in the room you are in. You will notice that your experience of reading this gains more depth. You might see things more clearly because you are more relaxed. You are no longer processing this article through the mind alone, but can feel more what is being said. You feel more aware, more energetic. You see, the question is **not only what you focus on but how you focus**. The less power you feel inside, the more you strain and try to grasp and grip what you are focusing on. The more power you feel inside, the more calm your focus is. Powerless people desperately grip and hold on. Empowered people release. They lack nothing.

You can learn to be alert but still relaxed. This is the ideal state in waking life. In society, we are conditioned to think that relaxation is related to lack of alertness and getting sleepy. We believe that high productivity is related to being alert and that this means being tense and rigid. So we shift back-and-forth between exhausted slumber or tense alertness. But the ideal state of waking life is relaxed alertness. It is in this state that we are creative, productive and happy without waste of energy.

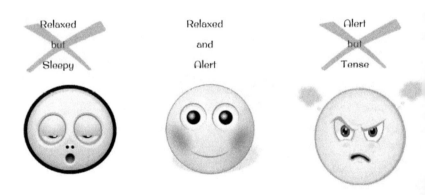

Most of the time and in most places, it is not necessary to be in "emergency mode" or "survival mode". Most of us are not in a war-zone. But we behave that way. Relationships or daily life at work are not war-zones, where one has to be aggressively prepared for the worst at all times. Rigid Attention is developed at times of danger (or perceived danger) or throughout emotional abuse (or perceived emotional abuse). You will notice that people who have experienced severe trauma tend to have the most rigid Attention. The problem is that these styles of Attention become locked in and are replayed even in times that no such rigid Attention is needed. For example, while reading this, no rigid Attention is needed. And you will retain the information herein to memory more easily, when Attention is more open and relaxed. "Being alert but relaxed" is the secret to rapid learning; the perceiving and processing of information and emotions. "Rigid Attention" is the cause of most of our ills.

As you read this and de-pressurize your Attention, your breathing will have relaxed and your muscles loosened. Please note that you can open your Awareness anywhere you are and with anything you are doing, and it will free your mind. It will make you more healthy. More successful. More anything. Narrow Attention will narrow your experience of life. Most of us are too narrowly focused all the time and on almost anything. Some will even take this article as another cause to narrowly look for some problem and try to "get it right". And then there are others who have no focus at all, no alertness at all. They appear to be relaxed and chilled-out, but they are actually half-asleep. Their "relaxation" is merely a rebellion against tension. So they suppress their tension and then go into this sleepy daze, where they appear to be "peaceful and chilled out", but are actually not really present. But that doesn't describe most people in "modern society". Most people are subconsciously stressed out to the max and super-rigid, as if their lives are at stake.

Rigid Attention is facilitated by strong desires and resistances. When you enter a room with a group of people…is your Attention open and aware of the general ambience of the place, or is it rigidly preoccupied with trying to avoid certain people or win the hearts of others? You know from experience that open and free Attention gives you a positive and happy state, but this type of charged Attention can make you quite unhappy. Anytime you notice stuck-Attention, you can deliberately open-up a little, and become aware of the periphery of whatever you were focused on. The periphery always includes other objects as well as empty space. The whole physical universe is solid objects plus empty space. Sounds are solid objects, surrounded by empty space (silence). Thoughts are semi-solid objects, surrounded by empty space (pure Awareness). And then there is you…who experiences the Universe through Awareness, gently drifting in-and-out of different experiences. So am I saying you should stay neutral all the time and never get involved or attached with anything? No, that's not what this means. You can immerse yourself fully and passionately. That does not make rigid Attention. Free Attention means you can shift and travel easily between all *Modes of Attention*. This is some of the most precious knowledge you will ever learn.

Attention Overload

I'm not a fan of over-attentive waiters. I recall one particularly overstaffed hotel some time ago. I went for some coffee. I was the only person in the breakfast room, but there were at least ten staff waiting to serve me. One greeted me. One showed me to my table. The other arranged my table. Another one poured my coffee. Another one was making an omelet, although I hadn't asked for one, and no other guest was in sight. The others stood around eager to run to my service when I only lifted my head. One waitress continually asked me what I wanted and what she could do for me.

"Just a cup of coffee, that's all." I really just wanted to have my peace and quiet, not this overkill. She then listed countless coffee variations. "Just coffee and milk please." Meanwhile, one of the service staff was acting all busy, unnecessarily removing clean forks and knives from my table and a table beside me and arranging them on another table. The waitress stood nearby, I could almost feel her breathing down my neck or peering into my smartphone. "Could I have some privacy, please?" I almost asked, but didn't. I had some yogurt, and the very instant I finished it, the bowl was whisked away by the waitress. "Anything else sir? Our special today is the omelet with seasonal..." – "No thanks!" I interrupted her. I really just wanted a cup of coffee. Next time 'I'd have it in my room. The very instant I finished the coffee, the waitress, standing right beside me the whole time, impatiently motioned to another service staff to refill. "Any more, sir?" I actually tried to pour the coffee myself, and he forcefully insisted to pour it for me. "Next thing 'I know, they'll be spoon feeding me breakfast," I jokingly thought.

The staff here, reminded me that there is such a thing as too much Attention. It's like watering a plant with a hurricane. The hurricane destroys the plant, it doesn't "water" it.

Too much of anything is disempowering. If I give someone in need some money, at first I empower him/her. But if I keep on giving him/her money, while he/she does not generate any him/herself, it becomes disempowering. He/she then becomes dependent on my money; dependent on external sustenance.

Giving someone Attention energizes and supports him/her. Giving him/her too much Attention disempowers him/her, he/she'll often run away from you or rebel. When a lover's Attention is too strong and intense, you tend to withdraw. When a mother's Attention to a child is too much, to the point of obsession, the child will eventually withdraw (or get "Attention deficit disorder").

With any skill, be it bike riding or piano playing, you'll notice that beginners always put too much effort into it. You can always tell someone is an amateur when he/she focuses too hard.

When you focus on your goals, you achieve them. When you focus on them too much or too strongly however, that's not a sign of calm confidence, it's a sign of desperation. Focus on your goals, yes, but not too hard. Have other projects to focus on too, so that there are phases of letting go and letting the subconscious work things out by itself.

Excessive behavior (especially when not consciously chosen), tends to unbalance you. It is good to give, but don't give all the time; do some taking as well. It's good to be available, but not too available. It's good to play your cards openly, but don't play all your cards at once. Do not depend on only one resource; do not put all your eggs in one basket. If you notice yourself becoming too attached to something, do without it for awhile. Giving Attention to something naturally creates an attachment, and you can once again detach by shifting Attention elsewhere for some time. Then, when you put your Attention back to the person, place or thing, you will have more enjoyment with it because there is no fixation.

With anything in life, you can learn to invest just the right amount of energy and Attention. If you give too little, your connection to the person, place or thing will dry-up. If you give too much, it will drown. Gently sustained Attention without fixation however, can create a perpetually positive flow (regardless of the object of your Attention).

It's All a Matter of Focus

One of the most popular exercises from my seminar works as follows:

Person A is to keep his focus on his good-feeling-thoughts by describing them in detail or imagining them. He is to stay with the desired final result until he feels it and is fully immersed. Person B tries to prevent and break that focus through negativity. He is to question, doubt, mock, attack and insult Person A and his positive thoughts. The purpose of the exercise is to see whether Person A can stay attuned and loyal to his stated intention and positive state in spite of the onslaught of "the world's" negativity (Person B is in this case playing "the world".) The exercise is immensely valuable in that, rather than trying to avoid negativity or allow oneself to get hurt by it, you learn to define your emotional state from within, not from external reality. It is how you react to negative realities that contradict your self-chosen new reality, that determines how quickly your new reality manifests. Can you maintain your new state and focus or are you easily distracted and hurt by various garbage coming at you?

Some students find being the negative "Person B" side very unpleasant. They don't want to hurt the other. I explain to them that they are helping the other by being hurtful within the context of the game. Why? Because it's not your job to help the other maintain their focus, it's his/her job, and it lies within his/her power if he/she can only maintain focus. Some people, who were already familiar with the exercise from previous courses, were quite good at this. No matter what insults you hurled at them, they stayed poised, happy and humorous.

I recall a student who was actually seriously hurt by what "Person B" said to her. After the exercise, her sense of fear and doubt lingered. What had happened? It's simple: The energy or focus of Person B had been stronger than her energy and focus. So I decided to run through the game with her again. I asked her to focus on one object in the room and to keep her focus there no matter what. I began insulting her, calling her weak, ugly and stupid. She was to maintain calm and remain aligned with the object no matter what. Then I directed her to focus back on her desire with the same intensity she had focused on the object and to not be distracted by my negativity. She managed to do it because she had the strong intention to stay aligned with her vision regardless of anything. Had I thrown those insults toward her outside of the game-context (without her prior intention to maintain calm), I may have seriously hurt her. She learned that if she will not allow it, nothing can get her down. She also learned that eventually, intense focus on what really feels good will neutralize any bad thing anyone might say. And with that, a new, powerful reality creator was born.

If negativity or rejection are thrown at you, and you can maintain Awareness of that which feels empowering, true, good and right, the negative event or person will lose steam. They might even reverse their rejection of you.

The next step was to learn that this pleasant state – while being bombarded by trouble – can be maintained without focusing too hard. Focusing too hard will in fact make you tired. "Maintaining focus" does not require all that much effort. It is simply putting your outer or inner sight on that which you prefer and keeping it there. It's more of a being-present-with-something than an act of concentration. A general air of non-resistance and acceptance of the negative while maintaining positive-focus will make it even easier. It is the pushing against the negative or the rigid maintaining of the positive that weakens your ability. All this and more is contained within this very simple exercise that I recommend for your exploration. The game should be played between two until it's clear that nothing at all can "get you out" of your positive state...only you can do that by the way you choose to direct your Attention. In fact, the pressure from the other can be used to make your own positive-focus stronger. From that point forward, you don't have to fear or hide from the negative, you make use of its energy and transform it to your benefit.

Put simply, if I say to you "You are such a loser," you have no obligation whatsoever to buy into that or sink into hurt. You could be thinking of someone you love, of a beautiful scenery or of your amazing success, and my "you are a loser" wouldn't even register. Not only that, you could even take my "you are a loser" and label it a confirmation that I am envious of you being a winner. That's how you'd use my negative energy to your positive benefit. It really is all a matter of focus.

Freedom of Choice

Freedom of Choice

Too Much Choice

I thought I had already ordered my meal, when the waiter asked me about 10 additional questions culminating in at least 50 choices of spice, food, toppings, types of meat, types of side-dishes, etc. I was starting to get annoyed and wanted to say, "Just give me some damn food." Even just the sauce became a marathon of choices:

"Do you want garlic, bbq-sauce, mustard, mayonnaise, salsa, chili-sauce, tomato-sauce or... (a few others I didn't even know)?"

"Just bring me whatever sauce normally comes with that meal."

"Well, you can have any of those sauces with that meal."

"OK, I'll take garlic."

"Alright, should that be garlic-yogurt, agliata or honey garlic?"

"I don't know."

The waiter stood there impatiently waiting on my choice, as if I knew better than the chef what type of garlic is used with that food. The same was then applied to several other aspects of the meal I thought I had already ordered. Even the coffee I later ordered couldn't just be a simple coffee:

"Skim milk, half and half, or whole milk?"

"Uh…whole milk."

"Cold or hot milk?"

"Cold."

"Would you like some chocolate on top?"

"Sure."

"What kind of chocolate? We have…"

It suddenly dawned on me that I would not visit this restaurant again.

The restaurant prided itself with giving the customer choices of every specific. I guess I just wasn't in the mood for spending that much Attention on food. I'd like to save my decision power for more important business. I was relieved when, one week later, I visited a restaurant in which I had the choice of three meals. I pointed at one meal, and it was delivered, no questions asked.

Too Little Choice
A couple of weeks ago, I was coaching with a piously religious woman who had been unhappy with the sex-life within her marriage. She complained she hadn't had good sex in twenty years. I realized that anyone who was willing to suffer for that long had severely limited her choices.

"OK, have you talked to your husband about it?"

"He won't talk to me. I have to figure this out myself."

"Yes, OK. How about seeing your husband as more attractive?"

"No, I don't want to."

"Alright. How about making yourself more attractive?"

"I can't. My husband does not want me to do that."

"Yes alright. But these are things you have to discuss with him. You are unhappy with the marriage and that's both of your business."

"I don't want to talk to him, I hate him."

"You hate him? Have you ever considered separation?"

"I can't divorce him. Our families wouldn't allow it".

"I didn't say divorce, I said separation, temporarily."

"No, I can't afford it. And it would be a scandal in the family."

"OK...why don't you talk to family members about your marriage issues?"

"I can't. I have to uphold the image that we have a good marriage."

I was starting to become a little frustrated because of the complete (perceived) lack of choice.

"OK...how about you first explore your own sexuality, by yourself?"

"I can't. My religious values forbid masturbation."

Every single option I was pointing out was discarded right off the bat.

"Why did you marry him?"

"It was forced marriage. I had no choice."

"What exactly do you want?" I finally inquired.

"I want to have a good marriage and good sex within that marriage."

"And can you imagine that?"

"I don't want to imagine that with my current husband."

She knew what she wanted, but she wasn't willing to move *one inch* from her many fixed positions. She thought she had no choice but to shut-up and put-up. "I can't stay with him, I can't leave him." Before she was to make any improvement, she would have to increase her perception of options available to her. She would also have to value her own dignity more than her image.

These two stories show how having too few options causes constriction, and having too many options can cause overwhelm. Sure, it is better to have too many options than none. And yet, option-overload can stifle decision-making. Driving on a highway is so relaxing because you have only one road to go on and one exit to leave from. , Although you can choose from many different exits, these do not all show up at the same time, but in intervals.

A metaphysical viewpoint: When we were born on planet earth, we forgot all other realities, dimensions, existences, afterlives and before-lives…in order to focus on this one. You can't easily focus on one piece of music if you have several pieces of music running at the same time. I have come to believe that **the better a person is able to focus and choose, the more options and choices he/she will be able to handle**. In other words, how many choices and options will drag down your mood depends on your current level-of-energy. While visiting that restaurant, I was in a tired mood. I wanted stuff to be done for me, not make my own choices. On another day, feeling more zestful and creative, I might have welcomed the endless detail in which I could specify my preferred "lunch-reality".

Freedom of Choice

In the last fifteen years, my options have steadily increased. I no longer feel restricted by external realities...which has led me to deliberately restrict myself. Back in the days when I felt restricted in my options, I always strove for having more options. Now that I have as many options as I like, I keep it simple. This is one of the little paradoxes of life; consciousness strives for a state of balance. I prefer having only one or two friends, not many, just a few seminars a year, not many, just one car, not two, just a few basic clothes, not many, and so forth. When Facebook founder Mark Zuckerberg was asked why he wore the same gray shirt all the time, he posted a photo of his wardrobe:

This guy is a billionaire with billions of options. Why cut down his choices to only one shirt? His explanation is remarkably similar to my attitude in the restaurant: He said he wants to focus his decision-making on business, not on clothes. In other words, at some level, he realizes that the millions of options we have as humans expend some amount of Attention-energy, and that we best prioritize where we put our Awareness. While I wouldn't like having such a bland collection of clothes, I understand where he is coming from. Similarly, Facebook is more successful than many other social media outlets because the options are neither too many nor too few: You can post, like, comment and share and that's it.

The image above is meant to teach the peculiar fact that, as your options grow you get happier, but as they grow beyond a certain tipping point, dissatisfaction sets in. Put simply: Having two houses for your private use is great. Having fifty houses for your private use could become a real burden.

Needless to say, deliberately choosing less options is very different from being forced or manipulated to less options. Higher consciousness has less to do with the amount of choices and more to do with **freedom** of choice. Infinity is like a vast supermarket-playground in which you have an endless amount of realities to choose from. "Evil" or negativity always involves your choice being manipulated, controlled or forced to a certain, pre-defined option. "Good" or positivity always involves you being able to freely choose from the many options there are. This includes **the freedom to make bad choices**. Why? Because we learn from bad choices and can then self-correct. Making good and bad choices are the basis of inner-growth and self-development. The only exception to this are children (and perhaps the mentally ill). We only let children make their own choices after they are experienced enough to know the consequences of what they choose.

A matured consciousness has **total freedom of choice** but also the ability to **pick a few options to focus on**, from the vast infinity of options. Where too many realities are focused on, not one reality can fully manifest because Attention (energy) is too widely dispersed. Similar to the highway, I recommend you choose one reality at a time, take that highway exit, manifest it, experience it…before going back to the highway and choosing another exit. If I either prevent you from taking an exit, or present 10 exits at the same time, your consciousness will shut-down, and no new reality will be experienced.

When we grow older, there is a tendency to want to make choices for others because we believe "we know better". I might say to my younger sister, "Don't choose this man, he is not good for you." And I might be right. But beyond a recommendation, I would not actively try to prevent her from making *her* choice. If my recommendations have proven trustworthy, she might listen to my advice. Or I might be wrong and she might have a good experience. In any case, she will grow and learn, no matter if her choice was good or bad. Actively preventing her from making her own choice stunts her growth, and disables her from becoming a responsible adult. Of course in reality, you cannot really prevent another's choices, nor can they he/she yours. You might temporarily stifle my choice to climb a certain mountain by pointing a gun at my head. But if it is my strong choice to climb it, I will eventually do it. Other people's attempts at preventing our choices are merely tests of our determination.

One of the principles of reality creation is: If you have a lot of other people doubting or trying to prevent your choices, it is because you have not yet really chosen within. If you've made a strong decision within, nothing in the world can stop you from achieving it.

The Sense of Being Stared At

Looking for consciousness in the brain is like looking for the announcer inside the radio. One of the pioneers of consciousness research is Rupert Sheldrake. One of Sheldrake's best known experiments was proving that the majority of people could *sense* if they were being stared at. He wrote a whole book on his scientific research titled *The Sense of Being Stared At*. While this is nothing new to us common folk, it was new in that it could be demonstrated in experiments with relevant results. In these regards, I recommend a video on YouTube that demonstrates these "staring experiments" conducted at Eton University.

I have myself replicated the staring-experiment in three (different) of my own seminars. The results of which have always been a "hit rate" of around 70 to 75%. That's clearly not the result of chance, and settles the case for me. I'm pleased by this because it solidifies what I have been teaching for the last 20 years: That **Attention itself is an energy-form that can be sent and felt by others.** Attention is consciousness in its active form.

The idea that consciousness may not be limited to the brain is still so "controversial" within the "scientific community" that various lobbying groups (of the materialist-skeptic faction) have gotten Sheldrake banned from universities, citations removed from Wikipedia, and even a harmless TED-Talk of his removed from their website. TED purports to be the leading edge forum for uncommon presenters. Their motto is "Ideas worth spreading." Their nervous removal of Sheldrake's 20 minute presentation titled, "The Science Delusion" sparked a lot of controversy at the time (2013), as did their banning of a few other of my favorite researchers – among them Graham Hancock, Russell Targ and Larry Dossey. All these scientists were blocked from TED or upcoming TED-Talks for the same reason: Believing that consciousness is not located in the brain. Despite mounting evidence to the contrary, this idea is still considered "pseudoscience" and its proponents "pseudoscientists" (even though all the gentlemen mentioned have science degrees and impeccable reputations). For those who want to know more about this recent controversy there is a book on it called *PSI WARS: Ted, Wikipedia and the Battle for the Internet* .

Emotion or intention is the wave, Attention the carrier. So whatever you are feeling when you put your Attention on someone is transferred as non-verbal and non-physical communication. Eyes (or staring) needn't even be involved. If your Attention is well-developed, he/se can sense it even if you are not directly looking at him/her but only thinking of them. This idea is worth many more social and scientific experiments, but it may take another while before it becomes mainstream.

From Restless Mind to Peace of Mind

If you experience a restless mind you can solve that by either *letting go, shifting focus, or by completion.* In this section we'll look at completion. Incompletion nags at your Attention. Incomplete things keep circling around the mind, running over-and-over, until they are completed. Examples of things that create big and small incompletion:

* Having a fight with your partner, then separating. The mind keeps rerunning the upset until what is between the two of you is resolved amicably. So if you are going to separate, it's best to separate in peace.

* Promising to deliver goods at a certain time, then not delivering. Here you create incompleteness in both yourself and another, and it occupies people's Attention until the goods are delivered.

* Having loads of unanswered or unhandled emails.

*Having something in your life that isn't working, but not addressing it.

* Being unclear about the terms of business with someone. This is a popular one. Lack of clarity scratches at the conscience, creates confusion and possibly even unexpected outcomes. (Hence the "Terms and Conditions" you sign for various items are often so complicated that you don't bother reading them. The company you are signing the contract with, is then in control of the outcome.)

* Having an urgent desire to ask someone a question, but not asking it.

* Having an important piece of information, but not sharing it (keeping many secrets sifts away at your energy.)

* Having a dozen browser windows open.

* Having a number of aborted goals and unfulfilled dreams.

* Wrongdoing without making amends.

* Owing someone something (Attention/energy is most free when you don't owe anyone anything.)

* Having someone owe you something

* Not acknowledging what someone says or thinks (when someone is unacknowledged, he/she will keep repeating their complaint until he/she finds some acknowledgement.)

* Having too many unknowns about something is a type of incompleteness.

* Pain is the most intense form of incompleteness. It being intense we usually strive to fix pain as quickly as possible. However, all the lesser pains of life mentioned above, can also be completed...the faster;   the better.

I could list hundreds of examples more but these are enough to get an idea. Anyone interested in being a whole and free person aims to reduce incompleteness. When nothing at all is nagging at your Attention, that's when you are most free to create. An old friend called me yesterday and asked me what I was "up to." It was amusing because my mind was utterly blank. "Nothing," I said. *So what have I been doing?* I don't know. *What's next on the agenda?* I don't know. That may sound like an unproductive state of mind, but the opposite is true. The sheer emptiness of mind allows for boundless creativity and productivity. Having a mind full of unfinished tasks, projects, unspoken things, conflicts and regrets, doesn't.

So go ahead and complete the incomplete. What is then left are a few ongoing projects plus peace of mind. If you wish to take this a level deeper, you can see recurring thoughts and emotions as "incomplete items that have not been acknowledged". If you deliberately repeat such thoughts several times, while acknowledging them, they begin feeling "complete" and stop bothering you. Recurring thoughts can be like nagging children. So let's say you have the recurring thought, "Am I good looking?", And it's been occupying your mind for many years. The way to bring that thought to completion is to voice or repeat it many times. "Am I good looking?" "Am I good looking?" "Am I good looking?" "Am I really good looking?" "Now, am I good looking?" "How good looking am I?" "Say, am I good looking?" "By the way, am I good looking?" "How do I look?" "I hope I am good looking!" "And am I good looking?" "Again, am I good looking?" "Good looking?" "Me, am I good looking?" "Do people like the way I look?" "Am I considered good looking?" "Tell me, am I good looking?" "I desperately need to know…am I good looking?" "Am I good looking?" "Am I good looking?" "Am I good looking?"

You continue this mimicking of your recurring thought until it is "at ease". There is no more emotional "charge" associated with it. It was previously subconscious. By deliberately creating it again-and-again, you made it conscious. It no longer controls you, you control it. "Am I good looking?" "Am I good looking?" When it becomes funny or boring you naturally let go. This is one way to bring a recurring thought (that cannot be completed in external reality) to completion. You will notice a pleasant sense of "peace of mind". And what could be more key to a good life than peace of mind?

There is much more to say on this, but being the reality-creator that you are, you can extrapolate your own methods based on the knowledge already given here. Have fun walking around as a person who is already whole and complete.

2

Secrets of Awareness and Attention

Contents of this Chapter:

People, Objects and Issues Require Space Time and Attention

No matter what improvements you seek, it always begins with creating time, space and Attention. When I was younger I thought I was not good at household repair jobs, I had no talent for writing tax-statements, I was not good at babysitting for someone and many other "I cant's". But over time I discovered the truth. The truth is that I was not willing to dedicate proper time and Attention to these things. Because of my lack of time and Attention, I was incompetent at anything that did not provide instant ego-gratification. I lacked an overall appreciation of life. Later in life I discovered that if I really wanted to, I could repair household appliances. If it was urgent, I could sit down, give it proper time and Attention, and I could fix things without having a repairman come in. An example: The TV was not working properly, so I sat-down with it and looked at it for awhile, became ever more patient- giving it the loving Attention it was apparently asking for - and soon saw that it was nothing more than a loose cable that was causing the trouble. Its "repair" only took 10 seconds, ultimately saving lots of time and money.

A repairman once confided to me that half of the repairs he is called to do could have easily been fixed by the people he'd been called to help, had the owners paid just a little bit of Attention.

That's the way it is with everything, universally. If you have a child who keeps causing problems, that changes if you, for once, dedicate *proper* time and Attention. That requires giving up your ego for an allotted period of time, giving up your sense of ego-related activities being "more important", and truly dedicating yourself to that other person. You can help solve anyone's problems by dedicating time and Attention. And if you do so without resistance, you will magically and miraculously have more time for your own goals and priorities. Paradoxically, because energy was preserved, your own goals will take less time to manifest. This is not to imply that you should neglect your own tasks for the sake of another. Balance is key.

I had a student who sought to solve a skin irritation problem. For this he got my audio program called *The Bliss Course*. He completed *The Bliss Course* within 3 days, then wrote to me complaining that his skin problem was still there. Seeing that he did a course that is supposed to take a month or more, in 3 days, I realized he lacked time, space and Attention, which is actually a lack of **love**. "Did you take notes during the Course?" – "No". – "Did you repeat the Course?" – "No." I told him to spend significantly more time (love) on his skin irritation issue. One week later he came back complaining that it still wasn't fixed. You could feel his impatience. Impatience constricts and contracts energy. It creates dryness, tension and stuck-ness. I told him to open up even more and dedicate himself even more fully to the dissolution of the issue. "Repeat *The Bliss Course* a third time, and do the entire course ONLY with that issue," I told him. I didn't hear from him for a few months. So I wrote to him: "What's up with the skin irritation?" He wrote back: "Oh that? That's no longer an issue. The irritation has receded. I've been dealing with other issues though, namely…" – "And these other issues require the same thing: time, space and Attention," I told him.

Not dedicating the proper time, space and Attention to things comes from the mistaken belief that one circumstance is significantly more important than another circumstance. For example: "Completing my project is much more important than my relationship. I already have the relationship, but I have not completed the project yet," While it is true that prioritization helps you to achieve goals, it is also true that, "The way you do one thing, is the way you to anything." For example, if he would open up to his relationship more and invest time into that, he might discover that his relationship-partner holds the key to the completion of the project.

Slowing down, becoming more comfortable with the eternal NOW and whatever daily-life thing is at hand now is almost always beneficial. Without losing sight of your goals and priorities, always make sure to take proper time for the "little things". Put differently: *"Take care of the little things and the big things take care of themselves."*

Life Is a Fantastic Work of Art

Next time you see a painting, move up so close to it that your nose almost touches the canvas. What do you see? Probably some chaotic blotch of color. You certainly don't see the overall intention of the artist, the overall context of the chaotic blotch; the bigger picture. But if you move your face away a little, you begin seeing outlines. Move it away a little more, and you see objects and figures. And move away enough to gain a perspective of the whole picture, and you see it in all its magnificent beauty.

Both life in general and your life in particular are a work of art. Sometimes you narrow your Attention down to look at one spot on the canvas-of-life in great detail. You filter out one aspect of your life, and make it very important. Then life may look like that chaotic blotch of colors and make no sense at all. You might start complaining about your bad situation. But if you take a step back, regain perspective and look at the overall work of art, your appreciation for its magnificent beauty will return. What then looked like a pointless blotch of color begins to look more complete. Whatever may be happening in your life, do not be too quick to judge it, because everything that happens is part of a greater work of art; a greater puzzle. Try seeing it from the eyes of the artist.

Secrets of Attention

Energy flows where Attention goes. How long can you focus? Did you know that single-pointedness clears your mind, and helps you feel more stable and awake?

Can you see how the people, brands, companies and countries of this world are in a kind of competition for Attention? So who hogs it? Who demands the most Attention? And who actually commands the most Attention?

Even giving someone negative Attention equals giving them energy. Whichever politician gets the most positive *and* negative Attention, usually gets voted for. Check this out of you don't believe it.

What is the connection between Attention and perception? Well, you only perceive what you give or have given Attention to. Retrieve Attention from it, and it stops existing…until you put Attention back to it.

What is the connection between pain and Attention? Yes, obviously when there is pain, Attention keeps going back there. But if you have a pain in your arm, and I step on your foot, causing a larger pain, the pain in the arm might disappear because you are distracted. Or if you have a pain in your arm and then fall in love, the pain in the arm might disappear because you are distracted. Or if you have a pain in your arm and there's a nuclear explosion nearby, the pain in your arm will disappear because you are distracted.

But did you know that you can dissolve emotional and even physical pain by the use of Attention? Go to the center of the pain, duplicate it. Then go elsewhere. Then go back to the center of the pain, duplicate it. Then go elsewhere. As you go back and forth in this way, you should be able to at least reduce the pain or even make it disappear completely. Yes, that is possible. And yes, knowing that liberates you from total reliance on pharmaceuticals.

What is the source of Attention or Awareness? Where does it come from? I'll let you figure that one out yourself.

What is the connection between Attention and love? Does the familiarity created by prolonged Attention to someone, create love? Think about it.

What attracts your Attention and why? Are you only reading these questions or are you actually taking them for contemplation? Answering the questions in this section alone could teach you everything that one could possibly need for life. Or is your Attention-span not large enough to take your time with this type of thing?

What repels your Attention? And why?

Where could your Attention go right now?

Where was it just a minute ago?

Where would you like it to be right now?

What is the connection between resistance and Attention? Have you noticed how wanting to change a problem, wanting to solve a problem and wanting to heal a problem actually puts your Attention where you *don't* want to have it? Isn't that amazing? That's how all viscous circles are run.

What fixes Attention? What gets Attention stuck? Can you see how desire, resistance and trauma play a role in stuck Attention?

What is something that repelled your Attention and no longer does?

What causes a change in whether your Attention is attracted, repelled or neutral?

What controls your Attention? Is your Attention controlled by television, the Internet, telephoning, your job, your relationship, your career, your marriage, your body, books, celebrities, your children, your friends and/or the media?

Where has your Attention been recently?

Where could your Attention be now?

Where would you like your Attention to be now?

How can you better control your own Attention? And how is that connected to discipline?

What is the connection between Attention and overwhelm or stress? Is stress not simply having to deal with too many impressions, thoughts and expectations at the same time? Could you reduce stress by slowing-down and doing whatever you are doing now fully, while parking all other issues?

What is the connection between Attention and health? When you are healthy, you have no or not much Attention to the body. That's a hint. On the other hand, giving loving Attention to certain body parts can have a healing effect.

What is the connection between Attention and exhaustion? Have you noticed how you can extend your athletic performance by Attention to the here-now?

Did you know that what people call "belief" is highly concentrated Attention?

What is the connection between learning and Attention? How does it overwhelm Attention if the schoolteacher moves along more quickly than Attention is able to process the information? How does relaxed and receptive Attention accelerate learning?

What is the connection between desire and Attention?

What is the connection between identity and Attention?

What is the connection between habit and Attention?

I am asking you these questions in order to direct your Attention to things most people never think about their entire lives.

What is the connection between time and Attention? Does time not only exist when Attention goes to a thought about the past or future, away from the experience of the present moment?

What is the connection between priorities and Attention?

The state of "free Attention" means that there is nothing at all unfinished, nothing at all expected, nothing resisted and nothing desired. One is completely open and free.

Focus on one thing and all else recedes into the background. What could that mean for your life? You can draw anything closer or make it recede. Any reality at all.

What do people want? They all want Attention. But what is the difference between wanting Attention and giving it? Giving it is the powerful position. Because you are giving people what they want. Interesting people are the ones that are interested. The people who seek Attention appear uninteresting. Those who give you interest, appear interesting.

How might a publicity hound benefit from negative Attention? Do you think there are organizations or countries that create their own enemy in order to control the negative side?

What is the connection between Attention and power?

What do mass-media, politics, sports and show-business do with the Attention of crowds?

Do you realize that large crowds and audiences can give a sports-team the energy necessary to win a game, and that this energy is an invisible life force that is transferred through Attention, injected with excitement?

How does Attention filter reality?

If you think this is all mystical hocus pocus, think again. Yes, it may be mystical, but it's also very practical. You can use it on a day-to-day basis for learning, giving, for profit and for pleasure.

How does Attention relate to viewpoints, opinions and beliefs? Do you realize that the more often you think a thought, the more it de-intensifies and solidifies into a belief? And that even more Attention to it has it solidify into a behavior, action and ultimately your reality?

Can you make imagination solidify into reality through Attention plus belief?

How does a young child play Attention games?

How do adults play those games too, but more subtly?

What happens to Attention when you try to keep secrets? Does your field of Attention become constricted?

What happens with Attention in very reactive or paranoid people? Can you see how they look for threats everywhere, and actually find them and thereby confirm and solidify their own beliefs?

What happens with Attention in very pro-active people? Can you see how they are able to create something out of nothing?

What is the behavior of Attention in a relaxed state? When do you just sit there and observe?

What is the connection of Attention to extrasensory perception? Can you put your Attention to another place and perceive what's there if you so intend?

What does "losing yourself in something" mean? Have you lost yourself in a book, a movie or an entire reality? Have you become so immersed in a relationship that you have forgotten your friends? Have you become so immersed in your job that you have forgotten your relatives? Have you become so immersed in your search for knowledge that you have forgotten how simple life is?

What happens with Attention during sex?

Is there ever a time where there is an absence of Attention?

How about you spend a little more time on the questions in this section? There is more to discover with more Attention.

Attention Flow

Flow of Attention and Energy

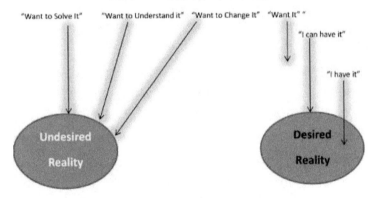

As you can see in this illustration, wanting to solve, understand or change an undesired reality focuses your energy on the undesired reality. Wanting the desired reality instead, puts your attention in the right direction but it stops halfway to the desired reality (want equals lack). "I can have it" brings you significantly closer. "I am that" and "I have it" puts your energy right into the desired reality and begins attracting it closer to you.

Attention Shifting

About five years ago I programmed an iPhone app that would turn on automatically every few hours or days and ask you:

"Where is your Attention right now?"

And

"Where would you like your Attention to be right now?"

These are two of the most important questions any human can ask, yet the app was rejected by Apple as *"having no information or entertainment value"*.

The reason for rejection was funny because it's actually true: It was not supposed to have any "entertainment" or "information" value. It was supposed to have Awareness and empowerment value. I guess that went over their heads...literally. Maybe this world is not really designed to empower its people, but rather to in-form (indoctrinate) and entertain (entrain) them.

To craft good conditions for yourself, simply have more Attention on what is good rather than on what is not. Each new day offers temptations to become preoccupied with things that are not good for you, to become an energetic muddle of random things, and then attracting a muddled mix of random things...some of which are commonplace, some of which are simply undesirable. When turning on the TV, you might accept the offer of negative news. When conversing with someone, you might accept hundreds of words that are not of the quality your soul prefers. When getting up in the morning, you might feel compelled to just go into the habitual morning-routine without conscious thought. Fortunately, a good night's sleep resets your energy.

You wake up in the morning re-set, all thoughts/emotions, except the most dominant ones, are cleaned and cleared up and you can start anew. **Things you give the most Attention to become dominant energies.** It behooves you to guide your thought process on a daily basis. You could write lists daily. Lists of what you like and appreciate. Why daily? Because the state of the world is just not that good. It's kind of pathetic, really. So, you counter the daily onslaught of non-good influx with your own good tidings. Your mailbox, the conversations in the train, the newscast, the radio, the newspapers - are all sources of never-ending mediocrity that have nothing to do with your soul's intentions. But it's not only external. Once the world has had its say, your own mind will play tricks on you, convincing you of limitation.

But it's not these things you have to change, (thus giving these things even more undue Attention) you need only to guide and handle your own thought process. You needn't find out, justify, research what's wrong, but merely indicate, notice, think about, study, consider, look at what's wanted, preferred, liked.

It really is as simple as this. Looking for more complex truths or techniques takes you away from the very basic and essential truth that ultimately your thoughts create your world.

Attention Shifting Technique

Write the following questions to yourself on a card:

1. *Where was my Attention today?*
2. *Where could my Attention be?*
3. *Where would I like my Attention to be tomorrow?*

Discipline yourself to look at the card and answer the questions every day for some time. These questions will have you confront your weaknesses and strengths, let you see what you are doing with your precious time and thoughts, and allow you to make small improvements every day. Ultimately these three questions will teach you how to create reality. To succeed at anything, you need to put Attention there. If your Attention is already occupied by many other things, you won't have the capacity to put it on something new. Sometimes old things must be shed, especially those that do not serve you. The Attention you invest in something, gives you a return-on-investment. But Attention must be given to the *end result* that is wanted, not to the *lack* of what is wanted.

Expanded Attention

Being too concerned about yourself is a limitation. If you release your concern about your reputation, or how you look to others, or whether you will succeed, or what others think about your work, you gain creative freedom. Attention is no longer stuck on a small sphere around your own head, no longer stuck on worry. No longer strongly identified with "I" and "me, me, me"; your sphere of influence expands to things "outside of yourself". "Paradoxically", the more concerned you are about yourself and your influence, the less you have. A few small exercise that will expand your sphere-of-influence and perception, and help you get out of identifying with that tiny body and head you call "me":

* While taking a walk, notice when you are preoccupied with thinking. Release that tendency and instead shift your Awareness to your surroundings; the objects, plants and people in your surroundings. Become interested in the world. Every time you have a relapse into thinking, return to extroverting your Attention again.

* Anonymously make someone a gift or an act of *secret* charity.

* Genuinely forgive and then publicly praise someone you've held a grudge against.

* Spontaneously give up trying to solve something you've been thinking about for a long time, and just forget about it.

Enjoy the expansion.

Stuck on Something? Improve Something Else!

Some subjects for improvement are:

Health/Body
Money
Career
Family & Friends
Romance & Sexuality
Mind & Spirit
Learning & Abilities
Energy

If you have been feeling stuck on one subject for a long time, I recommend you improve another. If for example, you have been trying to heal a health problem for a long time but to no avail, release the Attention stuck on that subject by improving another area...your relationships for example. If you have been yearning for a love lost, release your Attention stuck on that and improve something else...learn a new skill for example. Where you improve one area in your life, others improve. You are a holistic being. By letting go of the stuck subject, you can allow it to improve naturally and "by itself", while you look into other areas. It is important that you look at what you CAN improve and not always stare at those things that do not seem to be improving. You can make small steps of improvement in any area every day. Generate and maintain momentum.

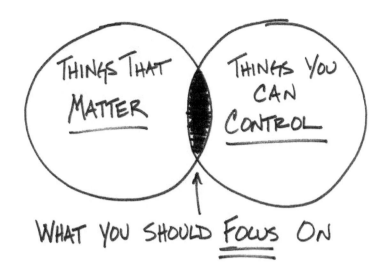

Keeping Your Focus After Setbacks

A losing-pattern I frequently see is how people react to setbacks. A setback is only a setback and no reason to give up the entire project or dream. You set out to lose weight. You change your eating patterns. Then, one evening, you make an exception to your new eating pattern, and eat something you are not "supposed" to eat. Unfortunately, most people take this as a setback and as a reason to stop their project altogether. They say, "Ah, what the heck. I failed so I might as well enjoy any foods I want." They usually then eat more than they did before.

This losing-pattern is connected to the labeling of the setback as a "failure" instead of a mere stepping stone on the path to the goal. See blocks not as interruptions, but as catapults toward achievement.

The error lies in seeing the snapshot instead of the whole movie; seeing the short-term, not the long-term. Seen long-term, a little deviation from the set goal is no big deal. Seen short-term, it *is* a big-deal, and the person feels they have "failed". If you have a setback now and then, it's not a problem. The problem is in your reaction to the setback. A setback can be an excuse to say, "I failed," or merely a reminder of your overall goal.

The Power of Single-Pointedness

"The degree of freedom from unwanted thoughts, and the degree of concentration on a single thought, are the measures to gauge spiritual progress."

"No one succeeds without effort… Those who succeed owe their success to perseverance."

"The adequate evidence for the fact that God, which shines
as the Self, resides in the hearts of all, is that all people indicate
themselves by pointing to the chest when saying 'I'."
- Ramana Maharshi: Collected Works

Single-Pointedness or One-Pointedness, is the ability to focus Attention on one thing and one thing only. This could be one thought or one object. This very simple exercise caused me to have the most powerful experience I have had in my entire life thus far – the state Easterners call "Enlightenment" or "Cosmic Consciousness". I think today, decades later, I understand why I had the experience: The one-pointedness stopped all thought, causing me to de-identify from my normal body/mind leaving me in a state of total Awareness of the whole Universe. But back then, at the age of 14 when I focused on a single thought for 7 hours, I didn't understand it. I hadn't read all these eastern books yet. But "something within me" must have understood it, otherwise I would not have done something as crazy as focus for that long. But even if you do not experience that very intense and special state, one-pointedness as a meditation has many hundreds of other beneficial effects, a few of which are: Total peace and calm and training your willpower. I´d recommend at least 10 minutes of one-pointedness now and then, for anyone. It will do more for you than any book in the world. You could do it with an object, with a spot on the wall, with a single thought, with anything as long as you stick your Attention to it and just keep it there, no matter what. Back when I did this for seven hours, I went through many different stages and levels of emotion. I recall going through some melancholy, some frustration, impatience, fear (of going insane), intense boredom – but I kept on. I also recall going through various states of joy and elation. But I kept on anyway. Something within me knew that if I kept focusing, I would finally go through all levels of energy. And so it happened.

Holding Your Gaze

Generally speaking, in an unloving state you can't hold your gaze. You tend to want to look away, look down or shift your eyes back and forth. To cover-up their unloving-state, liars try to fix their gaze on the other, but their expression is more often a frozen stare than a natural gaze. The truth of one's attitude is communicated through the eyes, so those who do not want to communicate their actual feelings, wear sunglasses when there is no sun, or cannot keep their gaze for very long. People who are freshly in love can hold their gaze for minutes and even hours, indicating that they are totally open to...whatever! Being able to hold your gaze in someone's direction in public indicates willingness to communicate. You can more easily pick up conversations with strangers if you can hold your gaze. By "gaze" I do not mean to stare like a psychopath. A gaze is a soft, natural, non-invasive look in someone's direction. They will smile or return your gaze, or, if they are not in a resourceful state, they will look away. If they look away you might want to send them a tel-empathic wave of compassion. Telepathy is actually tel-empathy because it requires empathy with others in order to be able to read their mind and emotions.

"Holding your gaze" as well as "withholding your gaze" can be useful in all types of competitive games and sports. At the onset of a game, you might hold your gaze to indicate no-fear. During the game, you might hide your eyes as not to communicate your true intentions to the opponent.

While negotiating contracts, both your eyes and your voice are key components. By withholding your speech in silence, the other becomes uncomfortable and starts talking. If you can, at the same time, keep your gaze extroverted to the other for most of the time, this signifies truthfulness. The opposite would be to talk a lot but look away at the same time, which is not necessarily a winning strategy for business.

If you are working as a teacher or healer, you can send tel-empathetic commands through your eyes. You can intend for another person to get better and hold your gaze with that intention. This sounds somewhat far-out, but it does lend great support.

Holding your gaze without intention can be used to find out more about someone. You can actually find out everything about anyone by extending your gaze on them. The longer you actually look, the more you "just pick up" about them. All you have to do is really **look.** And if you think that most people do look, take another look, because....they don't! People's eyes move here and there and are rarely really extroverted, focused and clear. But by actually really **looking** at people and things, they could slow-down their mind and feel a whole lot better about a whole lot of things.

The Value of Closed-Mindedness

In my view, the "Oversoul" or "Higher Self" actually experiences hundreds of lives simultaneously. For you these are "past lives", "future lives" and "parallel lives". You are currently living one version of many versions of your current life. I believe we can reincarnate into the same life and body many times to try it differently than before. I believe this is one of the interesting games of the Universe. We can also reincarnate into past lives and different versions of past lives. And we can reincarnate into future lives and the many parallel versions thereof. The potential is **limitless** and awesome. The reason a human being is so closed-minded and limited is so that he/she does not get all those lives mixed up! So next time you see a human being who is solely focused on this physical and material life and nothing else, don't judge him too harshly, for he is playing the game of life correctly. We often see people condemning others because of their disinterest in certain matters. But seen from a multi-dimensional and multi-existential perspective, they are doing their best not to mix-up levels and parallel lives. They are "maintaining their frequency". You need to maintain your frequency to create any sort of stable reality. Any stable reality is a miracle of focus. Even negative realities that remain stable are miraculous because it requires a lot of effort to build such a stable structure of habit and daily life. The only reason to change your frequency, leave stability, and open up to more than mundane daily life, is when your reality is not to your liking. Then it's time to explore other options in order to loosen your narrow definitions. One of the ways to do this is to travel to other lives, to explore parallel versions of yourself, or to imagine a higher version of yourself over a time-span. Then, you can enter a new version of yourself.

Reactiveness vs. Attentiveness - The Power in the Question

The words "question", "quest" and "request" in their original Latin, mean to "make a journey of inquiry", "to seek knowledge", "to ask" and "to gain". As a coach, I gauge a student's potential for growth by the questions they ask. If someone asks no questions at all, I know there is little interest and no learning potential. Where one asks many questions, I know they are still eager to grow. Children ask so many questions because they are on a journey of progress. They are not in the "I already know" frame of mind that leads to stagnation.

People are very happy to answer questions because they can search their mind and offer from their experience and expertise. Like a little child, I love jump-starting my curiosity and asking a whole host of questions. My experience is that anyone who is alive has a lot of interesting things to say from their perspective.

Having "all the answers" or fixed positions on things tends to create some mental stability, but having too many fixed positions also leads to a stop in expansion, as if there is nothing new to learn about a subject matter. Too many fixed positions as in, "I already know all about this," can generate blind stupidity, as can often be seen in school, in the media, in science and especially in the political arena, where "left wing" and "right wing" advocates see the world only from their particular pre-set cast in stone . Clearing one's mind of preconceptions and looking at some event, situation, or topic anew...with fresh eyes...with "tabula rasa" has the tendency to allow you to find out much, much more about something than if you were looking at it from some fixed position. I am talking about fixed mental positions here, but if I talk about it in terms of physical positions, it might be easier to understand: If you view the building across from you always from the position of your own house, you will always notice the same things about the building. In order to learn something new about that building, you would have to leave your position, at least temporarily, and view it from another perspective. You could view the building from a helicopter, from the back, from the sides, from the street, from within the estate and dozens of other positions. Each would reveal something new.

One good way to expand your perspective is by asking questions. Why? How? What? Where? Who? When you are with someone who has a lot of experience at something you are interested in, ask them questions. Take the answers that are helpful to you and make use of them. Even take some of the answers you don't like and ponder them. "I don't like that answer," indicates that you have a fixed/stuck position from which you are unwilling to deviate. Maybe you are unwilling to deviate from your position because it has brought you relative success or because entertaining too many different ideas can be confusing. But you can re-occupy an old position any time. If you deviate from your position and return back to it later on, you will be able to hold that position more strongly. If something is really true or effective, you don't have to worry about positions that contradict that view. Contradicting positions will then only strengthen your truth. Enjoy reading things that contradict your positions.

You can steer your own focus and the focus of others by the type of questions you ask. "Why am I so miserable?" for example, is a less potent question than, "How can I find more joy?" An even more potent question would be, "How can I enjoy finding more joy?" and even more potent would be, "How can I enjoy finding more joy today?" By the questions you ask yourself, you navigate where Attention goes.

Write down some questions you have been asking yourself. Then see if you can re-phrase your questions into more potent questions. Notice how that gets you going toward more positive, life-sustaining directions.

Assume that anything can be known. There are no "secrets" as such. Any supposed secrets are merely things you are keeping from yourself.

Asking questions can help you gain wisdom. In the ancient world, wisdom was symbolized by water and the river; getting you back into the flow of life. Remnants of this can still be found in many languages where the words "water" and "what" sound similar. In Italian it's "que" and aqua (similar in all other Latin-based languages). In German it's "was" and "wasser". In Hebrew, it's "ma" and "mayim". In Arabic, it's "ma" and "maa". Asking good questions can get you back into the stream of consciousness; the flow of the Universe; the river of life.

Attractions and Aversions of the Ego-Self

Ascending in consciousness means herding the ego-self, while letting more spirit shine through. This is easier when you know what exactly the ego-self / animal-self is attracted to, and what it has an aversion against:

It desires to **get,** and it resists **losing**.
So it is good to learn to *let go*.

It desires what is **known/familiar,** and resists what is **unknown/unfamiliar**.

So it is good now and then, to go into *unknown territory* (especially mentally),

It desires what is **easy** and resists **effort**.
So it is good to invest *effort* into your goals.

It desires **freedom** and resists **confinement**
So it is good, now and then, to embrace *confinement* (as in a commitment for example),

It desires **security** and resists **insecurity**
So it is good now and then to be OK with *uncertainty*, be OK with not knowing the future, be OK with *not looking perfect.*

It desires **more** and resists **less**
So it is good to sometimes do with *less*. Sometimes "less is more" and can bring forth the more creative and spiritual side of you.

The ego-self does not have too much energy of its own, so it attempts to create what we would call "negative emotions" as a fuel for survival. But when the spiritual-self awakens and grows, you no longer require such emotions as fuel because you have more than enough energy all day and every day. Don't allow the Attractions and Aversions of the Ego-Self to dominate your entire day. Let your spiritual-self be the boss.

Reality – A Trick of the Mind

When you look at this picture, what do you see?

Well?

I'm pretty sure 95% of all people would say, "I see a white dot". They would think that the picture is about the white dot. In reality, the white dot only makes up 1% of the image. 99% of the picture is black background.

So why make it about the white dot? Because the mind is used to focusing on figures, movement, contrast and shiny bright things that stand out rather than on the background. The mind is used to focusing on content rather than context.

This is of course the #1 reason human Awareness of overall reality is so limited. If a guy sits in a cafe, and I want to photograph him undetected, all I have to do is send a really good looking woman to walk by and his Attention will be zoomed for the duration of that time, while my activity goes unnoticed by him. In society, this is how organizations operate when they want to keep their activities secret – they just distract the crowds with something bright and flashy to focus on. Like naive little children, mass-Attention will then move in the direction of the bright and flashy, loud and boisterous, amazing and dangerous thing, while the keepers of secrets can operate completely undetected.

The mind has difficulty seeing the bigger picture. If it could see the bigger picture, it would see things more the way the soul/higher-self sees them. While talking with someone very good looking or fascinating, have you ever tried not to zoom into their talk too much, but remain aware of the rest of the surroundings or other people at the table? Try it out...it will free your mind. While a favorite sports-event or show is happening, have you ever just tried to temporarily reduce the importance of the game or show and remain aware of other things? I don't mean being distracted or unable to focus on it. I am talking about the ability to be able to focus on something but also retrieve that focus and become aware of the greater field, the greater context; the background of things. When walking through the woods are you more aware of single trees or the whole forest?

The background or canvas within which all of life arises is consciousness – the presence that permeates everything. You can experience some of this timeless context by stepping back a little and viewing not in zoom-focus-mode, but by getting a sense of background and the overall ambiance and setting and deeper meaning of things. What you consider "reality" is merely a trick of the mind. Its trick is to be super-zoomed and super-focused in all kinds of ways every day. There is nothing wrong with that, of course. But if it is overdone you may lose sight of the overall context of life, and lose yourself in too much detail.

As you sit there reading these words, at the same time become aware of your body and of the things to the right and left of your computer and the things above you, left and right of you and even behind you. Allow your Awareness to be 360 degrees aware rather than only focused on these words. You just expanded your field a little. You begin feeling a little less tense and contracted. You just became aware of things you were not aware of before because your entire Awareness was fixed on these words and the computer screen. And you notice how you can simultaneously stay aware of this text as well as your surroundings. What can you do with this knowledge? You can become aware of so very much more. The more you are aware of, the more your competence, ability and inner state improve. Put differently: Take care of the context from which you operate, and the content takes care of itself.

Feeling Energy Fields

I once took a student to a local museum. I walked around fairly unimpressed until I felt a sudden "air pocket" as if walking through a field of energy. I stepped back and forward a few times and waved my hands through that field to make sure I was feeling what I was feeling. So I had a looked around and discovered that we were in a room full of relics, and I had just passed by the bone of some saint. I realized the energy-field was emanating from that bone. So I asked my student to wave his hands in front of the bone to see whether he could feel the difference. And he could. Holding his hands there he felt a tingling. Holding them elsewhere he felt no tingling. ("Elsewhere" in this case being the wall or wooden frame and glass of the display.) I am not even sure he knew what relics are, but he could feel the difference.

And that would make sense, wouldn't it? A simple piece of wood or glass would have to have a different residue energy-vibration than an enshrined and revered bone of a saint, wouldn't it? It was the Nobel prize winning physicist Max Planck who first proved that every single object radiated its own distinct energy. Hence, every object, place, plant, animal, person, thing, thought would have to feel different than another one. How many differences are discernible? That is a matter of how deep ones Awareness is.

Do not underestimate the importance of **nuanced and discerning perception**, thinking and feeling. Life can be experienced as many colors and frequencies of energy. But when people are depressed, they feel everything as "the same" and somehow flat and grey. They'll say: "What difference does it make whether I ride the bus or take a helicopter?" But if you are into reading energy and just a little choosy about your reality, then it does make a difference.

The dictionary defines "nuanced" as follows:

1: A very small difference in color, tone, meaning, etc.

2: A subtle distinction or variation

3: Sensibility to, Awareness of, or ability to express delicate shadings (as of meaning, feeling, or value)

You can only perceive the nuances of a person, place, subject, belief-system or thing after you have given it enough thought and Awareness. Eskimos might be able to discern 40 types of snow, whereas we can only discern three types.

The societal "mainstream" has a generally low Attention-span and will tend to "dumb things down" and use shorthand opinions and labels to categorize the world. It will "take a side" on various political, religious, economical, societal issues of the day. That "side" will usually be pre-determined by some kind of ideology or belief-system. There is a lot of stereotypical-thinking going on. Even on my website, easily digestible and easy articles are popular, whereas highly nuanced and intricate pieces are less read. This is due to a general laziness of Attention that goes through all of society and applies to anything in life. So, there are two important points being made here:

1. If you do not dedicate focused Attention-to-detail to anything, you can never learn deeper layers of reality, nor can you become expert at anything.

2. If you view topics through the glasses of an ideology or fixed belief-system, you cannot perceive or respect anything outside of that belief-system.

Perceiving in a nuanced manner is closer to truth and also allows you to feel and see more. Seeing a piece of art is more enjoyable if you focus on all of its details instead of just walk past and perceive it in a generalized manner. Writing a book or painting a picture is much more enjoyable if you pay Attention to detail and make even the small parts of it the best you can. Skiing is more fun if you are familiar with many different kinds of snow, and what these kinds of snow feel like compared to others.

"Lots of Chinese tourists here..." someone I was walking with recently said to me. "They're not Chinese, they're Japanese," I responded. "How can you tell?" he asked. "By the shape of their faces and by the way they dress," I replied. In this example you can see how lack of nuance leads to generalizations, inaccuracies and ignorance. But while my discerning perception may have been greater than his, it still could have been much deeper. I was, for instance, unable to tell the difference between northern Japanese and southern Japanese, or between a Tokyo and Sapporo dialect. The fun thing about anything in life is that you can get into deeper and deeper levels of nuance, or greater and greater levels of generality. Someone even more general than this guy could have said: "Chinese, Japanese, Thai... it's all the same to me."

In terms of thought-forms the following rule of thumb applies:

1. To dissolve a thought-form, go more general

2. To intensify a thought-form, go more detailed

So if there is a thought bothering you, instead of imagining it in all its gory and painful detail, instead of memorizing every aspect of the painful event, you would see it more as a vague fog in black and white, "just a thought", "one of many thoughts", "one of many realities". And if there is a thought you would like to energize and magnetize, you will visualize it in all its wonderful detail (as taught in the Imagination Training Audio-Set).

If you wished to learn and master a skill, you would explore it in all its delicious detail.

If you would like people to love a product you produce, you would manufacture it with love to detail and near-perfection. If you do that, you don't need any marketing because your product will attract people no matter what. What all this invested-Attention does is it "loads the object" with your energy. Thus the object has a "glow" to it that may be invisible to the eyes, but its visible to the heart. It then becomes magnetic to others, and they feel attracted to it because it is glowing and represents a state they would like to achieve. They can feel the difference.

Keep the Mystery Alive

I'd like to talk about a style I have never shared publicly. It's called "keeping the mystery alive". It is useful for self-marketing, going on dates and fiction writing. Creating and maintaining mystery puts an audience's Attention into a suspended state that causes them to keep interest until the mystery is solved. Once solved, relief is felt and Attention retreats from that which it was focused on.

This is why TV shows usually end with "cliffhangers", which are unsolved issues that compel the audience to tune in again for the next show. This is also why you shouldn't reveal everything about yourself "on the first date", lest the other find out you are just as boring as everyone else. This is why, as a public person, I almost never talk about myself. People will spend an entire seminar with me, talking to me, and mostly we talk about their issues, never about me or my issues. This way nothing much is ever known about me, and I remain a mystery.

Creating and keeping mysteries is not a "bad" or "manipulative" thing. It trains people's creative imagination and ability to learn and discover for themselves. Frankly, I don't want to be told everything, I like to find out how stuff works, how things are done. Learning, to me, is pure joy. "Why don't you outsource your website-work?" someone recently asked me. "Because I love learning how all this stuff works!" I responded.

For precisely the same reason, I don't really enjoy nude beaches. Where everything is completely laid open for all to see, there is no more mystery, no more discovery, no more excitement over nudity.

A lot of my favorite self-improvement teachers know how to weave a good yarn; tell a good tale; deliberately create mystery. Sure – this is used as a marketing device because nothing sells better than fascination – but it's also a tool to school the audience in attentive study and figuring things out for themselves. Mystery is fun, and solving mysteries is satisfying.

The happiness associated with not-knowing and then-knowing, the sheer excitement of discovery, seems to be part of what this whole universe and life-on-earth set-up is all about. If we were originally in an infinite and all-seeing, all-knowing state, then we may have deliberately split into many separate, individual viewpoints and parts, hiding our wholeness from ourselves, only to gradually unveil it again. Maybe this is why "peek-a-boo" is an infant's favorite game. We're playing a gigantic, multi-universe-spanning game of peek-a-boo.

Awareness Training as a Key to the Mysteries of Life

What is life all about? What is going on? What do things mean? Who am I? Why are we here? Where are we going? Is there any purpose or pattern to all of this? Any sentient being asks these questions now and then.

I still don't know definitive answers to those questions. Neither do I wish to provide those answers for you. The whole fun and adventure lies in finding out the secrets and mysteries of life for yourself.

One thing I do know is that Awareness Training has given me more choice, depth, health and well-being. Life is experienced through an experiencer, through a sense of "I am". While you may be uncertain of numerous things, the "I am" you can be certain of. You can be sure that things are *happening* (I think this we can all agree on) and that there is someone or something witnessing and experiencing them. That "something" is a field of Awareness that is not confined or limited to the brain or body. Stop to look and really examine reality, and that's what you will notice.

Do it. Right this moment...what is going on? What are you aware of? If you slow down to become fully present, what are you aware of? Notice the sounds, sights, smells, textures, the breathing, the body and the thoughts. Those are some things one can be aware of and experience. Those things cannot experience themselves, they require an **experiencer**. Furthermore, the experiencer/witness/observer cannot **be** that which it is witnessing. In order to observe something, there must be a time/space separation between object and observer. You are not the brain, you are not the body and you are not even your thoughts. You are that which is witnessing them.

Most of the popular views of who we are, are a dead end, literally. The current scientific dogma is that you are a body or a brain; a coincidental result of chemistry, and that there is no reason or purpose for your existence, and when the body dies it's all over. If you think this view of reality through – like I have, thousands of times as a child in school – you will find that it doesn't make any sense at all. And I'm sorry to say, but I don't think you are too bright if you fully subscribe to that view. Believing in the doctrine of scientific materialism is only possible on a level of consciousness that has not experienced a sense of existence independent of body/brain. Luckily, because you can experience yourself as Awareness, you needn't rely on either of the "two pillars of civilization" (science and religion), and can make advances in your understanding of reality with the tool of in-depth-Awareness. **You have been given a precious tool that cuts through all delusion like an unbreakable diamond. In its numerous variations, that tool is called Attention, witnessing, looking, Awareness, examining, observing, sensing.**

An interesting quality of *neutral Awareness* that I discovered in meditation:

It tends to dissolve that which is negative/false/unreal and to let grow and expand that which is positive/true/real. That means if you put neutral Awareness on something that is good for you, it grows. If you put neutral Attention on something that is bad for you, it diminishes. For example, you would like to get rid of a nasty habit and simply mark down in your calendar every time you act out that habit (such as overeating or smoking), that is giving it neutral-Awareness and the habit will diminish over time and without much effort. It may take a few months to diminish, but recede it does, because that is just how the light of Awareness affects the negative. And if you likewise make just a brief diary entry of every time something good happens to you, that is applying neutral Awareness to the positive, and thus it will grow and grow and grow.

Why not try this out? When I make such an extraordinary claim, it's up to you to test its validity and whether it works for you.

I am relieved that I really have found THE primary key in life. The big elusive "secret" everyone is looking for is actually Awareness. It's the trump card that overrules all other cards (with the possible exception of love).

They say "knowledge is power", but Awareness trumps knowledge. In fact, without Awareness (in the form of Attention) you would not have acquired any knowledge. What use is knowledge you are not aware of when you need it? The main tool I use to help people release bad behavioral patterns is *to be aware of them while they are happening* (not later while regretting them). The mere Awareness of an unhelpful pattern while it arises de-automates the pattern, and one can let go of it.

When you want something in life – anything – you will have to increase your Attention on its fulfillment and become aware of the factors that lead to having it. When you want to get rid of something in life – anything – you will have to become aware of what is creating it and release it. If you missed a crucial detail in a contract you signed, it was because of unawareness. If you wish to be a good salesman, increased Awareness of other's desires is crucial. If you wish to appear attractive to the preferred sex, behaving in a mindful and deliberate manner can make you irresistible. If you wish to be a book author, dedicating plenty of Attention to your writing is required. Awareness is universal; it permeates everything. There is no situation that cannot be improved by the injection of more Awareness. Is your relationship going sour? Dedicate more Attention to it. Are your emotions in turmoil? There is something nagging for your Attention. Want to learn a skill? Put Awareness to it. Is there something you think you don't know? Put more Awareness toward it.

Becoming increasingly aware of greater and greater nuances of everything in life – your body, different types of bread flavor, the many personalities of your spouse – anything, is also the key to joy. The Infinite is aware of everything. As a mini-god, you are merely aware of small aspects of everything. The more you expand your Awareness, the closer you come to the Infinite. What follows are a few exercises to experience intensified Awareness.:

Your First Day on Earth

This is a walking meditation. Take a walk and look around you. Pretend it is your first day on earth. You are seeing everything for the first time. How would you be looking at things and feeling things if it were your first day here?

On the in-breathe think "I am" and on the out-breathe think "amazed". Repeat that a few times throughout your walk. Walk around in gratitude and silent wonder. There is so much going on in each and every moment. Wake up.

Let go of all preconceptions and judgments about anything at all and just walk and look. It is your first day on earth. If you notice any impatience or judgment arising, breathe it in and let go of it on the out-breathe. Practice viewing life with amazement.

Or go to a place where people walk by, sit down and observe. Notice something about a person. Notice something else about that person. Notice something about another person. Notice something about your surroundings. Notice how many things you learn just sitting there being aware. Notice how much you sense and feel when there is nothing you want from these people and just take your time to silently observe them and their world. This silent meditation is for compassion, wisdom and Awareness. It can be done for a few minutes or many hours. It will alter your world.

Expanding Consciousness Exercise

Beyond all the slogans and books on "expanding consciousness" this little eyes-open meditation will expand you immediately.

1. Look at the walls of the room you are in, and notice something about them you have not noticed before.

2. Look out of the window, and notice something you haven't noticed before.

3. Examine the skin of your arm, and notice something you haven't noticed before.

4. Examine the keyboards of your computer until you become aware of a function you were not aware of before.

5. Examine an object in your surroundings until you notice something about it you haven't noticed before.

6. Look at your stream of thoughts until you think a thought you haven't thought before.

7. Focus on feeling something you haven't felt in a long time for a minute.

8. Look at a person you think you know well until you notice something about them you haven't noticed before.

9. Open up wikpedia.org and learn something you did not know before.

10. Walk through your living spaces, noticing things you haven't noticed before.

11. Look up a correspondence you have been having with someone, and notice something about it that you missed the first time reading it.

12. Taste a piece of food and notice nuances in it you have not consciously been aware of before.

13. Make the intention that today you will experience something you have not experienced before.

14. Listen carefully and hear something you have not consciously listened to in a long time.

15. Notice something about yourself you have not noticed in a long time or ever before.

Carry this on throughout your life. What people call "the normal state" is actually a state of hypnotic and habitual blindness. There is so much more to notice, discover, learn and experience.

Segments of Reality

Awareness being essential to everything, these are a few segments of the day you can deliberately improve or set intentions for, especially if they are not to your liking or make you over-reactive. As you go through the list, for each point consider what your own emotions have felt like in these segments, and perhaps think about how you would like to respond or be in these situations in the future.

* When you wake up in the morning

* Taking a shower

* At breakfast

* Throughout the day

* At work

* With employees, superiors or colleagues

* With children

*With friends

* With old friends

* With new friends

* At lunch

* At dinner

* When going out with someone

* During sports

* In the living room

* In the kitchen

* In bed

* In bed with someone

* At night

* At the computer

* While having a conversation

* When meeting new people

* When having an argument

* After alcohol intake

* When someone praises you

* When someone blames you

* When you hear good news

* When you hear bad news

* Among friends

* In the basement

* While doing household chores

* At your relatives house

* At someone else's relatives

* When you are alone

* When you are not alone

* While surfing the Internet

* In the living room

* In the bathroom

* When there is a lot of noise

* In town

* After work

* On your way home

* In your yard or garden

* On your balcony

* On Monday

* At an event

* While performing

* At a spa

* In the country

* When approached by a stranger

* While taking a walk

There are many of other segments of reality you experience on a regular basis. You can bring conscious Awareness into every aspect of life and improve it. Becoming mindful of these segments as segments that are improvable is in itself a valuable realization.

As You Do One Thing, You Do Everything

Either you are on top of your game here and now, or you are not on top of your game at all, across the board, regardless of external circumstances. So if, for example, you are unemployed and would prefer employment, you should not wait until you get employed to be the best you can be today. If you are in a job you dislike, you should not wait until you get a better job before performing well. Regarding the whole, as you do one thing, you do everything. As above so below, as in the macro so in the micro. Whether on the highest or lowest levels, everything follows the same principles. The difference between the levels is how rapidly these principles play out. Only success attracts success.

Sex, Politics and Extraterrestrials

This section is about the artificial creation of importance in society and subjective vs. objective importance. First I would like to demonstrate how easily importance and unimportance can be **created**. Creating importance binds Attention, de-creating importance releases Attention from a subject.

Extraterrestrials Are Unimportant

In our times there is a lot of preoccupation with the search for extraterrestrial life, contact, invasions, UFO-sightings. In my book, *Parallel Universes*, I describe my own real encounters with extraterrestrial life forms. I have however, not really been interested in extraterrestrials in more than ten years for the following reasons:

1. If they are extra-terrestrial, they are part of the physical universe. My interest however, lies in ascending beyond the physical universe to the spiritual universe.

2. At least half of the beings who pose as extraterrestrials are actually astral-beings. This is why they only appear at night in people's bedrooms – because in the twilight of waking from sleeping is one of the only times the door to astral-realms is open.

3. Most science-fiction movies and documentaries focus on incredibly ugly beings as extraterrestrials. This must be either a superiority/inferiority complex of humans or some kind of sensationalist hunger for cheap horror movies. The beings I encountered were of breathtaking beauty.

4. Preoccupation with extraterrestrials can become a distraction from the tasks at hand in daily life. It can become a projection of glory and adventure being *elsewhere* rather than available to you here and now. You need not believe that fun and excitement lie elsewhere or that your own life is small and insignificant compared to the supposed adventures of aliens.

If you release your preoccupation with that which is not readily available in the here and now, that leaves more time and energy to craft your today-reality.

Extraterrestrials Are Important

Awareness of extraterrestrial activity is very important to your personal enlightenment and to society as a whole. Awareness of that which is beyond earth releases your earth-centric preoccupation, allowing you to see all events on earth from the perspective of a wider universe, in the context of a much, much greater game being played. Researching extraterrestrials may reveal not only a grander scheme but even the possibility of manipulation of ET-forces throughout the history of humanity. How many historical and ancient events were influenced by some beings, lights and phenomena coming from the skies? If such intervention took place, wouldn't you want to know? What if the world is their laboratory? As the world becomes more and more populous, it would also be wise to start thinking about establishing bases of humanity on other planets where we can also try out new forms of life and society.

The things we can learn from other civilizations are numerous. Learning an advanced civilization's engineering methods, biology and way of life can greatly benefit us. Focusing on extraterrestrials means focusing on the advancement of humankind.

There are few people that look beyond the self and much fewer that look beyond the planet. Looking for and at extraterrestrial civilizations is part of the natural progression of our species. When we see how vastly different the others are, it will also bring us humans closer together.

You just saw me first creating extraterrestrials as unimportant. This would result in my Attention (and those who agree) releasing from the subject. Then you saw me creating extraterrestrials as important, which would lead me (and those who agree) to dedicating more curiosity to the subject. Those who understand how to create and de-create importance are manipulating the reality you live in.

So what is it, are extraterrestrials important or unimportant? Well, that's for you to define for yourself. The objective truth probably lies somewhere in the middle: Keeping some Awareness of what might be going on beyond earth is a good idea, but if we overdo it, we lose focus of our life here. Because you have just read both sides of the coin; both dualities, it is more likely that you arrive at such a middle-ground attitude. People who like to tread the "middle path" in things do so because they are aware of different sides of a story They are aware that life on earth is split into many, many dualities, and that merging such polarities allows for a better overview of a subject as a whole and releases undo preoccupation on the one hand and undue disinterest on the other. Undue preoccupation with a subject can tend to generate extremism and hubris. Undue disinterest in various viewpoints can lead to apathy and a full-stop to learning/growth. Hence, long-time meditators keep talking about the virtues of balance and moderation. **Whether something is "good or bad" usually depends upon the dose in which it is prescribed**. A medicine in the right dose can be good, but if you overdose on it, it becomes poison. An ideology applied in small doses may have a healing effect on a country, but overdone may ruin that same country. Hence, any given ideology cannot be seen as either "good" or "bad". Its goodness or badness comes from a larger context: To which country is it applied? In which dose is it applied? Extremism usually fails, while the more balanced attitude usually succeeds.

Sex was mentioned to create artificial importance for this section. In reality, this has nothing to do with sex. It doesn't really have much to do with extraterrestrials and politics either. It has to do with **importance**. You can dissolve and release issues that are bothering you by reducing their importance. You can intensify your experience of various realities by increasing their importance. You do so my putting Attention there and finding plenty of reasons why something is important. Writing down what you have been preoccupied with, and making notes of what is important vs. not important to you is a helpful exercise of self-guidance.

Here is something to think about for yourself:

What is important?

What is not important?

What is subjectively important, and what is objectively important?

What are your values and principles in life, and how do they direct what you label as important?

What used to be important to you 10 years ago and no longer is?

What used to be unimportant to you 10 years ago and no longer is?

How to Attract and Not Attract Attention

I was sitting with a long-time student in a restaurant. We left without paying. "What was that all about?" he asked surprised. "I wanted to make a point on how easy it is to be invisible," I replied. I then went back into the restaurant to pay. The people at the cash desk were surprised because they hadn't noticed me. Normally, one takes food from a buffet, then goes to the cash desk to pay, and then sits down to eat. But I had gone straight from the buffet to the dining tables because I noticed the staff were inattentive and complacent and wouldn't notice. Thus, they too learned the lesson that anyone could enter their place, eat an entire meal and leave without ever being noticed.

I had been teaching this student a module on "attracting Attention and not attracting Attention".

I pointed to a woman walking down the street who was wearing a bikini top. She was attracting the Attention of several drivers passing by. I asked my student why she was attracting Attention. He assumed it was because of her bikini top. But that was not the case. Can you guess why she was attracting Attention?

It is because she was wearing a bikini top on a normal street of the neighborhood. If she were wearing it at a beach, she would hardly attract any Attention at all because everybody else would also be dressed that way. In other words: It's the context that determines whether the bikini is considered within the norm (unworthy of Attention) or outside of the norm (worthy of Attention).

If you cut up a piece of cheddar cheese into cubes and put toothpicks through them, they suddenly look like fancy "finger food" and attract Attention, whereas otherwise they wouldn't. In any normal context, it's just a piece of cheese.

My student, who managed a retail shop, experimented with these ideas. At regular intervals, he placed products on a pedestal right beside the entrance. These were sold much more quickly than if they were on the shelf among similar items. He reported the success to me with shining eyes, as if he had discovered one of the secrets of the universe.

Both attracting and not attracting Attention are useful skills at different times. If you are a marketer of a product or service, or looking to increase your popularity, you'll want to study the attraction of Attention. If you are an undercover agent, a celebrity hiding from the paparazzi or an employee avoiding the boss, you'll want to study how not to attract Attention. To attract Attention, be unique and different. To not attract Attention, represent the norm or be similar to others. Some people think that all they have to do is dress flashy and crazy and that'll attract Attention. But if they go to a party where everyone is dressed that way, being dressed modestly will actually attract Attention.

U.S. Presidential elections are won by emotions, not by facts. The candidate who attracts the most positive *and* negative Attention, wins. Reasonable and moderate sounding voices drop out of the race fairly early, because being sane and balanced does not attract that much Attention of a populace conditioned to seek "entertainment". Thus, our "mass-media" is designed for low-Attention-span and high-adrenaline, and we are left with the lurid machismo of Donald Trump and the phony sob-stories of Hillary Clinton as our leading "presidential candidates".

Those most skilled in *not* attracting Attention are secret intelligence agencies. During the cold war for example, a CIA agent stationed in Moscow was routinely instructed on how to stay undetected by surveillance operatives of the KGB, by staging a "normal life routine" in all its elaborate details. He'd dress like the people in the area dressed, and followed a daily commute around Moscow for months before engaging in any espionage. Through repetitive "normal behavior" the alertness of potential watchers dropped. Then, after many months of unchanged patterns and travel routes, the CIA agent might disappear during his normal commute for a very short time to conduct his secret act – such as delivering goods or dropping off a letter – before reappearing at his habitual destination only a couple of minutes behind schedule. Surveillance teams would not be alarmed by the short gap in routine – if they even bothered watching him after such a long period of routine behavior. Intelligence operatives say that "a larger action covers a smaller action, as long as the larger action itself does not attract suspicion". By this method, any clandestine act can be carried out in plain sight, and nobody will notice. Thus, most secret operations are carried out by people who appear entirely normal, not by those who appear interesting or mysterious.

Another common method of not attracting Attention is by diverting it. Politicians and stage magicians use this method routinely. They know that the eyes move quicker than the body. If I say to you that there are a hundred dollars on a table nearby and you should walk over to get it, what do you think will move first? Your feet? Your shoulders? No. Your eyes. An interesting side-note: Professional athletes have learned to make their bodies move before their eyes (and the connected mind) move. A tennis or basketball-player will go by body-sense and intuition first and by mind and eyes second. A stage magician will always move his eyes and hands very slowly. When he fools an audience, the eyes only observe what the magician wants them to observe. He will make their eyes go in a certain direction while performing his trick out of sight of the audience. Because the mind can only focus on one thought at a time, if the magician can control the audience's visual sight of events, he can implant a false image and memory. One example: Lightning a cigarette with a match with one hand, provides the opportunity to drop an object from the other hand. The audience's eyes are on the flame and incapable of also noticing the object (unless their Awareness remains open). Thus, both the magician, the spy and the politician use a bunch of props that are meant to capture people's Attention, so that they can do something else in the background.

While doing my "trick" in that restaurant, I realized that actions that are expected by the staff, would not be noticed. Walking with my food to a table in a leisurely manner was not noticed. Any unusual or surprising action would be noticed (unless the action is followed by a "rational explanation", by which it will soon be forgotten). Had I taken up eye contact with the staff, I'd have been instantly noticed.

Let's say you are sitting in a cafe and do not want to be noticed by other people there. You want your privacy. In that case, you'd have to get interested in something, to immerse your Attention into the work on your laptop for instance. Calm and absorbed people don't attract Attention. But if you wish to attract Attention, then be interested in your surroundings, interested in the other people or looking around as if you are waiting on someone. If you are looking around the cafe in an interested manner, you will quickly attract others Attention. Put differently: People you are interested in, become interested in you. Moreover, interested and fully present people appear more interesting.

An exaggerated preoccupation with trying to attract or avoid Attention is rooted in insecurity. A confident person does not much care whether he is getting external Attention and validation or not. One type of insecure person will try to stay small and unseen all his life (and call it "being humble"), as well as not being "figured out" by others. He'll mostly dress in grey, never get loud, never ask anything of anyone and never exert enthusiasm. In this way, he'll sabotage any sort of success he might have, because success can only come with showing up, presenting yourself and your ideas and values and sometimes becoming a public target. The other type of insecure person will do the opposite and try to make himself big and flashy, saying, "Look here, look at me." He'll go to great lengths to be different, famous, higher and better. He'll talk loudly, make constant demands and generally be a pain in the ass. Both the egomaniac and the person with false humility have issues with Attention. These issues derive from childhood where Attention from either parent was or appeared to be withheld. In a confident person, both getting Attention and not getting Attention are "just fine".

What attracts your Attention? What repels it? What keeps it neutral? Some people are attracted by dogs ("Soooo cuuuuuute!!!!!!"), some are repelled by dogs ("Get that filthy thing away from me!"), some remain fairly neutral at the sight of dogs ("Those are dogs."). Why? It is your inner-ideals, beliefs and values that determine what you give importance and what seems unimportant. To attract or repel Attention (which are both actually *attracting* Attention), you'd therefore have to present something consistent with what a certain amount of people love or hate. To not attract Attention, you'd have to present something people neither like nor dislike. When someone who is desperate for positive Attention (love, acknowledgement) fails to get it, they will usually resort to negative behavior to at least try to attract negative Attention (criticism, anger, pity).

Beyond all the games around Attention however, is the emotionally healthy person who:

1.   Does not *need* anyone's Attention
2.   Openly says so if he or she *prefers* to have someone's Attention

3.   Gives others Attention freely, without intentional withholding or expecting something in return
4.   Also gives plenty of Attention and love to him- or herself.

In other words: At a higher level of consciousness, the question is not on how to avoid or attract Attention, but how to give more Attention to yourself and others.

From Thinking to Awareness

Life is energy that is always flowing. As you resist that flow, your breathing becomes shallow, muscles contract and more thinking happens. As you go with the flow of energy, your breathing becomes slower and softer, your muscles relax and you feel more.

Letting go of compulsive and incessant "thinking-ness", and letting go of looking in the mind for answers will not reduce intelligence or make you dull. It will put you more in touch with life and energy as-it-is; unfiltered. The mind-aspect of you is useful for a number of tasks of daily life, but it does not know or understand happiness and life-energy. Likewise, a computer does not know how to feel. Letting go of seeking answers, trying to understand everything and trying to grasp this and that with your intellect will actually make you smarter. Have you ever noticed how the more someone applies mental exertion, and tightens his forehead in an attempt to figure things out, the more stupid he becomes? It is a common misconception that thinking gets things done and solves issues. Even scientific research is best done with a mix of thinking and receiving, of mind and emptiness, of concentration and release. With a fairly empty mind, the obvious can be perceived and universal answers received.

Somewhat reducing thinking will increase your clarity and well-being. Trying to suppress thinking will not work, but Awareness will. When you notice yourself get tense or unwell, notice how you are into too much thinking and wanting, (both go together; wanting = lack, thinking = unsuccessfully trying to get out of the state of lack) then shift to *Awareness* or to *feeling*. By "feeling", I don't mean becoming all emotional and sentimental, but rather becoming aware of the energy-of-the-present-moment, your breathing or physical body or becoming aware of your present-moment-surroundings. This is also called "getting out of the head – to let go, to relax, to regain your most effortless and natural state and to put an end to all worry.

So rather than being preoccupied in thought and having Attention in the head-area, you redirect your Attention to your stomach, chest, arms or legs, or simply to feeling. Feeling what? Just feeling whatever is there. Whatever you are feeling right now. The mind will say that you are "supposed to" feel this or that way, but that's just its usual commentary. The mind always provides commentary. You can't stop the mind. Meditators try to stop it, but that's quite challenging. Just let the TV set run, it's not important. Do not resist your current state, but relax with it. If you resist it, you go back to thinking-mode. The way you have been brought-up as a human being, 90% of you is resisting what you are feeling in this moment. Alternatively, you can also become aware of your present surroundings as-they-are. Becoming fully present raises your well-being, clarity and energy because it takes you out of the narrow confines of that thinking-ness. You can either be lost in thought or you can be aware.

So take a deep breath and just feel what you are feeling right now. Feel your life energy right now. When you feel life, you feel all the energy passing through without filters. Thinking-ness is like putting filters on that energy. After awhile you only perceive a tiny percentage of all the energy.

Sit in an upright position. Watch your breathing. Do this for a minute or two.

Notice how just watching your breathing calms your mind and lifts your mood.

Breathing is connected to feeling. Cutting-off the breathe of life is connected to thinking.

The mind is similar to a recording machine. It records information, then plays that information over and over. This mind-function can be useful to draw upon a large amount of information and make decisions of daily life. But it can also become a burden when you keep playing the same old negative records. The funny thing is that it thinks it's helping and protecting you by playing these old records. It thinks that fear protects it. But fear is only useful in instances of real danger. Because we have created a society of harmlessness, called civilized society, fear as a daily companion is no longer necessary. At a more evolved level of consciousness, fear is no longer the best way to protect yourself, because fear tends to more strongly attract that which is feared. Dogs can smell fear for instance, and are more likely to attack you when you have it. A bully is more likely to attack and a rapist is more likely to rape when there is a radiance of fear. What you radiate out into the world, tends to come back to you.

Likewise, too much Attention on problems does not solve the problems. When you have a problem, it can be very empowering to *let go* of trying to solve it, grasp it, understand it, figure it out and to simply return to feeling-what-is and Awareness-of-what-is. What will then happen is that it will unravel and solve itself in many cases.

The practice suggested here is to return to resistance-less Awareness and/or sensing/feeling every time you notice yourself drift into an undue amount of thinking and wanting. Let all energies that are present simply come-up and pass-through. If you do not resist, they just pass-through. When something painful comes up, there is the tendency to stop that energy or try to push it back down. This doesn't get rid of it, it just puts it back into the subconscious. In this way, you may not feel it anymore, and you do not have a gain in energy but an overall loss. If you let that "painful" emotion come-up and out it may be more painful than usual, but in the long run there is a gain in calm, a gain in lightness and a gain in **emotional clearing**. People who practice this may be experiencing more emotional "pain" than other people because they are letting it come up and out. All other people keep it down in their subconscious. They will have to face it someday. But in reality there is no such thing as emotional "pain". It only feels like pain if there is still a part of you pushing it. Just let it completely come up and out.

Try this: Feel into each body part before going to sleep. Have your attention be in your right foot and then the left foot. And in this way gently through the whole body. Because of this Awareness/feeling-ness you will experience an obvious increase in energy and aliveness again.

Remember that 99% of real life is completely invisible. It's the energy all around. The mind is always preoccupied with the visible; with the 1%. If you wish to access the 99%, stop resisting life and instead feel it.

Stop & Start

You can increase Awareness by not having all of your movements and actions run on automatic; by controlling some of them. A practice I've once seen Japanese monks do is "extremely slow walking". Starting in the morning, they walked 300 feet by evening. This amount of self-control seems impossible to most of us. But even only taking 1% of this attitude will enhance your Awareness greatly. Enhanced Awareness equals an improved life.

Choose a day on which to do everything just a little more slowly. Down the stairs more slowly. Turn the ignition more slowly. Shower more slowly. Drive the car more slowly. See how life seems to get better and easier, how the "time-pressure" of modern life subsides. *"Haste makes waste,"* is an old saying that always holds true. Haste is created by the ever needy and ever lacking mind/ego in an attempt to "gain" something it thinks is missing. But spirit/real-self/higher-self is *never* in a hurry. It is never under pressure and it is never lacking.

Another way to increase Awareness is to deliberately start or stop something. Have you ever, while walking down a hallway at work, just stopped in your tracks, right there and then? I suspect you have probably almost never because you're on autopilot. You are running like a wind-up-toy according to what is expected of you or according to what everyone else does. When you stop in your tracks, you stop the movie of life and allow a space of silence to open. **From this stillness it is easier to determine what the next part of the movie should be about.** Otherwise, the movie determines what your life is about, and you lose your position as movie-director. If you normally smoke after eating, why not just stop that today and not smoke after eating? Or if you normally never have a cup of tea after eating, why not just start today?

The easier it is for you to stop and start things, the more creative control you have over reality.

Stopping and starting things may bring up various subconscious resistances. That's alright, just let them pass by. If you never say hello to strangers, say hello today. If you always say hello to strangers, don't say it today. You can change the script your life runs by at any time. Even small changes are helpful in that they introduce an element of choice and free will into your reality.

This is one of my favorite meditation-techniques to experience 100% Awareness for a few minutes. I call it "Being Source": Say what you are going to do next and then do it. For a few minutes, don't do anything without deciding to beforehand. "I am going to walk over to that window," (do it). "I am going to touch that window," (do it). "I am going to sit down," (do it). Fifteen Minutes of this puts you back into a state of full control of your reality. I recommend it especially when life is seeming to become confusing, exhausting or overwhelming. It will put you back into the driver's seat rapidly. The advanced version of this exercise is to watch out for automatic behaviors (during the exercise), and to step-back and do these behaviors intentionally. So if I say, "I am going to the window," and I brush through my hair while going there, I would stop and say: "I am going to brush through my hair" (do it) and then again: ""I am going to go to the window."

You will notice that most things in your life run on automatic. That is not a problem. You don't need to do everything intentionally. It's fine if the hundreds of movements required to drive a car go on automatic. The problems come-up when **too much** of your life is running on automatic. Then every day is the same as the day before: Get up. Wash. Drive. Sit in office cubicle. Drive. Watch TV. Sleep.

Having just a little bit more self-control will help you be both more calm and also more productive. You will make better decisions because you are coming from a place of clarity, not from the rat-race people call "normal life".

Exercise your ability to stop and start things. You are able to stop talking when you like and start talking when you like, to stop biting your nails and to start, and to stop drinking coffee and to start etc..

Love Is to Give Attention, Time and Space Attention

Love is life's primary lesson, all other lessons are secondary. If you have solved the Love issue, that covers all other issues. Where there is lack, any lack at all, **lack of friends, lack of joy, lack of money, lack of health, there was always lack of Love first**.

You can actively give yourself or others Love by giving Attention, time and space. The Old English word for fear (which is the opposite of Love) is *angst*. This word comes from the Germanic word *"eng"*, which means tight, narrow or contracted.. Anytime a tightness arises it is because you are not giving yourself or others enough time, space or Attention.

When a client of yours starts complaining, it's because you have not given that client Love. Give that client either more time, more Attention or more space, and they will stop complaining.

When a spouse starts becoming a stranger in your own house, spend more time with him/her. Or, if you think you don't have time, then give more Attention in the little time you do spend. Or, if you don't have Attention either, give your spouse the space to say, do and be whatever he/she wants. If you have neither time, Attention nor space, relax for goodness sake!

If your body is feeling unwell, open up and give it more love. Sit or lie many an hour with your body only. That's the whole purpose of going to bed when you fall ill. Going to bed gives you the opportunity to send Love and appreciation to your body. It's the purpose of lying around in a sun-chair at an outdoor spa.

If you lack income, open-up and send more Love to yourself, others and the world. Release your resentment of rich people, of success, toward working, your resentment of everything. Give the issue some time, space and Attention.

Giving Space: Allowing things to unfold naturally. Allowing others to be who they are, without trying to change or control them; allowing life to unfold naturally.

Giving Attention: Looking at, listening to, thinking about something or someone. Being with someone or something, without constant preoccupation with yourself or your own "issues".

Giving Time: Spending an amount of time with someone or something. Patiently resting with someone or something. Enjoying time spent with someone or something without restlessly going to and fro.

Pleasure Delay

Most children are not able to delay gratification. If you offer them a small candy bar now or a bigger one later, most will choose the smaller one. This tendency to want immediate and instant results and gratification lessens with maturity. Unfortunately, some adults still display this. I recently watched a grown man pay $700 more for a gadget because he couldn't wait a week, for the gadget to be reduced in price by 50%.

I frequently refer to "being source". "Being source" means being *cause* of your Attention and emotions rather than letting the world play you like a ball. If you *are source* of your energy, you don't desperately "need" anything. You have no problem delaying so-called "pleasures". In fact, since you know that all happiness comes from within, nobody can control or lure you with all of these supposed "pleasures". Does this mean you no longer strive for pleasures? No, it means you are no longer a slave to them. And because you are no longer slave to them you enjoy them so much more than someone constantly seeking instant gratification.

Do not turn your spiritual journey into seeking ultimate or rapid results, but into a *long-term lifestyle of growth*, appreciation and constant learning. There is no "ultimate goal" to "reach". If there were, you would immediately stop learning and stop growing. All challenges are fantastic opportunities to grow; opportunities to embrace whatever comes up.

Replace gratification with gratitude. **Seeking gratification is what makes you weak. Giving gratitude makes you powerful.** Seeking gratification implies lack. Giving gratitude implies abundance.

There are many ways to implement this lesson into your life. You don't have to have sex on your first date, not even on the second. It's so much more intense if you can delay it for a bit. You don't have to have chocolate right now, you can have some later. An experiment: Try to have your favorite food when you don't want it, and don't have your favorite food when you want some. That would completely break your conditioning regarding food, putting you back in a source-position rather than being a victim of your cravings.

Awareness Intensified

Exercise "Intensifying Attention": Examine any object in detail until you "lose yourself" in it. Become aware of details you had not noticed before. You know you've lost yourself within the object once you forget your daily life, time, space, your surroundings, and urgencies. After you've lost yourself in that "reality" to a certain extent, "wake yourself up" again by releasing Attention and looking around. Repeat this a few times. This can also be done with thoughts. As elaborated on in many of my books and articles, intensifying focus and the release of focus are valuable psycho-spiritual abilities that can be used for many purposes. I will leave it up to you to find out what those purposes might be.

Exercise "Intensifying Awareness": Look at something. But while looking at it remain aware of other things outside of the periphery of your view. All you're doing here is focusing on something while remaining *aware* of other things. Focus without fixation. So you might be looking at a car, but at the same time remain aware of the tree at the border of your vision and the other cars outside of your field of vision. This can be done with objects, thoughts and even with people. While they talk to you, you remain aware of other things and do not become hypnotized by the person.

Levels of Awareness

There are three basic levels of Awareness:

1. Thinking

2. Imagining

3. Observing

Thinking-mode can be split into a lower-level of reactive, unconscious and negative thinking and a higher-level of intellectual reasoning. The thinking-self is predominantly concerned with its survival and gain, with avoiding pain and getting pleasure. The thinking-self is the mode of Awareness most people are on. They can be easily manipulated by appealing to their wants and worries. The thinking-self (ego/mind) only gets its data from what the mind has recorded throughout life. Within normal thinking, there is hardly any access to the soul-plane or the real-you. This level of self has assembled thoughts and identities taken from others or in resistance to others. Although the thinking-self is an elevation from the purely instinctual animal-self (which would be a level zero on the scale above), it is still pretty muddled and chaotic. As one progresses in energy and ascends through higher levels of Awareness, some of the thinking-self is still left, but that thinking is more refined and creative.

The second level of Awareness is imagination. In order to activate it one must access frames of reference and information outside of that which the mind has recorded in the past. One begins defining one's own thoughts, making one's own choices and assuming responsibility for where one's Attention goes. At this level of Awareness, one can imagine or think of something different than the circumstances are presenting, and therefore move forward with more optimism than if one were only a reactor-to-the-circumstances. There is still a lot of thinking-ness mixed in with this level, but now that thinking-ness accesses some of the soul-plane.

The third level of Awareness is observation. Rather than contracting and trying to dissect reality through thinking (which is actually a subtle form of resistance), one is simply open, aware and looking at what is happening. The thinking-self can be utterly oblivious to what is actually happening (especially when in a state of fear) while the observing-self is acutely aware of what is **really going on** in any given situation. This observing-self is beyond the body, beyond the mind and even beyond the imagining-self. Nothing can ever hurt it because it is infinite and eternal. It is the only stable and reliable part of your overall persona and energy-field. This aspect of self is awoken in the Infinity Course. To activate the initial levels of the observer, you need to slow-down to observe what is happening independent of the constant stream of thoughts. You need to take a time out and see if you can just be-with-what-is and observe it. Under observation-without-thinkingness (judgment, labels, resistance, memories) anything not true dissolves, anything not real dissolves.. This is how the observer-mode can be used to dissolve difficulties. In this state you realize that the way you thought things were…are only the way you thought they were…that they are not fundamentally real. At the lower levels of the observer-mode there is still some thinking-ness and imagining-ness left. There is also a distinct and unique identity present...the more real YOU, beyond all the superficial masks you wear. This state and viewpoint is more relaxed, more humorous, more able and more far-sighted. At the higher-levels of the observer-mode there is hardly any thinking-ness at all, it is replaced by bliss.

Peripheral & Detailed Awareness

Awareness can be *detail-focused* or *peripheral*. Both modes are of distinct value. Peripheral Awareness is more open and deals more with context than content. Peripheral Awareness is to de-stick Attention from what the world thinks you should be focusing on and to become less of the effect of those things. People habitually stick Attention to what is being shown and rarely become peripherally aware of the *space* which allows for the content. For example, the content called "sound" and "noise" can only appear in the wider context of silence. Buildings and trees (content) can only appear in the wider context of air and space.

If you watch a disturbing scene on a movie screen, and you would like to reduce the impact of that scene, stop looking at detail and look what else is going on in the scene. The center of the screen may feature a gruesome monster, but the scenes backdrop may have some nice flowers and buildings. Or you might become even more peripherally aware by noticing the frame of the movie screen itself or the movie theatre audience. The same technique can be used with movies of the mind, where you can learn not to zoom into the habitual focal point, but become peripherally aware. This frees you from the need to keep re-creating negative mind-content. For meditation-practitioners it is also important to note that the mind runs on by itself and is not really that relevant. Trying to "stop thinking" only involves you more in the contents of the mind because it is a reaction of the mind. .

If you close your eyes and look at a thought, notice the empty space around that thought. Reduce your reaction to thought. That is peripheral Awareness of context rather than content. From here it is easier to shift to a better thought or not stick to any thought at all.

When people enter a room full of people their Attention usually goes to people they deem important. What you can do instead is remain aware of the room in its entirety or of what else is going on.

If you talk or think about the same things all the time, you have been brainwashed. That is a state of "compulsive Attention". You may have set out to consciously focus on something, but it may have become obsessive. What are the things you have been thinking about and involved in the most?

Even if these are things or people you love, constantly having them on your mind is not necessarily beneficial. Anything other than the Infinite is destined to change, so by always thinking of something or someone, you are placing your reliance on that which will fade away. Life is full of phases, and the phase you are in right now will likely be irrelevant to you in 10 years.

So what is it you think is so important that you have to focus on it all the time? Some person? Some subject? A job? A goal? Money? The idea here is that you do not have to keep thinking of these things for them to go well. Actually, too much thinking can be an obstruction to those things flowing in your life. Quit thinking about money in a resistant or worrisome way, and money starts flowing. I say to people who want more money: "If you can't think about money positively, don't think about it at all.".You can deal with things while they are happening and not weeks before. If you have an important meeting in 2 weeks there is no use in worrying about it until that time. You can deal with it when and if it comes up. Big performance tonight? See if you can spend the morning and afternoon completely unconcerned about tonight's performance (unless you are preparing, of course). Once you become too preoccupied with something, you turn it into an obsession or some cult to follow. You make something external more important than your internal state. Don't.

To become peripherally aware would mean that while you are with a loved one, you are focused on him/her, but maintain some Awareness of the rest of your life. Or while you are at work you are focused on work, but still aware of the rest of life. By that I don't mean that you think about other things while doing one thing. You should be focused on the thing you are doing at the moment, but not always to an extent that you lose yourself in it completely. It's like a wonderful book: You can lose yourself in it, but you don't become obsessed with the book. You could put it aside any time and do something else.

Detailed focus is of more value if it is done intentionally, instead of getting sucked in by something. Focus-to-detail is the main factor of success in life. If you want to become a well-off lawyer for example, the studies required for that are mostly concerned with focus-to-detail to a much larger extent than any normal human being would do. And that is what makes you competent and trustworthy in the eyes of your clients.

Good meditation is to either have full peripheral Awareness, which is Awareness of the ultimate context (infinity), or full detailed focus which is single-pointedness. These two modes slow-down the thinking process allowing you to become more intensely aware.

Questions for Higher Awareness

These are questions you can ask yourself throughout a week, month or lifetime. They will naturally increase the depth of Awareness and sense of meaning and aliveness in life.

1. What value does my life have?

2. How can I be of service to the Most High?

3. How can I be of service to humanity?

4. If I lost my job, position, status, what meaning/value would my life still have?

5. What would I do if I lost everything?

5. What would I do if I already had everything?

6. What or who, if anything, would I die for?

7. What could I let go of because it no longer really serves me?

8. What has and has not worked last week?

9. What are my intentions for next week?

10. Where or with who could I practice being more loving and kind?

Slowing down for More Mindfulness
To increase mindfulness, take the steam out of stressful situations or regain control of something, deliberately slow-down your body movements.

In the recent Live Course, I had a student who felt nauseous on uneven surfaces such as boats and planes. Incidentally, there was a huge super-trampoline in the backyard of the house, where we could practice breaking through his limitation. As is his habit he became nauseous and got a headache once got on the trampoline. So we slowed down and broke down the whole thing into very slow movements, thereby desensitizing him to the experience. It was only after half an hour that we made our first tiny jump. And another half hour before we made a big jump. Because of the extreme slowing down and walking around in slow motion, he gradually regained control of his mind, emotions and actions, so by the end of the exercise he was able to jump on the trampoline without getting a headache or feeling like he had to vomit. A problem he had been carrying around ever since a traumatic event on a carousel in childhood was beginning to unravel. Some might consider this a "miracle cure", but it's actually nothing special. Any slowing-down equals gaining control over a reality. Imagine someone who is learning to dance. In order to master it he/she would first start with the movements very slowly and as he/she gained control, he/she would gradually speed up. And if it became too fast and he/she began to feel overwhelmed, he/she would just slow-down again and then gradually speed back up. Likewise, if your child feels overwhelmed in school all they have to do is slow-down and go back to what they missed and apply slower mindfulness to their issue.

Interestingly, life is like a hologram and slowing-down in one area improves other life areas too. So if you walk up the stairs in slow-motion, this will also have an effect on other things that occur throughout the day. You are then practicing mindfulness and being in conscious control of what is happening. Learning to slow-down is a gateway to more personal power.

Millions of parents struggle with "learning disabilities" of their children, but from my perspective, there really is no such thing. In my experience, there is no need to administer drugs against "ADHD". Instead, children *should be given,* and *give* themselves more **time, space and Attention**. They will then have no more "Attention deficit". It may take more Attention to prepare a proper meal for the child than to simply drop them some sweets. It may take more Attention to play with them personally than always let the TV entertain them. So, "extra" Attention reduces "Attention deficit".

Throughout the last 20 years I've helped numerous people overcome "learning disabilities" and "hyperactivity", by addressing their personal interests and likes, and by slowing the learning process down. If information is presented more quickly than the mind can process, the mind goes into freeze or stress. Relaxation and enjoyment are keys to learning. When I learn a foreign language, I simply slow-down my mind to a point where I fully grasp a grammatical concept or word, and then I move on. This saves me the effort of having to repeat the concepts over, and over, and over again...which also works, but takes more time overall. Constant repetition is a method of indoctrination of the mind, whereas proper perception is a method of learning. It is because of our inattentiveness that we get stuck or require repetition. Repetition is beneficial but only after one has already lost the natural ability to learn by perception alone. For example, in order to perceive a chair in your room, you don't really have to concentrate or repeat that there is a chair standing there...you merely "allow" perception of the chair, no effort required. The states of boredom, stress and impatience are overlays of the restless ego/mind. It is this part of yourself that you need to calm in order to fully dedicate yourself to whatever you are learning. If your child has learning difficulties, teach him/her to slow-down, to breathe, to be happier here-now. Usually there are emotional issues or unexpressed desires that are preventing the child or teenager from becoming fully present with the task at hand. If he/she him/herself is unwilling to become present, he/she can be tricked into presence with entertaining and interesting learning devices. But in time, he/she should also learn to become present of hihs/her own power, without the need for entertainment. Entertainment is actually a crutch a human being uses until they have learned to relax from within.

Slowing-down the mind can be done in several ways: By slowing-down body movements, by slowing-down one's breathing, and by slowing down speech. It is not that the slow-motion state doesn't get things done or makes one lazy. It only appears that way short-term. Long-term, the slow and deliberate person, the mindful person, gets more done because less effort is needed and thinking becomes more clear and vivid. Society's tendency not to slow-down and just-perceive, can be seen in the way they walk when they walk. A person will usually walk from A to B, without ever stopping on their path to have a look around. If someone were to secretly follow me and watch me walk, he/she would notice that I sometimes stop in mid-track and just stand there. As I just stand there, I look around and notice the area I am in. Only then would I resume walking. This behavior, perceived as "strange" by onlookers, puts me firmly in control of the overall flow of energy...be it my physical body, the mind, my emotions, my speech or anything else. Hence, I never feel rushed, out of control, overly emotional or worried. Neither criticism nor praise will get me out of my centered poise, and no opponent in the world will ever exhaust me if I am identified with the inner-calm of the witness/observer self, rather than the up-and-down waves of the ego-self.

"Time" is somewhat of an illusion. The mind perceives sequence, then superimposes the idea of some sort of linear time-track onto what is actually infinite and eternal Awareness and presence that is radiant and timeless. As you slow-down in daily life, you lessen the degree to which the rat-race has control of you and get more of a sense of this **timeless presence that permeates everything**.

Being too caught in the ego/mind and on some kind of "time-track" with deadlines has an abrasive effect on oneself. Slowing-down time by slowing-down your mind, your body movements and your speech, not only increases your deliberateness and control of any reality, it also allows you to perceive your surroundings with more **depth, color, texture and vividness**. People who practice meditation or mindfulness see "normal physical objects" differently than the rest of us.

I repeat it: "Slowing-down" does not mean becoming a lethargic person who doesn't get anything done and misses appointments. "Slowing down" is an inner state of mind that can "paradoxically" make you quicker externally. Quicker in productivity, creativity, more quick-witted and quicker in thought. Being inwardly restless (quick) does not make you quicker in external life.

You can leave the time-illusion any time by dedicating yourself more fully to whatever it is you are doing. Let's say you are sitting with some person you deem "unimportant", and your mind is wandering to "more important" people, or to your dog or to a friend, or to some other activity. In that instant, you are creating a time-track; creating an Attention-split. If you were to **breathe out your tension and dedicate yourself more fully** to the person in front of you and the task at hand, you would step-out of the Attention-split, step-out of the time-track, and total well-being would be the result. Every day offers many opportunities to be and become even more timeless. The opposite of wandering Attention is over-fixated Attention. That's what might happen when you sit across from a person you deem "very important". Attention then becomes fixed and frozen on that person at the expense of all else. The way to release this is to remain aware of your surroundings and other things happening in your life. Things and people are neither "very important" nor "unimportant", and Attention neither need to be fixed nor wandering but simply a calm and natural Awareness.

Could you be complete and happy just sitting there? I frequently asked this question in my workshops. It's a key question of life. Can you be happy before you get, before you have, before you do, before you acquire, before you know, before you see, before you meditate? If so, your meditation has slowed-down the thought-process to a point where you suddenly realize that happiness has nothing at all to do with external events. From that arises the essential happiness which is the **joy-of-being-alive.** This state need not be created, it is naturally present when your mind and stream of thought have been calmed. One way to slow-down your stream-of-thought is by retrieving importance and interest from it, just like you would retrieve importance and interest from a boring show on TV. Ninety percent of the contents of the mind are actually repetitive, narcissistic and boring anyway. Those who meditate can clearly see how irrelevant much of the mind-contents are. But we keep the babbling mind alive by thinking it's "mine" and what's mine is "very interesting". As you let go of this tendency, the surface-mind is at rest, and what then surfaces is higher-quality thought along with a lot of silence and peace of mind. There are few things more precious than peace of mind. Peace of mind brings a new experiential-quality to any situation you are in…whether you are driving your car, playing a ball game, on a date, working at your computer, repairing a bike, having a conversation or standing in a line at some counter, you take either tension of mind or peace of mind along with you everywhere you go.

Group Games for Awareness

These are "group games" you can play as a facilitator, coach, or teacher in your workshop or seminar to increase Awareness and creative consciousness in a playful and fun way. I have used these games to break the ice and demonstrate important principles at the same time.

1. Simon Says

I have played this one in nearly every seminar I've conducted because it teaches powerful lessons on reactive-ness vs. self-determined and aware consciousness.

The leader or coach gives various commands such as "stand up" or "put your left arm out" or "sit down" or "walk around" or "put your right hand on your nose and your left hand on your right ear" (next command: "switch!"), etc. But the group does not obey all commands. It only obeys the commands that begin with the words "Simon says".

So if I say, "Simon says sit down," the group sits down. If I say, "Sit down," they are not supposed to react. The game is continued until all participants are in a non-reactive state and not following any of the commands that "Simon didn't say." They are in a state of conscious Awareness, present, focused and clear.

Most groups are easy to "get", but there are some groups that are a little more evolved and will get it right on the very first or second round. Such groups require additional tricks to get them to lose concentration. A few examples of such tricks: I get the group to run around ("Simon says run around.") and then I shout "Stop!" (Simon did not say stop,) Even in evolved groups, there will be usually one or two that follow the command and stop. Another one is to pretend the game is over. I'd, for example, have everyone raise their hands ("Simon says raise your arms and hands."), and then drop my hands while saying, "Alright, that's it." There will usually be one or two who fall for it. Another way to overwhelm Attention-spans is by speeding the game up. But after a few minutes most participants will have "gotten it", and no longer react to the tricks. Awareness of tricks makes you immune to them.

After the game you might want to explain the difference between being reactive (acting in a knee-jerk manner, without consideration, based solely on impulse) vs. acting through conscious decision or with forethought. That is one of the many things this game addresses.

2. Concentration-Clapper

This is another seminar-favorite. It is ideally played by a group of 5-7 people. So if you have 20 in your seminar, there would be four teams playing, then perhaps the winner(s) of those teams play in a final match.

The group sits in a circle tight enough so every person can *cross their hands with each other.* You cross your right hand with the left hand of the person sitting right of you, and you cross your left hand with the person sitting left of you. Everybody has their hands resting on the floor and crossed in this way. First make sure that everyone is comfortable in their positions.

Before the game begins, there is a practice round. If I clap my hand to the floor once, the next hand, clockwise of me claps. And the next. And the next.. Go through the whole circle at least once in this way. If someone claps to the floor twice, the direction changes. So "clap once" goes in one direction, "clap twice" changes the direction. Once this is understood, the game begins: Any hand that makes a movement out of turn or hesitates, is removed from the game. The hand left at the end of the game, wins. If there are two hands from different players left at the end, two players win. The person with the most calm will have the most concentration. Effort can also win the game, but effort will not win several games or long-term because energy is depleted. Effort needs to take frequent breaks before it resumes. **Calm, on the other hand, can keep Attention for very long periods of time**. Of course, those who invest neither tension (effort) nor release-of-tension (calm) will not win it. This game is also fun and appropriate for party-settings.

Those are some of the experiential lessons of this game. A scale of winning-potential from none to full, might look like this:

Level 1: Confusion/Distraction/Nervousness

Level 2: Boredom/Inattentiveness
Level 3: Effort/Concentration
Level 4: Calm/Awareness

3. Moods

Dozens of different emotions and moods are written on pieces of paper and then placed into a cup. The emotions are also written on a paper or chart for the group to view. If you like you could even write them as a scale from negative to positive. The first person whose turn it is, sits on a chair in front of the group and does their best to non-verbally occupy the state/emotion he/she drew out of the cup. It is the groups job to guess which state he/she is occupying. The person occupying the chair and the emotion is given some time to "get into it". Then, once he/she is in the emotion he/she gives a thumbs-up. The first person to guess the state correctly, is given a point. Depending on the size of the group the person in the chair then does another emotion (if the group is smaller than 7, for instance) or the next person comes up to the chair (if the group is larger than 7). Give the person who wins the game a prize. Also give the person who has the most intense emotional (a room changing wave of vibration!) a prize too.

Depending on how advanced the group is, there should be no acting, mimicking, talking or role-playing from the person occupying the emotion. Advanced groups will be able to **feel** the emotion in the room, without hints needing to be given. In groups not used to work in energy and consciousness, some facial expression is allowed. A variation of this game is that each person sitting in the emotion-chair is given a neutral and random text to read (such as from a book or magazine) and aims to "get into the mood" throughout. This is an easier variation that might be played with beginners.

This game addresses changing one's state (realizing just how quickly you can change your emotional state!), and sensing other people's condition. You learn that through mental focus alone you can not only change your own state, but also bring a whole group of people up or down with you.

4. Creating Definition

The aim of this technique is to develop imagination and inner will. As a game it can spark a lot of laughter.

A word that nobody in the group knows is chosen from the dictionary. Every person (or team) writes down what they think the *definition* of the word is. The person who read the word out writes down the correct definition (and if he/she likes he/she can also participate in the game and add an incorrect definition on a separate piece of paper). All definitions are then put into a cup or hat and scrambled. Someone then reads out each definition while the group takes votes on which definition is correct. Those who guessed it correctly score. The game is continued in this way for a number of words (which you can pre-define before the game) with each person getting a turn looking up definitions.

Creating your own definitions is a good exercise in higher-thought and reality-creating. We have been too reliant on the world to tell us "what things mean" and are, and it can be empowering to decide for yourself what some things are. In creating definitions and meanings, concepts and words, emotions and worlds are created..

5. Noticing Things

This game is about making changes to the room you are in, to your clothes or to an object, and then checking whether those temporarily absent notice the changes. Of all the games presented in this series it most directly addresses *Awareness*. There are many variations in which this game can be played.

In a group for instance, you divide the team by two. Team A is given a minute to look at team B. Team A then leaves the room while each member of team B changes something about their appearance, such as taking off earrings, removing a tie, untucking a shirt, swapping shirts with someone else, etc. Team A then returns and must notice what has been changed. The roles are then reversed. This variation alone can be played in many sub-variations. You may wish to keep score or not.

The other variation is to make changes to the room instead of the people. You might, for example, define that 20 changes were made and see if the person or group can spot all of them. Or you can have them score according to how many alterations they spot. If played in teams, every change noticed is a point for one team, any change missed is a point for the other team.

Most people are oblivious to most of the things happening most of the time. The purpose of this game is to help reduce that just a little.

You can also play this one alone by simply going for a walk and noticing what has changed compared to last time you walked there. Or, by going for a walk and simply noticing things you have not noticed before. In each case, you will have increased your sense of Awareness, and the world will look a little brighter and more interesting.

6. The Power of Poise

I developed this group-game based on the Reality Creation Technique. I've used it in every single seminar and course of the last five years. One person sits on the "hot chair" at the front of the room. That person's job is to "remain poised in their vision/goal/intention". So he/she will either visualize his/nher intention, defend it verbally, or simply feel it no matter what comes up. It is the group's job to flow negative energy and words, and try to get that person out of his/her state of poise and confidence. The idea of this game is for the person in the hot-chair to re-affirm and physically feel fulfillment, and for the group to represent "the world" that tries to "bring you down". There are many variations in which this can be played. For example the hot-chair person does not have to speak. They can simply remain present. Or they can talk themselves into a higher belief in their vision. The referee makes sure that the group drops sufficiently negative beliefs and the hot-chair-person stays in his/her power. If there is any indication that the hot-chair-person has been swayed to the negative, the game is interrupted and he/she is given time to re-align with his/her vision. It is continued until it is seen that the person can easily maintain poise no matter what negativity comes up.

This is a game in which the group is meant to have fun with negative-beliefs and objections, while the hot-chair-person is meant to grow bigger and stronger in his/her convictions and poise (instead of smaller and smaller as is "normal" with the onslaught of negativity). Done correctly and under professional guidance, this is the most powerful game I have administered thus far.

7. The Balloon Stomp Game

While winning this game does require a dose of heightened Awareness it is more of an icebreaking/fun-time game than one that specifically trains consciousness. It is best used after lunch or to get a group that has been sitting for too long into some movement. You need two balloons per participant and strings (such as strings with which you pack gifts). The balloons are blown-up and with the strings, tied to each ankle, so that a balloon is dangling from the outside of your ankles on both sides. Once everybody is ready you give the command: "The last person standing with a balloon wins!" The group then proceeds to stomp each other's balloons out. Those players who lose both their balloons retreat from the game.. Pushing, shoving and other physical manipulation apart from the stomping, is not allowed. Enjoy all the noise.

8. Blind Catcher

This is played in a group where the people know each other a little (not on the first day). One person is blindfolded. His task is to go looking for other players around the room. The players in the room are not allowed to move their feet, they must stay standing in their spot. But they are allowed to twist and turn their bodies so as not to be touched by the Blind-Catcher. When the Blind-Catcher does touch someone, his/her task is to identify who he/she is, by touching his/her face and clothing. If the Blind-Catcher correctly identifies the person at the first guess, he/she becomes the Blind-Catcher, and puts on the blindfold. If incorrectly identified, the Blind-Catcher must continue on elsewhere until someone he/she can identify is found.

9. Activity

This is based on the official board-game Activity. The game addresses creativity, Awareness, communication and role-playing. The group has to guess a word. The person performing the activity can do so in one of three ways:

- Make a drawing
- Act-it-out (charades/pantomime)

- Describe it (without naming the word)

Whoever guesses the word first (words may be drawn from a prepared box, a dictionary or given by someone) scores. Alternatively, you can agree to focus on only one of the modes of communication (draw, act, describe) per round.

10. Rampage of Appreciation

One variation of playing this is to have several groups-of-two sitting across from each other. Person A asks, "What do you like?" And Person B responds by naming something he/she likes in detail. Person A may prompt Person B to go into even more detail by asking, "What else about that do you like?" or, "Can you tell me more about that?" Person A listens attentively. Then Person A asks: "What else do you like?" to bring up another thing Person B describes in detail. This continues on-and-on with an increasing number of things Person B likes and describes in detail, until you can see a very obvious and marked improvement in the mental, emotional and physical state of Person B. Roles are then reversed.

The purpose of this exercise/game is a rapid improvement of a person's state. When positive things are elaborated on in detail, the mind tends to "lose itself" in that, resulting in emotional upliftment.

The Viewpointing Technique

Get comfortable and close your eyes. Extend your Attention to another person. Look at him/her from all sides: From the left, the right, from above, from close-up, from far away. Seeing from all viewpoints gives you a **complete intuitive knowledge** of him/her. Now look at he/she from the perspective of his/her father or mother. What opinion might his/her father/mother have of him/her? Then look at he/she from the perspective God might have of him/her. Next, look at him/her from the vantage point of someone who dislikes him/her. What negative opinion/s does he/she have of him/her? Next, from the vantage point of someone who likes him/her. What positive opinion does he/she have of him/her? Now from the viewpoint of someone who desires him/her. Next from the viewpoint of someone who does not know him/her. Experiment with a few other viewpoints.

The viewpoints you resist occupying limit your experience. You limit your soul by rejecting a number of viewpoints. The more sides you can see someone or something from, the more your intelligence, knowledge and intuition increase. Applying this technique on a person will help you to know the person more fully. It can be applied to a friend, a foe, a boss and employee, a spouse, a relative, a celebrity, a discarnate being or anyone else you wish to gain more intuitive "flashes" and knowledge about.

The Viewpointing-Technique and Emotional Releasing

Remember an event that was painful or emotionally charged. Put yourself back to that memory or scenery. Looking at that event as a thought-form or energy-form, view it from close up, from far away and then from the left, right, top and bottom. Rotate it so that you have viewed it from all possible angles. Next, view it from several mental angles: Look at it how someone who is very, very serious would see the event. Then look at it how someone very humorous might view the event. Then be someone indifferent and view the event. Be someone angry and view the event. Be someone bored and view the event. Pretend you are someone who wants more, much more of that. Pretend you reject it completely. Be someone who thinks it's dangerous. Be someone who thinks it's good. Be someone at peace. Finally, view it without any label or opinion whatsoever. You have no opinion on it. What happens?

Did you notice how your experience and feeling of the event changes depending on **your viewpoint**? Do you realize how powerful this lesson is?

Viewpoint Shifting and Labels

Look at an object in your surroundings. Next, label it as ugly. Tell yourself that it is very, very ugly. Look for evidence that it is ugly. Notice aspects of it that might be viewed as ugly. After 1 or 2 minutes of this, change your label and tell yourself that it is beautiful. Repeat that it is stunningly beautiful a few times. Look for evidence that it is beautiful. See its inherent beauty. Next, release that label, and simply view the object as an object, without label. Perceive what-it-really is. It is from the neutral perspective that you perceive its actual vibratory frequency and energy-level, without distortion. Your label of things changes the way you experience those things. Some of the properties of an object or event are inherent (absolute), but the rest of it is created by the meaning/s you assign.

It is your viewpoint, perspective, label or assignment-of-meaning that, in part, determines how you experience and respond to life. Only your soul is able to see things without label-distortion. The soul is able to occupy many different viewpoints and therefore sees the big picture. To expand consciousness, try to see your spouse as more than only a spouse...see them from the perspective of a friend, a lover, a parent, a child. Try to see your company as more than only one perspective...from the eyes of an employee, a boss, a customer. This enormously increases your intelligence. If you like politics, see an event from the perspective of many different political views. And so on.

One step higher, *presume no reliable knowledge of anything at all.* Allow Source/Soul/God to reveal the meaning of things. Any mind/body/ego perspective is incomplete.

Advanced Viewpoint-Shifting

Sit comfortably, having placed another empty chair near you. See an ideal version-of-yourself sitting in that other chair. When you have taken some time to get a clear picture of that person, walk over, take-in the seat of that person, take on the viewpoint of that person, become that person. Sit in that chair and feel what it feels like to be that person. Allow the energy field of this new you to stream through your body. Look at the world from the eyes of this person. Feel yourself as not only having a new present and a new future, but also a new past. Finally, it's nothing "new" because that is who you have been all along. Let go of the exercise and proceed to your regular daily activities. In your week's schedule, note down a few activities that this version-of-you would be doing, and actually go out and do some of them.

Radical Viewpoint Shifting

Remember an event that was painful, traumatic, emotionally laden or especially serious. Before reading on, please put yourself into that serious mood.

While having your Attention on that painful event, imagine the head of state or president of your country and another head of state both wearing dotted bikinis and playing table-tennis. View their semi-nude bodies while they are playing the match. Keep your Attention on the silly image, and at the same time on the problematic event.

What happened? Were you able to maintain your serious mood or did something shift inside? Keep practicing focusing on your seriousness, while at the same time looking at more silly images until you feel the shift. Seriousness keeps problems stuck. Surprise and humor shift consciousness.

In-Between Times

You may think that sitting in a traffic jam is no fun. You may think that it's a waste of time. You may think differently after reading this.

The part of us referred to as "mind" or "ego" is kind of restless and subtly irate. It thinks that life is defined by points A and B, not by the times in-between. Because it doesn't like the in-between-times, it will tend to go hazy in those times, and only reawaken to alertness again once point B has been reached. The problem here is that most of life is spent "in-between times", not at points A or B. The reaching of a destination or achieving of a goal is over within minutes or even seconds. What about all the rest of the time?

So there you are in a traffic jam. It's kind of muggy and hot and there is no sign of the traffic moving anywhere. You started somewhere at point A (home perhaps) and are traveling toward point B (work perhaps). The sense of impatience and frustration with the traffic jam comes from the mind drifting back and forth between points A and B, labeling those moments as "much better" and investing very little interest in the time in-between, as if that time were bereft of opportunity and energy. This traffic jam couldn't possibly hold any fascinating contacts, ideas, opportunities, riches, beauty, wellness...or could it? And it's certainly not OK to be here now...or is it? I have looked closely at the faces of my fellow traffic-jam-drivers. They seem to believe that frowning is obligatory.

The secret of lasting happiness? Knowing that the in-between-times are full of life and energy. Happiness is not at point A or B but in-between those, because that is where most of life is happening. Lasting happiness is knowing that ordinary life can be extraordinary. You can have an extraordinary ordinary life.

You may have noticed that the lower your mood, the more important it becomes to "get to some other place". My hypochondriac grandmother was often this way when she was in a bad mood. When I was young I recall us taking her for day-trips. We might be in the zoo, admiring a giraffe and she'd ask, "So where are we going for lunch?" Once we were at lunch, rather than enjoying it she'd ask, "Where are we going afterwards?" Afterwards we took a stroll through the town, and she'd ask, "What are we having for dinner?" My parents rolled their eyes because she was never really "being here now" but always with "what's next?" She was chronically unhappy most of the time. If you have ever experienced children in a car, train or plane, you'd know that the worse their mood and the less focused-on-something they are, the more they will be asking, "Mommy, when do we arrive?"

Some people mistakenly believe that being-here-now entails having no plans for the future, being dull, slow or being complacent. But that's a misconception. Calm is not dullness. A lot of people try to pass-off dullness as calm, but they are a different energy altogether. Here-now-ness does not mean being slow. As long as your slowness or quickness is deliberate rather than reactive, both are a product of presence and Awareness. For example: The other day I washed the dishes of 7 visitors after they had left (No, I don't have a dish-washer because I use dish-washing as meditation-practice.) I took great pleasure in doing it faster than I had ever washed dishes before. The whole thing was done in a record 15 minutes. But this quick-pace was not a result of reactive-ness or of worry, but of deliberate intent. See the difference? Likewise, when I slow-down in order to calm-down, it is usually the result of deliberate intent, not of dullness. There is this grocery shop nearby. I don't visit it anymore because the people working there are so slow, it's nerve-wracking. But they aren't slow out of a calm, Tai-Chi-like Awareness and here-now-ness, they are slow out of a tired dullness. Big difference.

Right there where you are…right now…it's OK to be here. If you're sitting in the park at a fountain, don't pull-out your smartphone so quickly…see if you can first get a sense of the sights, sounds and smells around you. When you rest into the here-now you start **feeling more real.** That's what this is about. There is no need to escape from the moment. There is nowhere else you "need" to be. If you "needed" to be elsewhere, you would be elsewhere. As you **allow** yourself to be precisely where you are right now, no matter where you are, stress and tension are reduced. Sure, you might *prefer* to be elsewhere, but it's not what you *need* or *must* have. Sitting in that traffic jam is a good chance to release all sorts of unbecoming thoughts.

I am grateful for my education in meditation. It's allowed me to learn to, "Let the experience be what it is." This reduces resistance. Resistance reduction reduces pain. When nothing is happening within you, meditation becomes unbearable. Sitting in the here-now becomes unbearable. But where a lot of energy is pulsating within you, you can be happy with wherever.

What if you were caught in a time-loop where you experience every single day twice? So you wake-up in the morning, and it's the same date it was yesterday all over again. So you have a second chance at everything. You could undo awkward or unconscious moments and behavior. The result of this would be that, the second time around, you would be much less tense and more conscious. But here's the trick: You don't have to live everyday twice to become more conscious. You can live *this* day as if it were your second chance to do it better. What if you were given a second chance at life? What would you do better than the last time? Well...you can already start doing that now. You can begin to cherish the ordinary life in-between-times. What if it were the last traffic-jam you ever experienced in all of eternity? Or what if the traffic jam was a secret gate to a higher-state of consciousness?

Life is not at all about the "high points" but about all the rest. If we can find serenity in those moments and not only when something extraordinary is happening, we have reached an awesome state of consciousness.

Here's why we subconsciously suppress higher Awareness: When you are surrounded by foul smells for a long time; you learn to suppress your ability to smell. When your heart is broken; you learn to suppress your openness toward love (so that it doesn't get broken again). When you are surrounded by falling bombs; you learn to suppress your enjoyment of life. When what you see is horrible; you learn to suppress your clarity of vision. So Awareness and Perception gradually become smaller and smaller. Life being a perfect mix of nice things and not-so-nice things, we see, feel, hear, smell and taste many things we do not want to see, feel, hear, smell and taste. So we think that shutting-off Awareness is the best solution. But of course it's not the best solution because then we also fail to perceive the beauty; fail to learn and grow. The solution is not to shut-down Awareness of things, but to release them within. So, when there is a traffic jam for example, and it's been going on for 2 hours and you get all agitated and cranky, it's time to release those emotions rather than blaming the traffic. Then, you emerge from the traffic jam clear and happy.

See Things as They Are, Not as They Seem to Be

When we project, we do not see things as they are, we see them as we are. Projections are made up of secret inner-desires, expectations, assumptions, speculations and beliefs. Just because someone is wearing a doctor's suit, a police uniform or a priestly robe does not automatically mean that they are trustworthy. "They are trustworthy," is only a projection. You'll do better looking into their eyes instead of at their uniforms to find that out.

Have you ever found yourself walking the streets in the dark and seeing something in the distance that you think might be some kind of person standing there, but when you get up closer it's an object? That's projection. And if you have too much of that or perhaps even paranoid fantasies of some killer standing on the side of the street, and it turns-out to be a sign-post, you really should do some relaxation or meditation practice. "But won't this protect me from real killers?" you ask. No it won't. If you project too much, you no longer see clearly. Then, a killer could come in the guise of a policeman, and you wouldn't notice because your intuition is covered-up by too much thinking.

Have you ever experienced someone saying, "Yes" to a deal you wanted, and you then considered it a "huge success" before the contract was even signed? In that moment you were projecting and lost contact with reality. As long as the contract isn't signed, there is nothing at all going on. You'll notice that when a few days later, the person that said "Yes" suddenly changes his mind and says "No". The same thing goes for negative projection of course. Just because someone says, "No, you won't get the job," does not mean it is so. And if you actually believe that you won't get it, you might be creating that fact right in that moment!

Have you ever thought you have met the "love of your life" and later found out he or she does not care one bit about you? You were projecting.

Recently, someone shared how terrifying airplane turbulence "is". I told her that I had just stepped off an airplane that had experienced major turbulence. "Wow, really? Your life must have flashed before your eyes. I bet you were really afraid." But I hadn't been. I was just wondering whether my Coke Zero can was safely tucked-in. "But seriously though...you must have felt really terrible!" she exclaimed with a worried look on her face.

She was *projecting*, of course. She was taking her personal feelings toward airplane turbulence, and *assuming* that I shared the same feelings. But I don't share the same feelings about airplane turbulence. If I told her I don't mind a little turbulence, would it register with her? I don't know. What I do know is that psychological projection is a foremost problem in human communication...especially when it's not clear what's real and what's only projection.

For example, what is valid criticism and when is someone just being bitchy? Here's a good indicator: If you very easily and quickly lose calm at what he/she says, then at least some of the criticism is valid. It means he/she is touching upon something that is within your subconscious; your subconscious is a co-creator in their complaint. But if you remain fairly reasonable, and it takes a little more negativity to get you angry, then the criticism is likely invalid. Because it's not valid and you don't believe it, there is no initial reaction. Your mind doesn't compute with it because it has nothing to do with you.

Someone once suggested that I am psychopath or somehow criminally insane. This "criticism" of me, elicited no reaction at all. I was a little puzzled, but not at all defensive or hurt. If this person had continued to voice the criticism over and over again, I might have gotten angry at some point (due to the untruth of it), but the first time I heard it, it did not mean anything to me. Had that person said, "He has not properly prepared his seminar," that might have made me defensive, and I might have felt the urge to "set this person straight", and show he/she is "wrong". Why? Because he/she may have been right.

When one's own emotions are suppressed (consciously pushed away) and repressed (subconsciously pushed away) long and hard enough, a human being begins projecting negativity onto the external world, seeing danger, evil, bad intent and catastrophe everywhere else. After such deep-layered emotions, traumas and stresses are released, the person forgets all about those evils and once again returns to the fullness of who he/she is.

That is not to say that all negativity in the world is unreal and talk of such only projection. But there are plenty of bad things happening without the need for aggrandizing them with projection. What a projector does is go on a crusade of indignation, instead of simply acknowledging what is wrong and working to improve it.

What follows is an exercise to practice seeing-what-is. Seeing-what-is will help you navigate the oceans of life with more poise.

1. Look at something (a person, object, thought, place, thing, emotion, space, shape, etc.)

2. Notice what judgments, expectations, beliefs, labels, ideas, opinions and judgments come up while you observe it. Let these labels un-stack and run out. Let go of them.

3. View the item without label, opinion, judgment or fantasy...just-as-it-is. You will sense what its energy actually is intuitively and effortlessly.

Repeat this exercise with hundreds of people, objects, thoughts, places, things, emotions, spaces, shapes, etc. If you have the time, do this as a meditation for a full hour. It's very well worth it. Living in irreality costs you a lot of time, money and energy. If you are not sure what something is, what someone thinks and/or what a situation means, apply this exercise.

Body Posture and Well-Being

The last time I became aware of the connection between body posture and well-being was while sitting on my cruiser-style bicycle. Even though this bike is slower and less easy to ride and certainly more odd looking than a normal bike, I always feel much better on it. At first I didn't understand why. Why do I feel more clear-headed on this bike than on others? The answer came to mind promptly: *"It's because you are sitting **upright** on this one."* Wow. Could that be the reason? On other bicycles I am usually bending forward like a hunchback, but on this cruiser I sit upright, arms wide.

Body Posture from Inside Out

I've never practiced body-yoga, never been to the military and never took dancing lessons. My body-posture is lazy; I tend to lean on things. While working, I prefer lying on the sofa to sitting at the desk. Despite my shortcomings in this regard, I am fully cognizant that "stand straight, chest out, shoulders back!" changes my state of Awareness, provides more poise, strength and clearness of mind. When I really need to change my state for important events, I do put more Awareness to my body, its movements and its posture. On long trips by car, sitting upright will give me an extra hour of awake-and-alert time.

But these are deliberate efforts of will "from outside in", rather than natural or habitual inclinations "from inside out". Unless a certain posture-Awareness has been inculcated from childhood or drilled in practice-sessions, "good postures" won't be maintained. Nor do they have to be. I have found that the more well-being, the more I take-in good body postures effortlessly – without trying. Then it is coming "from inside out". A positive state of mind will have the body align and balance itself naturally. So you can drill yourself to have the proper posture – this is an arduous and lengthy process, or, you can simply increase your self-Awareness.

Self-Awareness includes being present in the moment, Awareness of your periphery and space-time situation, Awareness of your movements, Awareness of your emotional state and on-goings inside the body. For example, the body-scan meditation, available on my website is a good body-Awareness exercise. Because the body is always here-now, putting Attention to the body is a good way to get more into the now and away from past/future worries. All emotional pain comes from mental turbulence (thoughts that create mis-emotions). Entering the here-now reduces mental turbulence. This turbulence can, of course, also be reduced with focus-of-Attention. Being Attention-focused means you are able to stick to a task at hand, complete a project without distraction, follow a thought to its conclusion, quit looking for the next thing, and the next thing, and the next after that to do, say or purchase. For those who like browsing the Internet: Notice how when you are in a tired or uninspired state, you click and jump from page to page without being able to focus on one item exclusively.

There are a great variety of methods that offer a gentle mix of inside-out and outside-in body Awareness and Awareness-through-movement. A few of them are:

Tai Chi

Tai chi is an ancient Chinese tradition that, today, is practiced as a graceful form of exercise. It involves a series of movements performed in a slow, focused manner and accompanied by deep breathing. Tai chi, also called tai chi chuan, is a noncompetitive, self-paced system of gentle physical exercise and stretching. Each posture flows into the next without pause, ensuring that your body is in constant motion. Tai chi has many different styles. Each style may have its own subtle emphasis on various tai chi principles and methods. There are also variations within each style. Some may focus on health maintenance, while others focus on the martial arts aspect of tai chi (mayoclinic.org).

Feldenkrais

Feldenkrais aims to reduce pain or limitations in movement, to improve physical function, and to promote general well-being by increasing students' Awareness of themselves and by expanding students' movement repertoire. Feldenkrais taught that increasing a person's kinesthetic and proprioceptive self-Awareness of functional movement could lead to increased function, reduced pain, and greater ease and pleasure of movement (wikipedia.org).

Alexander Technique

The Alexander Technique, teaches people how to stop using unnecessary levels of muscular and mental tension during their everyday activities. It is an educational process rather than a relaxation technique or form of exercise. Practitioners say that certain problems are often caused by repeated misuse of the body over a long period of time, for example, by standing or sitting with one's weight unevenly distributed, holding one's head incorrectly, or walking or running inefficiently. The purpose of the Alexander Technique is to help people unlearn maladaptive physical habits and return to a balanced state of rest and poise in which the body is well-aligned (wikipedia.org).

…among many other methods. These days we are very much "in the head" because of our attachment to screens, computers and TV. But you are a physical being meant to experience reality, not only mentally but physically and that will increase your well-being.

You Have Options

It's good to have options. Not seeing them is the Top 10 List of "Common Problems People Have". If you have options, you have choice. Then you have less dependency on only one source.

When I was 19 years old I applied for a job. Then I sat around waiting for a positive message from that employer. Then I got rejected. Then I was disappointed. So I grew smart quick. Applying for only one job meant having only one option, meant having no choice, meant sitting around waiting, meant setting myself up for disappointment. So the next thing I did was to apply for close to a *hundred* jobs in writing and through going door-to-door. I wasn't going to sit around fixated on only one source. Lack of options creates fixation and dis-empowerment. I put my CV into a copy machine, made a hundred copies and sent it out with a short "application note". Of the 100 applications I had written, I got 5 positive responses back. So now I had five options and was **free to choose**. That felt much better. It felt better not to have to sit around waiting for "something to happen".

Even though ultimately I had no interest in being an employee, I learned my lesson about having options early-on. It has served me throughout life.

Granted, having too many options can be overwhelming and cause one to lose focus. That's why it's good to eventually choose one or two options of the many you have. But before that, it's good to have many options to choose *from*. And to have many, you either have to **see** them or **create** them (as I did by applying for a hundred jobs at once).

If you are often sitting around on weekends, waiting for your partner to show-up, it's because you are fixated on your partner, and don't see other options on how to spend your weekend. If you are looking for a relationship and only have one person in mind, I recommend you look at and talk to **hundreds** of potential partners, not just one (note that I said *look at* a hundred, not *choose* a hundred. That helps you be more discerning and less fixated. If you are seeking a new business venture, don't go for the first offer that presents itself, look at **hundreds** of options and then cut them down to the best three. Then make your choice.

Furthermore, there is not only one way to fix meals, not only one way to heal yourself, not only one way to respond to someone, not only one way to raise kids, not only one way to conduct your job, not only one way to use the day. You have plenty of options. Any difficulty you face is a matter of **constricted-Attention**; of being blind to the many possibilities and ways of seeing. When you change the way you see, what you see changes.

A recent student of mine sells services to companies. But he had made himself dependent on only ONE company. That company was the source of all of his income. Once he had landed a contract with them, he became fixated and quit looking at other options. That's a dangerous situation I will never allow myself to be in. When I was 19 years old and finally got a job, I didn't rest on that or become fixated, I kept on looking for better options. And better ones. And better ones. And I still do today. From this point forward (from ANY point forward) there are many paths I could go on. I can see them. I can imagine them. So if I can imagine them, then they are achievable. And I'll choose the ones that shine the brightest.

In childhood we are programmed for an extremely limited set of options. "You have to go to this school, there is no other," and, "You either eat your meal, or you get punished." And in childhood it's useful to limit options. Why? Because children feel safer that way. Too much choice overwhelms them. But in adulthood, this limited way of seeing things becomes an impediment to greater ability. In fact, **the more of an adult you become (also spiritually-speaking), the more options you can handle**. Much of society is run this way: "You can either pay your taxes by bank transfer or by credit card." Not much of a choice, is it? I'd love to get a list of items my tax money is permitted to be spent on. And if that's too much choice and overwhelms you, you could check the box "don't care".

So how do you see more options? You see more options when your Attention is not constantly occupied. When you take some time to sit-back and gain perspective. When you have some energy left over after you've checked-offyour to-do list. And when you're used to not becoming fixated, but remain aware of the periphery.

How to Stretch Time

The best ice-hockey player of all time, Wayne Gretzky, displayed a skill never seen before in any athlete, as if he was able to anticipate moves on the playing field before they happened. Gretzky himself claimed that when he played, "time slowed down". The same statement has been made by several other professional athletes. If they really experienced time in slow-motion, it would explain the crazy ease with which they outplay their opponents.

Today my eyes shifted to a ticking clock. Resting my Attention there, the ticking of the second-hand seemed to stop and time stood still. For a moment it was as if the tick wouldn't move over to the next second, as if the world had stopped. I wondered about this strange alteration of perception, so I checked online whether anyone else was experiencing it. To my surprise, there is an official term for this. The perception of time standing-still is called Chronostasis or "stopped clock illusion". This BBC article treats it like a common phenomenon:

Have you ever stared at a second hand on a clock and thought that time seemed to stand still for a moment? It's not just you. Sometimes, when I look at a clock time seems to stand still. Maybe you've noticed this to your bemusement or horror as well. You'll be in the middle of something, and flick your eyes up to an analogue clock on the wall to see what the time is. The second hand of the clock seems to hang in space, as if you've just caught the clock in a moment of laziness. After this pause, time seems to restart and the clock ticks on as normal.

It gives us the disconcerting idea that even something as undeniable as time can be a bit less reliable than we think.
This happened to me for years, but I never spoke about it. Secretly, I thought it was either evidence of my special insight to reality, or final proof that I was a little unhinged (or both). But then I found out that it's a normal experience. Psychologists even have a name for it – they call it the "stopped clock illusion". Thanks psychologists, you really nailed that one.

An ingenious experiment from a team at University College London recreated the experience in the lab and managed to connect the experience of the stopped clock to the action of the person experiencing it. They asked volunteers to look away and then suddenly shift their gaze to a digital counter. When the subjects tried to judge how long they had been looking at the digit that first appeared, they systematically assumed it had been on for longer than it had.

Filling Gaps

Moving our eyes from one point to another is so quick and automatic that most of us probably don't even think about what we are doing. But when you move your eyes rapidly there is a momentary break in visual experience. You can get a feel for this now by stretching your arms out and moving your eyes between your two index fingers. (If you are reading this in a public place, feel free to pretend you are having a good stretch.) As you flick your eyes from left to right, you should be able to detect an almost imperceptibly brief "flash" of darkness as input from your eyes is cut-off.

It is this interruption in consciousness that leads to the illusion of the stopped clock. The theory is that our brains attempt to build a seamless story about the world from the ongoing input of our senses. Rapid eye movements create a break in information, which needs to be covered up. Always keen to hide its tracks, the brain fills in this gap with whatever comes after the break.

Normally this subterfuge is undetectable, but if you happen to move your eyes to something that is moving with precise regularity – like a clock – you will spot this pause in the form of an extra long "second". Fitting with this theory, the UCL team also showed that longer eye-movements lead to longer pauses in the stopped clock.

It doesn't have to be an eye movement that generates the stopped clock – all that appears to be important is that you shift your Attention. (Although moving our eyes is the most obvious way we shift our Attention, I'm guessing that the "inner eye" has gaps in processing in the same way our outer eyes do, and these are what cause the stopped clock illusion.) This accounts for a sister illusion we experience with our hearing – the so-called "dead phone illusion", which is when you pick up an old-fashioned phone and catch an initial pause between the dial tone that seems to last longer than the others.

These, and other illusions show that something as basic as the experience of time passing is constructed by our brains – and that this is based on what we experience and what seems the most likely explanation for those experiences, rather than some reliable internal signal. Like with everything else, what we experience is our brain's best guess about the world. We don't ever get to know time directly. In this sense we are all time travelers.

As glad as I was to have found information on this, I think they got their interpretation all wrong: It's not time stopping that is an illusion. The real illusion is, that time is moving (in my opinion). And reality is not constructed by the "brain", but rather by the mind, which is a non-physical thing. I have experienced phases of complete timelessness in deep meditation. That is why I believe that consciousness itself is timeless. We experience the same timelessness when staring into the eyes of someone we are in love with.

If you have been studying Awareness and perception, you know that your sense of time can expand or contract. If you are focused on something, your sense of time stretches. If you slow-down your breathing, moving and heart-rate, you can even perceive events as your timeless consciousness would perceive them...in slow-motion. This can be particularly useful in car traffic, sports, combat, business situations, games and whatnot. If you are fully present and calm, it is much easier to handle challenging situations. In super-advanced versions of this, one may even be able to dodge bullets.

Professional tennis players, baseball players or goalkeepers in soccer all require some time-stretching – otherwise they couldn't handle the sheer speed with which the ball shoots toward them. No person in a "normal" state of Awareness could possibly hit a ball flying toward one at 140 miles an hour. These athletes are in an altered state of consciousness while playing. They are actually magicians. That's why we are so fascinated watching them.

So here's how to slow-down time and thereby your sense of well-being: Pay full Attention to whatever is happening right now. That's it. The more keen your Attention is in the now, the more your sense of time slows down. And with that, your sense of well-being and "being in control" increase. If you are too hurried or impatient to spend quality time with your friend, spouse, kid, boss or whoever, you are not really being present, not really being consciousness. You see, these athletes are just so invested into the present-moment that their mind stops, and they enter a new dimension. Their state is lucid, sometimes euphoric.

There are a lot of different techniques to experience time-stretching. I'll share one of them here:

Go for a walk. Notice something that is moving (it could be anything: a car, a bee, a balloon, a person, etc.). *Observe its movement* carefully. Sense where it came from and where it's going – when it's movement *started* and when it will *stop*. Continue to do this on many moving objects until time seems to stretch and you experience an altered state.

The closed-eyes version: Think of a phase of your life (such as your school-time, your time as a single, your time at a company, etc.). Spot when it started. Spot when it stopped. Continue this meditation with different phases of your life until you experience stretched time and an altered state.

These exercises can be done for minutes or hours, depending on the intensity you prefer.

It's Not About Knowledge, It's About Awareness

It is generally believed that "knowledge is power". Having been a success-coach for the last 20 years, I can assure you that this is not true. Society assumes that if there is an alcoholic, an obese person or a smoker, that they "don't have the knowledge" or "education" that drinking, smoking or overeating is harmful. As any of them could tell you, that's just not true. I smoked for many years when I was younger, even though I had been educated on the "dangers of smoking" many times. The *knowledge* of the ill effects of smoking was of no use to me. The Government wages endless "public information campaigns" to battle all kinds of "societal ills". The so-called "War on Drugs" for instance, has had no deterring effect whatsoever, quite the contrary. Why? Because knowledge alone does not create change. One would have to be **aware** of that knowledge at the right time, as well as **aware** of other behavioral options, as well as a commitment to act upon them. *Awareness, Energy, Behavior and Action* are three things that supersede knowledge every time it really counts. If knowledge and education really were the key, then the rise of the Internet, where we have access to more information than ever before, would have radically changed the kind of choices people make. The Internet and its Knowledge are a mere tool that can be used for good or bad. They are not the source or cause of change. It's about the user of the tool, not the tool..

Our culture keeps teaching us that education is the key, knowledge is the key and that with just enough information we can get the right job, find the right partner and be healthy, make money and live a good life. But if you look more closely, you'll discover that *your boss does not care how much knowledge you have, your boss cares about the results you deliver. Your customers don't care about your knowledge, but about the actions you take or products you have. Your future spouse does not really care about what you know, but whether you can make them laugh and feel good.*

Awareness trumps knowledge because it is that with which knowledge is acquired, sorted, prioritized and applied. Without that Awareness, I could just fill you up with a bunch of false data and you'd be unable to make the right choices.

Intuitive Awareness means to know things before you even acquired knowledge about them. An example: Awhile ago, I stumbled upon an internet article titled: *6 Intimate Details You Can Tell Just by Looking at Someone.* The article imparts some strange knowledge, such as being able to tell how much alcohol someone can drink by their eye-color, telling their sexual orientation by the length of their fingers, telling someone's political attitude by the movement of their eyes, etc. But the article wasn't all that interesting to me because I already knew all of that...through Awareness. Nobody taught me, and I didn't know there were scientific studies. Instead, working with people on a daily basis, makes a number of things "clear", even if you don't consciously learn about them. Through intuitive Awareness, you know a whole lot more about a person than these few trivial details. You can know everything about anyone the instant you meet them. The method of doing so is to just observe and perceive without pre-judgment or expectation.

Therefore, it is more important to learn about **Awareness than it is to accumulate knowledge. If you have high Awareness, there is really nothing you don't already know. And,** if you already know everything, what's left to do in life? What's left is to laugh, have fun, feel and experience. Learning happens all by itself, and much more rapidly if you focus on being alive and experiencing rather than accumulating loads of data.

"If you subscribe to this philosophy, why do you read so many books?" someone who knows me might ask. The answer is: When I read books I either do so to train my **imagination** (fiction), or to **implement action** based on the information (non-fiction). Neither is for mere knowledge acquisition. In addition, knowledge is only applicable when it's true and unbiased....which rules out a big chunk of data right-off the bat. Knowledge that is not applied, is not real knowledge. It's just superfluous mind-stuff that has no use or consequence in daily life. Knowledge becomes a good thing when it is applied. And yet, many of us feed ourselves with unapplicable knowledge every day. About a week ago, I read a newspaper article which said that Jennifer Aniston was hanging out with Angelina Jolie's father. It said that Angelina Jolie was not happy about the friendship between her father and Jennifer Aniston, because Aniston is Brad Pitt's (Jolie's husband) ex -girlfriend. Jolie has therefore not invited her father to join them on a trip to Europe. Other than showcasing the infantile mindset of some "celebrities" (or, if untrue, the dishonesty of gossip-journalists), of what applicable use is this trivia? Of none at all. So why did I read it? The honest answer: I was bored while sitting in a public waiting room and enjoyed the Attentiondiversion. You see, even if I don't think that such data is of any value, I'm not going to turn my philosophy into a religion and forbid myself from a little garbage now and then. In the same vein, I don't think alcohol, cigars or sweets are of any value, but that doesn't mean that I will guilt-punish myself if I try them here and there. That's the difference between smooth non-judging attitudes and rigid right/wrong thinking (The moment you feel guilty for eating sweets, you set yourself up for doing it more often than is good for you.)

Our evolutionary path is to become increasingly aware of the Universe. That includes knowledge, but is not limited to it. Put a little differently: Awareness is the cause, knowledge is the effect. Instead of emphasizing the importance of the effect, pay Attention to the source. The other day I spent a few hours with people whose language I did not understand. One could say I was lacking knowledge of what was being said. But through Awareness (cause), plenty of other types of knowledge were acquired (effect). So instead of being upset that I didn't understand the language, I picked up on the different tones of the voice, including the mood and mentality that generated such a tone. By the objects hanging in their house, I picked up on their spiritual beliefs. By seeing that the married couple never touched each other, I picked up a little on the nature of their relationship. When I told them the price of my services, I could see by the movement of their fingers, whether they were comfortable with it or not. And all of that doesn't even include psychic information yet.

Some of you might be thinking: Isn't it scary for people to be sitting with someone who is aware of all of that? And the answer is: Not if the person is less judgmental , non-manipulative and open. Some people try to use Awareness to influence or manipulate. I know a guy who calls himself a "mentalist", who is continually trying to use "seduction techniques" to influence, control and manipulate. The problem with that is, people who are fairly aware themselves, don't feel comfortable around him. His circle of friends is therefore limited to people who want to be manipulated. With people who are super-aware but non-manipulative, we usually feel much more warmth because we can let down our guard. Since they "know everything anyway", there is nothing to hide and no fake-self to assert. I have sat with enlightened teachers who had such super-Awareness. It is with those that I felt the most comfortable and at home, even though they "knew everything about me". Why? Because they had the only quality that supersedes total Awareness: Total Love.

3

The Power of Appreciation

Contents of this Chapter:

Cherish the Little Things

Quality of life is amplified by increasing the amount of undivided Attention given to things. Another way to say this: Savoring things increases your well-being. To intensify the point, here are some synonyms of the word "savor":

Cherish

Delight in

Luxuriate in

Relish

Revel in

Sip

Taste

Experience

Feel

Appreciate

Enjoy

Honor

Treasure

Bask in

Regard

Many of us have no difficulty cherishing the big things. It's the little things that are too often taken for granted. I was watching someone have coffee the other day in a most exquisite 20s-architecture poolside cafe. I'm not sure she even tasted the coffee because she was fondling her smartphone, while at the same time chatting to someone at the table. Her Attention was split three-ways: the drinking, the chat and the smartphone. The coffee was emptied in three large swoops. I wondered whether she was even aware of the magnificent setting she was in.

Lack of Awareness-depth diminishes one's perceptual experience. There are several levels of depth in which the coffee could be tasted. At the most superficial level you would not even take notice of the cafe because you are caught up in mind-stuff. One level deeper you might take brief notice of it and comment, "Oh, it's nice here," but that's still superficial. At a few levels deeper you would sit in silence for a few minutes and marvel at the beauty of the setting, enjoying the cup of coffee as if it were your very first or very last. At a deeper level still, you would feel the entire history of the setting, and the coffee would make you ecstatic.

I sense that when we leave this planet to the afterlife, we'll miss those many "little things" that are so unique to earth and will have wished we had more thoroughly savored them. Savoring things means to slow down, to allow yourself the luxury to expand time and become centered and to bring more quality to the present moment.

The Radiance of Appreciation

As most of you have noticed, appreciation is an actual energy; an actual frequency. It's deliberate radiance benefits all endeavors, and its importance cannot be over-emphasized.

Think of a person, life-form, place, object or thing that you appreciate. Now describe it in as much **detail** as possible.

Do that before reading on.

If you have done so, you just had a noticeable mood-shift upwards. Within only a few minutes. It awakens the **heart**, and detailed-focus allows the energy to accumulate. A good exercise on any given day is to take note of things you like. To write lists of what you appreciate. To speak about and mention what you appreciate. To get specific about what you like and why you like it. In those moments you are **sourcing** energy directly from a higher realm.

In this field-of-energy all takes care of itself – just the right contacts, projects, ideas and events flow into your life. There is no reason to withhold appreciation. It overcomes resentment, burnout, illness, exhaustion, emptiness, stagnation and any other malady. The mini-version of appreciation is **respect,** which is also well worth cultivating. The premium version of appreciation is **Love**.

Feeling unwell is due only to the contraction or stress you feel when you resist things. And you only resist things when you focus on what you *do not* appreciate, or on the *aspects* of something you do not appreciate (every person, place or thing has **aspects** of value). The instant you condemn something, as in a strong "No!" your Attention *sticks* there. Appreciation is the opposite of that, it is finding things you can say "Yes" to, or even more powerfully, finding aspects to *anything* you can say "Yes" to. Lost your suitcase? That's GREAT! It gives you an opportunity to radiate more strongly, independent of the clothes in your suitcase. Such is the attitude of appreciation. The Universe is non-dual, so it understands "yes" and "no" as the same thing – as a focusing of Attention. So whatever you say "yes" or "no" to, you gravitate towards.

Falling in love with existence increases your handle over it. Pushing against it alienates you, and makes you unable to have any effect on it. You cannot control a dancing partner that you push away. Your personal energy field lights up with the admiration and gratitude you radiate.

Regard vs. Neglect

I stood in front of two houses that were in stark contrast to each other. One was in a state of neglect, the other was well cared for. I enjoy contrast. It is rare that two things so dissimilar stand right beside each other. This was a few years ago, I was on a coaching-house-call, and I thought I would be entering the nicer house. The plants and garden were cultivated, the windows were spotless, the kids toys in front of the house were looked friendly, and I thought, "Good, I look forward to this."

Then I realized it was the wrong address, and my job today would be in the house that looked neglected. "Uh-oh," I thought. In fact, it looked so run-down that I at first thought it was abandoned. Frankly, it looked like a haunted house. Shrubs were growing so tall and wild that they covered the porch. Windows were either broken or dirty. There was also a child's toy, but it was broken, dirty and just lay there decaying in the shrubs.

For a moment, I wondered whether I should even enter the house because what I saw spelled trouble. Why? Because when personal belongings are in a state of neglect, it indicates a lack of love. And where there is a lack of love, there is a lack of *everything* else. This has nothing to do with being able to afford a nicer house. Even without a cent of money, the owner could have thrown the broken toy away or cleaned the windows.

Compassion got the better of me, and I entered the house. Inside was no different than outside. It was a perfect reflection of the person's inner condition, which was *resignation.* After her husband died, she had lost the will to live. Having lost the will to live, she developed various illnesses. Having developed various illnesses she no longer had the energy to get things done with the house or even ask someone else to get them done.

The coaching-session proved difficult. At first, everything I suggested was only replied with "I've already tried that", "I've already done that," "That didn't work, I tried that too," Being familiar with low-energy, these answers were not unexpected. When someone is depressed then it appears as if *nothing* will work, and as if "Everything has already been tried." These are protective statements because on some level, no change is desired. Movement upwards would only bring up the painful emotions she was trying to avoid.

One way to get out of such states is to work oneself up the latter step by little step, allowing **just a little** more love into one's life on a daily basis. One way to do so is to cultivate **regard instead of neglect**. So, I did something I had actually never done as a coach (and may never do again) and started playing "cleaning-service". While explaining to her the point of loving-ness as opposed to neglect, I cleaned one of her windows, threw piles of trash away, swept the floor. She was flabbergasted, and I was surprised by myself. "You don't have to do that!" she declared. But in this case I really did *have to* do it. She did not need "coaching" in the normal sense, she needed someone to **care.** She did not need any of my mind-techniques. A picture that her daughter had painted that was just lying around, was dusted off and hung up. This made her cry because it transported her memory to better days. Sadness and grief are quite an improvement to apathy.

Some synonyms for "Regard":

Cultivate

Devote Oneself To

Cherish

Foster

Nurse

Respect

Nourish

Take Care Of

And these are some antonyms of "Regard":

Neglect

Disregard

Ignore

Not care for

Indifference

Oversight

As you neglect people, their relationship to you will deteriorate. The skills you don't use, you may lose. If you don't give a hoot about your house, it will start falling apart in due time. All of this can be reversed of course, with care, regard and cultivation. Such love can be applied to anything for improvement. It can be applied to a garden, to a friend. It can be applied to furniture. I can be applied to a project, to your health, to a website, to anything at all.

Love It or Leave It

A common block for people is doing something they don't like. One of my current students keeps telling me how she is not enjoying her university studies at all. She relates it to a lot of boredom and frustration. So why won't she quit? Probably because she has already invested too much, and believes she needs those credentials for future success. If I don't enjoy a movie, I get up and leave the theater. Some stay because they have invested 10 dollars for the seat, but that is a double loss because they are also wasting two hours of their life. If I did not enjoy my studies, I'd either learn to embrace and love them, or quit. "Love it or leave it," – those are the only two options that make any sense if your aim is to have energy.

So if that student insists she is not going to leave her studies, then she should at least learn to enjoy them, embrace them and to stop complaining. If she is not willing to cut ties, then she could practice letting go of the subjective state of boredom, and mentally coax herself into enjoying, loving, embracing and saying "yes" to what is happening there. Higher-self is capable of enjoying almost anything, that's it's special capability. In the grand scheme of things, everything that happens is perfect, and there is no reason to assume that whatever does happen to you in life is inherently bad for you. Even illness and accidents can turn out to be a blessing in disguise for deeper soul-exploration.

Another person who has been writing to me for awhile about a physical disability, has been communicating the many different things she has tried to heal it. I applaud her willpower and drive to find a solution and to really be able to say, "I've tried everything." But her increasing frustration with not being able to find a solution indicates that she is strong with "wanting to overcome" it, but weak in the *acceptance* department. "Love it or leave it," here would become "Accept it or heal it." Since she has been unable to heal it for over a decade, the time has come to accept it. Not as a sign of resignation, not as a giving up any hope, but as an acceptance of the way things are right now, so that she can get on with her life instead of being preoccupied with only the physical part of it. Her disability is only the physical part of life. Being preoccupied with that means reducing oneself to the body. The lesson in this might be to be able to fully enjoy life in spite of a physical condition; to make the best of the cards one is dealt; to play the ball as it landed.

When you are no longer attached to the outcome of things, you become completely fearless and free. You are guaranteed that your goal will come true, or it won't. And both are alright. But that doesn't mean "no longer caring"- that's a misunderstanding of non-attachment. You don't detach because you don't care, you detach-from-the-outcome because you are optimistic that whatever the outcome is, is for the highest good. You have goals and dreams, but you don't ponder suicide if they don't immediately come true.

"Love it or leave it" can also be "Get it, or let go of it". To someone complaining about not finding a girlfriend I said: "Then get the girlfriend already or let go of the idea for now." It's this in-between-state that causes trouble. It's the needing and wanting rather than the having. If you cannot get something right now, let go of it. And if you can get something, then get it. But don't go around lamenting how you want it but can't get it. That's just wasted breathe.

Exercise: Love it or Leave It

Here's an exercise to teach this concept to your body/mind:

1. Write down things you want but do not have.
2. For each item on your list, write down either a)
how you are going to get it in the near future, or b)
deliberately let go of it mentally, and cross it off your
list.

3. Write down things you do not like in your life
4. For each item on your list, decide whether you
are going to a) leave it or stop investing time and
Attention to it, or b) mentally focus on it, and try to
embrace and love it.

Exercise: The Smiling Experiment

If you are of the reclusive and somber sort, you may
want to try the Smiling Experiment. Choose 3 days
in which to smile at all kinds of people...strangers,
familiars, the old, the young, men, women, the rich,
the poor, the in-between, the sad, the happy, the
neutral.

It can be a big smile, a soft smile or, if you do not
want to smile openly, just a friendly glance with your
eyes, an inner-smile or the sending of blessings to
someone.

Also smile or send blessings when you are not in the mood for it, because "acting-as-if" you are in the mood will uplift your mood. It is not a "fake" smile if your intention is good-willed. It is not the smile of a salesperson, who only smiles because he believes to get something in return. Fake-smiles come from masking one's intentions. Deliberate smiling is done with positive intent.

If you already smile a lot, then try to extend your smile to strangers, sending them blessings or well-wishes.

The world is a mirror of you. What you see in the world is to some extent a reflection of the energy you radiate. Hence, if you notice stupid, evil, ugly people everywhere, this partially says something about who **you** are being. And if you notice smart, good, beautiful people everywhere, this partially says what **you** are being.

In any scenario of daily life, there are millions of things to notice. If you always notice the same things, it's because you are always being the same attitude. You can see the very same scenario you saw yesterday, with brand new eyes. And that is something this exercise is meant to convey.

Having done the smiling-experiment for 3 days, notice: What has changed? What are some of the things that happened to you that are different from your regular routine? Why, apart from people in service-jobs, is smiling so rare around the globe? How would your life be if you treated all people kindly without expectation of something in return?

Exercise: An Appreciation Walk

Take a walk and **bless**, appreciate or acknowledge all that is nice, well done, well crafted, loving, beautiful, and representative of abundance and beauty. Deliberately bless, acknowledge or appreciate specific objects, people, places, parts of nature, scenarios, events, landscapes, buildings, pictures, cars etc. Take special note of nice sounds, colors, shapes, textures and hold them in observation for more than only a glance. The more you do this walk, the more your personal energy-field and aura expand.

Exercise: Giving Yourself Energy

Here is something to give yourself energy within only 5 to 10 minutes:

Place your right hand on your forehead and your left hand on your heart-region. Voice something you could forgive yourself for. Take a deep breath. Voice something you like or appreciate about yourself. Take a deep breath. Repeat. Continue.

Excessive self-criticism is self-defeating and unlikely to provide energy. Self-approval is rare with most people but will give you a real energy-boost. Some people have objected that self-love is selfish. To which I respond: "Humility is not thinking less of yourself, it's thinking of yourself less."

Self-criticism should only be practiced in the context of an official exercise – such as writing a list of your weaknesses – with the intention to correct them. The constant and excessive mind-based self-criticism of daily life really is de-energizing.

Exercise: Count Your Blessings

This exercise is great for anyone who experiences any kind of lack in their lives. A great way to start and end the day is to count your blessings. Focusing on what you liked about your day and what you have **already** received, takes your Attention away from lack-consciousness.

The mind/ego tends to take everything for granted after only a few weeks of owning it. Rekindle your sense of amazement and gratitude for all things you do have, and more will be given to you. If you focus properly, there is no limit to the amount of things you can list.

Exercise: Random Acts of Kindness

Examples for Random Acts of Kindness:

* Anonymously paying for someone's drink in a restaurant
* Helping an elderly person carry bags
* Letting someone pass you in the check-out line of the supermarket
* Paying the parking fee for the next person behind you
* Holding the door open for a complete stranger

In an infinite context, there is no difference between big things and the little things. Even small acts of kindness go a long way.

All people are "children of the Universe". The Universe and its many beings love it when you take care of its children.

Exercise: 10 Minute Shower of Love

In the **Downloads-Section** of my website, you will find a Audio titled "10 Minute Shower of Love". This excercise helps you shower yourself with love for 10 minutes out of which you will come out re-energized. The first minutes teach you how to shower yourself with three forms of love: Giving yourself **time**, giving yourself **space** and giving yourself **Attention**. The next minutes involve releasing judgments about yourself and your life. The final minutes are about embracing whatever is going on in your life and whoever is currently in your life. The audio elegantly solves all pressing needs and issues within a very short time.

The Joy of Travelling

"Once a year, go some place you have never been before." - The Dalai Lama

I'll take that advice. I love travelling and make sure to spend 20% of a year away from my "permanent residence". You can't really get a sense of the world through the TV news, the Internet, or YouTube. Learning is most rapid through direct, first-hand experience. So, I find out that many places are much, much nicer than their reputation (as crafted by the 8 O'clock news), and other places are not all what they were trumped up to be (noisy and congested Paris comes to mind).

"Travelling – it leaves you speechless, then it turns you into a storyteller." - Ibn Battuta

Of course, it's more cozy and safe at home. But too much comfort can make one a closed-minded, complacent slacker or even a screenaholic. On the road, we are cut loose from daily, routine, habit patterns, and so the mind opens up.

"A ship is safe in the harbor, but that's not what ships are built for." - John. A. Shedd

Travel need not be all risk-free and pre-planned. Sure, I understand that some planning is vital when a lot of people are involved, especially a busload of senior citizens. I meticulously plan, route and prepare trips now and then. But at other times, I don't. The human heart flourishes in surprise and marvels at the unexpected.

Travel long and far enough, and you meet yourself; you find out more about who you really are. When you change your location, you come to realize what habits, states and thoughts are yours and which ones are influenced by your surroundings. You can tell the difference now because your surroundings have changed.

Travel puts you in touch with peoples' kindness and generosity. Every place I have ever visited in the world, there is so much hospitality.

"Come sit on the porch with me, the drinks are cold and the friendship is free." - Unknown

You will feel places where you "belong" and places where you seem not to "belong". But even in the place you don't really "fit in" you will encounter kindness and hospitality, if you are yourself a kind person. Sometimes you come to places where it seems like anyone and everyone belongs.

"One belongs to New York instantly. One belongs to it as much in five minutes as in five years" – Tom Wolfe

You can usually tell whether someone has traveled a lot or not by this peculiar kind of "travelers aura". They have this look in their eyes like they have seen a lot. You take some of every country you have been to into your heart and it stays there for the rest of your life.

Sometimes it can get a little rough. Challenges can come-up along the way. Once your boat has left the harbor and the weather gets stormy, keep in mind that...

"A smooth sea never made a skillful sailor." - Franklin D. Roosevelt

…and that you will soon experience one of the best parts of traveling, which is homecoming:

"No one realizes how beautiful it is to travel, until he comes home and rests his head on his old, familiar pillow" - *Lin Yutang*

Forgiveness Has Miraculous Effects

The effects of forgiveness are nothing short of miraculous. I have seen people restore bad eyesight, tumors reverse, a sudden influx of fortunes; I've stood in awe at the spontaneous disappearance of family feuds and grudges decades old, the termination of insolvency proceedings and much, much more…just through forgiveness.

Letting Go of the Juice of Hate and Resentment

Resentment is a doorway to negative vibes. In phases of prolonged resentment, you weaken your energy-body and open the channels for negative energies to enter your body and being, attach to you and build a nest of sickness or inner oppression. That is why it is vital for you to release hard sentiments thoroughly and completely if you want goodness.

Forgiving people and groups does not mean you approve of what they did. This misconception keeps many from forgiving. They think forgiving is approving and say: "No way! How could I ever *approve* of that?" It is not the person's actions you are forgiving. You are forgiving the human; the soul behind the actions. You recognize that a human being is limited, prone to error and misunderstanding, and release your grudge against them.

Of course, if there weren't a seeming benefit to hate, there would be none. The secret "benefit" is that it gives the ego power. People "juice themselves up" with hate. When you have been wronged, sometimes it feels delicious to lose oneself in fantasies of revenge. But if you allow this to go on, without putting a stop to it through emotional releasing, it will turn into resentment, then rage, then cruelty. Not to mention what it does to your health. It gives one "energy" only at a very low level of overall energy. So if you are down and out, apathetic and depressed, lost and lonely, then hate feels like coming alive and rising above the muck. But it also prevents you from addressing the issues you are covering-up, and it takes away from your sense of aliveness and kindness. This is why all the big spiritual names in history taught forgiveness as their primary consciousness-liberation tool.

The following exercise will help you start cleaning up on self-destructive resentment:

Resentment Release Technique

1. List the people and groups you resent or have not forgiven.

After every name indicate how much you resent them on a scale from 1 to 10. 1 indicates "OK", 5 indicates a dislike, and 10 indicates hatred.

2. Hold them in mind until you feel their pain.

Think of the first person on your list. Hold that person in mind. Instead of holding what they did in mind, simply hold an image of that person or group. You do not have to approve of what they did or do. As you look at them release your labels and judgments while breathing softly. Try to feel the pain they are in. Without being in pain themselves, they would not cause harm to others. *Hurting people hurt others*. Once you discover the hurt or ignorance they must be in to behave as they did...

3. Forgive them.

Mentally or verbally forgive them. If you want, you can use this statement:

"*I acknowledge that you are a human being limited in understanding and therefore prone to error. I forgive you for what you thought, said and did. I release all and any resentment, wanting revenge or ill-will towards you. I release trying to change or correct you. I release all energies, emotions and beliefs connected to this from my whole body and being. May you find peace and happiness. I repeat: May you find peace and happiness. May you find peace and happiness.*

Repeat the statement, directed at the person mentally, three to five times and then let go. Quit concerning yourself with this person or group and direct your Attention at the nicer things in life.

If during the process you feel sickish or have aches, these are *parts of the process*. Allow all of that stuck energy to come up and release.
Repeat the process for each person or group on your list. You will experience a new surge of energy and possibly a kind of warmth or softness in the chest area.

You are releasing these energies for your own benefit, so that you don't hold them in your own field.

The Forgiveness Technique

The subconscious cannot tell the difference between resenting others and resenting yourself. It is therefore recommended that you release all types of resentment. This technique is another way of doing it. Feel free to use your own variations.

1. Write down the name of a person you would like to forgive.

2. Write down which thoughts create the feeling of resentment toward this person.

3. What problems must this person have had in order to behave that way? What do you assume are those person's feelings, thoughts and beliefs that compel him/her to behave in that way? And: If you were in this person's position, might you behave that way too? Write down your answers.

4. What negative energy came from you, prior to the other person doing that thing you haven't forgiven? Can you see how you were complaining, blaming or in a bad space before that person?

5. If you pretend for a moment that it's 10 years from now: Have you forgiven by now? How many years do you think is enough before you can forgive?

6. If you could forgive the person, how long would it take for that to feel natural?

7. If you could forgive the person, how would that make you feel?

8. Gently focus on yourself and the person. Ask yourself: Could I first forgive myself for resenting this person?

9. Focus on yourself and whisper: "I'm sorry. I forgive you. I love you."

10. Gently focus on yourself and the person. Ask yourself: Could I forgive this person?

11. Gently focus on the person and ask yourself: Have I made similar mistakes before?

12- Gently focus on the person and ask yourself: When could I forgive this person?

13. Focus on the person and whisper: "I'm sorry. I forgive you. Thank you."

You can also apply forgiveness to yourself. You can forgive yourself for your past mistakes and move on. If you have wronged yourself or others, you can also *make amends* to balance out the energy.

Your Critics Are Angels in Disguise

Who says criticism is bad? Who says that it's a bad thing when your customers complain? Who says it's a bad thing when your spouse blames you for things? Who says it's a bad thing when your boss or employee tell you what they don't like about you?

Where did we get the idea that those things are "bad"?

If you assume these things are "bad", it's time to fundamentally change your beliefs about how reality works – to boost your life energy and quit walking around like a victim.

Check if you can see critics as angels in disguise. All criticism – whether valid or invalid, as an opportunity to learn and grow. Depending on the way you **take it**, you can let it drag you down or use it to become quicker, happier, more efficient, and more zestful. The following (metaphysically derived) concept will help you tremendously in achieving this and other things:

Pain and suffering are not the same thing!

"Pain" is an emotion, a passing energy, a brief "pang" in your chest or stomach. The suffering only comes in when you resist it. When you try to battle it, when you start resisting it, rather than accepting or even enjoying it, the pain not only grows, but it starts sticking to you. But if you can break through the barrier of pain by non-resistance, you can "come out on the other side" feeling high.

I have experimented with this idea at the dentist, among other places. Unless the pain is excruciating, I normally won't take anesthesia, so that I can explore the dissolution of pain. Pain creates several layers of resistance, and if I can give them all up, onion-layer by onion-layer, I "come out on the other side" and feel vivid and high after my dentists visit. If I did not manage to release and surrender, I feel exhausted and tired from trying. Resistance wastes energy, surrender gives energy.

It's the same with criticism. There are various layers of your identity that despise criticism. These are layers of self-importance than can be given-up to unveil a higher version of yourself. This does not mean that all criticism is valid – mostly criticism tells more about the person criticizing, than about yourself! However, that's not the point. Whether they are "right or wrong" is not the point. The point is that every instance of complaint and criticism from outside is there to help you peel off another layer of victim-mentality and transcend your smallness. It therefore behooves you to look forward to criticism, because it's an opportunity to become happier. The untrained mind becomes more resentful with every complaint thrust upon it, the trained mind becomes happier and stronger with every complaint. But don't be surprised if nobody complains toward you anymore. It's no fun criticizing someone who **truly** appreciates it.

On the other side of the coin, you need not be shy of being a critic of others. It's in the way you say it – the "carrier vibe" which carries the words – that determines the results of your complaint. You can carry a message with anger, which will cause counter-anger. or you can carry it with decisiveness, which will cause respect. You can carry the same message with fear, which will cause the person to get back at you, or the carrier-wave can be love, by which your complaint will be heard.

Fight Back or Forgive?

"I know I should forgive him, but on the other hand it just feels like I have to fight back, otherwise he will do it again and again," some say. The question: "Should I fight back or forgive?" is quite common.

The answer I usually give is not an either/or. It depends on what level-of-consciousness I and the other are in. If I am dealing with a complete psychopath, the question, "should I forgive them or fight back?" ought not even arise because I have removed myself from his/her physical proximity long ago. But if I am dealing with your everyday bully, here are different levels of dealing with him/her (using a 1-1000 levels-of-energy scale as described in my book "Levels of Energy"):

80: Groveling and Afraid of the Bully: Trying to gain his approval by doing what he wants. "Please don't hurt me. I'll do whatever you say."

160: Enraged and Seeking Revenge Without Taking Constructive Action.: "How dare he bully me? I'm going to show him just who the *%$ck I am!"

200: Avoidance and Denial.: "Alright, never mind. I just need to shift my focus. C'mon. I can ignore this…again."

300: Fighting Back.: "I can play the games he plays too. I am going to fight for what's right and not let myself be bullied."

400: Neutral but Standing Firm.: "I will not bow to his demands, nor react to his antics. I will remove myself from his presence when possible. I will try to talk things out with him, but will never compromise my integrity."

500: Forgiving and Loving.: "I can see his suffering. While I don't approve of his actions, I forgive him and genuinely wish that he recovers from his emotional affliction."

From this scale you can see that both the "Forgiveness" and the "Fighting" options could have a positive outcome that it is not "either/or", with one being negative and the other positive, but simply dependent on context. If, thus far you have always been afraid or angry, then actually "Fighting Back" is a step upwards. If, on the other hand, you are used to fighting back and restoring justice, then the next level for you is to practice Forgiveness instead of Fighting. Every level has other lessons to learn. Not all people want forgiveness instantly, even though it's the most powerful option. Some want to learn to fight for what's right first.

The best option for most readers here is probably a good mix of 300s-500s: To *always* forgive, but at the same time not becoming a doormat for people. I can forgive and extend compassion, but that doesn't mean I allow someone to scam me for thousands of dollars. He/she will probably be hearing from my lawyer…while at the same time I forgive. Of course, the high energy of forgiveness can often "miraculously" turn events so that lawyers are no longer necessary. The important point here is that the external action of "Fighting Back" (with a lawyer for instance), need not be accompanied by feelings of resentment (thus producing bad vibrations for all involved), but can be done in a state of calm. Or as Jesus said: *"Be peaceful as doves but wise as serpents."*

Instant Forgiveness

It has become habitual for me to apply instant forgiveness when I am "wronged". This is made possible by quickly seeing the hurt condition someone is in when he/she "wrongs" or "attacks" me. From a higher perspective, there is nobody who is actually "wronging" or "attacking" you. All they are doing is calling for Attention. That loving Attention can be sent, as a wave of acknowledgement and kindness, immediately. When you learn to do this strongly, you can wipe out someone's irate mood within seconds.

The Gratitude Attitude

A few days ago in a museum a kid damaged a vase. I saw a complete stranger walk up and take responsibility for it. He said to the warden: "I'm sorry about the vase, I'll pay for it." The kid stood at a distance amazed and humbled. The stranger gave the kid a wink. The parents remained oblivious to who knocked-down the vase. I was deeply impressed because I was seeing someone who was willing to reap disapproval from the museum wardens in order to protect a child he didn't know. The small-self would do anything to avoid disapproval. It would spend more time seeking gratification than extending gratitude. More time demanding respect than being respectful. More time seeking recognition than recognizing. Of course, doing just the opposite of what the small-self urges, facilitates quite a boost in Consciousness-Level. Let's look at just one aspect that the small-self lacks: Gratitude.

Gratitude is an energy-form that can be developed for the purpose of healing and well-being. A few different ways in which Gratitude can be increased:

* Meditations on Gratitude
* Meditations on what you are Grateful for
* Writing lists of what you are Grateful for

* Finding what you are already Grateful for and increasing that feeling
* Expressing your Gratitude to others
* Deliberately remembering things you are Grateful for
* Finding out how even things you thought were "not good" turned out to be helpful in retrospect

Or why not just do the entire list? There is no point in holding back. You get more of what you focus on, therefore increasing the energy-field of Gratitude will bring more into your life to be Grateful for. One great way to start and end the day is to count your blessings. Focusing on what you have **already** received takes your Attention away from the pervasive lack-consciousness. The small-self tends to take everything for granted after only a few weeks of owning it. Rekindle your sense of amazement and Gratitude for all things you do have, and more will be given to you. If you focus properly, there is no limit to the amount of things you could list.

As Gratitude and appreciation grow stronger, they can be felt as a real warmth in your physical body. As they grow stronger still there is an actual heat emanating from the solar-plexus. This is quite amazing because it demonstrates the effect of inner attitudes on physical reality.

So what prevents Gratitude? Well, it's simple: The small-self or mind/ego-complex has ZERO interest in anything but survival. It's comedic how little interest there actually is, and how this interest is faked when the ego wants something from another. Like a carnivore, the small-self is only interested in devouring something for personal benefit and then discarding it when finished. So when eating food, the ego is focused on the food itself, not on the occasion or conversation. In business the ego is focused on "getting the money quickly", so it can then "relax" and forget about the customer (which is a formula for poverty because good business only comes about through good relationships to others, not looking at them as a source of sustenance that is discarded after the transaction). In relationships, the ego wants relief through sex, and then rapidly loses interest in the partner – until the next time it wants sex. The big-self or higher-self lives in a larger context. It's primary aim is not to "get stuff" out of others, but to experience others and enjoy the time with them…in Gratitude and recognition. Gratitude and recognition must be consciously and deliberately developed to grow.

5

A Training in Flow, Energy and Happiness

Contents of this Chapter:

A State of Flow

The picture below is from a chart drawing I made at a recent private coaching. It shows how the state of "flow" works. It contrasts the challenge or difficulty-level of a task with your skill set. If the challenge is much higher than your skill, you experience overwhelm, stress, tension, strain and frustration. If the challenge is much lower than your skill, you experience underwhelm, boredom and lack of learning. If the challenge matches your skill level or even better, is just **slightly above** your skill level, you experience the state of flow, fun, growth and a general inner fire.

It's safe to say that anyone unhappy in his/her job is either over- or underwhelmed. Either he/she has tasks way above his/her qualification, or he/she is given tasks way below his/her ability. Neither achieves much. If you are a beginner at a sport and play against a professional…what are you going to learn? Nothing. You'll be wiped-out. And if you are a pro and play against a beginner, what will you learn? Again, nothing. The beginner will be wiped-out. **It's best to play against someone at or slightly above your skill level.** If he/she is slightly above your level, you feel challenged but still believe that you can achieve his/her level. That's where the fun comes in. There is a challenge, but it's not out of your range.

And that's how to maintain a flow state. By giving yourself challenges that are not too high and not too low, but only slightly above you.

The flow state is an enhanced feeling and perception in which reality seems to be more fluid, effortless and synchronous. When you are "in the flow" good things happen; you are riding a wave of positive momentum. Then you seem to magnetically attract just the right people. The flow state is not experienced perpetually because every wave arises and falls again. However, like a surfer of life, you can learn to ride numerous waves as they rise and fall, rather than getting caught up in maelstrom.

I've found that "the flow" is rarely something that just shows up by itself. It is not something you start out with. It is something you can **get into**. Whether you are practicing for a theater-play, involved in a sports-match, starting a new project or creating a romantic evening for you and your partner, these things usually don't start out flowing and effortless but require some time/effort to **get into**. You can get into a mood, get into a game, get into a role, get into a project, etc. And the way to do so is through will/concentration. So if for example you are in the habit of fighting with your partner, it may take some mental discipline not to fall back into old patterns of conversation and really get into the flow of a more pleasurable evening. But once that flow starts, no more discipline is required and reality becomes **fluent**. Accumulate a lot of reality-fluency and you become **affluent**. If a sports-team has had a losing streak, it may take some mental discipline not to remember that, but instead to shift focus to winning...until they get into a new flow. Another word for flow is **Momentum**.

When you first learn to ride a bike it takes concentration and effort to balance the bike, to pedal and to stay on track. But as you get into it, riding becomes easier and easier. And if you put a little effort into pedaling, you will notice the momentum of the bike speeding you along, and your legs can take a rest. This is essentially how all of reality works.

The streaming state of flux and flow is also related to being so properly focused on **one** task that you lose track of space and time. A deep relaxation ensues as you lose yourself in some project or item, and sensory perception also changes. Things look brighter in this state. You **remember things you had not remembered while in your normal state**.

So you'd like to induce a state of flow. Well, then you first have to choose something to get into the flow about. And then you consistently repeat that, focus on it and do it. And as you break through the various barriers of resistance, you finally break on through to the other side, where there is flow. But that requires deliberately embracing things you were previously resisting. Then, whatever it is you are doing just keeps pouring out, consistently, with no sign of letting up. The task then becomes not only effortless, but almost an addiction. Let me assure you that anything you'd like to do but feel too lazy, tired or untalented to do, can be turned into an addiction. Too lazy to go jogging? You have the potential to turn it into an addiction. You feel you don't have enough talent to become a film-director? With dedication you could turn it into an obsession that makes you wildly productive. You think you don't have what it takes to be a public speaker? As you begin there will be some resistance. As you repeat, and repeat. and repeat, and repeat resistance eventually turns into confidence, then into joy, and then into an almost addictive habit. I use "addiction" and "habit" in a positive sense here to convey that you can really turn any sort of dullness, idleness, sluggishness, and

inert phlegm into states of heartfelt joy, brightness,

zestfulness and reality-fluency. "But what if I don't know what to choose or what to focus on?" some might ask. To which I respond: Then choose anything that interests you. Because you can get into the flow on almost anything. Your state is not created by an external item. Next time you see a river, stream or current, meditate on it. Identify with it. Feel what it would feel like to **be a flowing river**. Contrast it to the immobile stubbornness of the surrounding earth. That earth may provide more stability and security, but it too needs flowing water to produce. The qualities of water as compared to earth give you a good idea of how to get into flow. It may be required to loosen the grip on stability/security (element earth) a little and instead take on the non-resistant, softer and lighter qualities of flowing water. And should you ever "get into deep waters", you simply go back to the earth-qualities.

Elevate Your Level of Consciousness

Getting into a more positive flow entails raising your consciousness. By writing down responses to the following list, you will gain an accurate map of what to work on to raise your level. This map will elevate your energy-frequency no matter who or where you are.

1. Write down how you have **transgressed** against other people, treated them unkindly or betrayed them. After each item write down a way you might be forgiven or make **amends**.

2. Write down every minor and major **resistance** and aversion you have in life. After each item write down how you might soften the resistance through understanding, releasing, **letting go** or mental neutralization (as taught in the "Bliss Course").

3. Write down how you have been **doubting**, giving specific examples of your doubt and inner conflict. After each item, write down how you might turn your doubt into trust. Alternatively, write down what you would be willing and able to **trust** in today.

4. Write down how you have put **wanting-ness** over **joy**, money over relationships, and material objects over inner state. These are formulas for failure. Write down how you might practice putting that which **really matters** first, how you might put love and joy over external factors.

5. Write down how you have been **thinking small**. After each item write down how you could **think big** instead. Move from seeing problems to seeing opportunities. Move from seeing problems to seeing them as challenges. Move from being a miser to being generous. Move from being "realistic" to dreaming. Move from lack to abundance. Move from fear to courage.

6. Write down how you have been **dissociated**, alienated, remote or distant from yourself and others. After each item write down how you could become more **present**, aware, engaging and authentic.

7. Write down how you have been **complaining, criticizing** and **blaming.** After each item write down how you could assume **responsibility**. In addition, write down something to **praise** and **appreciate**.

After completing this little exercise: How do you feel? I expect nothing less than a new feeling of elation. That feeling will increase as you look at your map regularly, and check off the items you have improved.

Seize the Day

It's not the best of habits to "save energy for later" in the mistaken assumption that energy is limited. If you act from that assumption, guess what? You won't have quite as much energy. To help you see pattern, here are some examples:

* "I will withhold my best performance for a customer who is paying more."

* "Maybe someday a better partner will show up, THEN I will give everything."

* "I will give my best in the next game because the next game is more important."

* "I will save this nice shirt for a more important day."

* "I will withhold love because I must keep my energy for work."

With the athlete who says: "I am saving my energy for a more important game," the following is going to happen: By the time that more important game comes around, he will not be in the *momentum* of high performance and will have a harder time in accessing *peak state*. Had he accessed peak state in the previous "unimportant game", he would be in the habit and flow of it, and easily do well in the current game. Taking the example of the relationship: There is no future day in which it is more appropriate to give love. No energy is "saved for work" by withholding love to your partner. On the contrary, giving love energizes you for work. Everything is ONE energy, and as you approach one thing you approach everything. The amount of energy in the Universe is unlimited. And if you give it all today, you will have more tomorrow, because the sleep in-between re-energizes you. Seize the day, and you'll be right back in a state of flow

Feeling Alive and Energetic

That feeling of sheer exuberance we felt in our childhood...we wouldn't mind a little more of that, would we? As children, we rarely if ever felt burnt-out, depleted or wasted.

There is a Spanish word, "duende" that originally meant a higher spirit entering you and causing you to view your surroundings, other people and nature with awe and wonderment. According to the dictionary today the word refers "a mysterious power a work of art has to deeply move a person". But I prefer the original definition. If you are infused with spirit, anything, not only art, has the power to deeply move you. Art and music are used to reconnect *after* soul is lost.

You can experience "duende" if you move from your **concept** of life to the actual **experience** of life, if you see the world from soul-eyes instead of mind-eyes. There's a difference between your concept of the chair you are sitting on, and its experience. There is a difference between your concepts of other people, and the actual person. For a moment, forget all of your memories about chairs, about what chairs are and what they mean. And just reduce all expectation you have about chairs. Instead, put your Attention into the chair (or sofa, or bed) you are sitting on, and feel it; be the chair fully and without boredom or resistance. You are now actually experiencing the chair instead of conceptualizing it. Try the same with another human being - notice how intensely you can encounter them.

One of the core-statements of the mind/ego goes something like this:

"Nothing is happening."

"There is not much going on."

"Nothing is moving."

"Nothing is changing."

"Things are mediocre."

"Things are boring."

The mind/ego sees things this way because it's a recording device that is meant to record events throughout life on earth. Having seen everything thousands of times, it gets bored. A good example is of the way it sees the moon and the way a child (or the soul) sees the moon. Already having made thousands of recordings of the moon, it's nothing special. *"It's just the moon. So what? There is nothing happening here. Nothing moving. Nothing changing."* Hence, the ego-self always strives for "change" but never gets it (wanting change = lacking change). A child who looks at the moon for the first time is awestruck: "Wow! The moon! The moon! Look at that mommy!" Until about the age of three, the child is ECSTATIC about seeing the moon. And there is a lot happening, a lot moving and shifting around, but ego-self doesn't see it because it lives in past-recordings, not in present-time. The child repeats: "It's the moon! The moon!" and mommy says, "Uh-huh…the moon. Yeah."

If you could take some time, now and then, to just sit and observe for a few minutes. Observe what is happening. There are trillions of things happening right now. And it's ALL incredibly beautiful. But the mind says, "I already know." This viewpoint is actually a subtle block to expansion, discovery and adventure because if you "already know", there is nothing new to see. Considering that infinity is infinite, you don't actually know much of anything. "I already know" is a lie that manifests itself in statements such as:

"I've seen it all."

"You can't teach an old dog new tricks."

"I have already read so many books."

"I have already done so many things."

"I have already been through all of that."

But have you "been through all of that" from the eyes of Love? There are millions of ways to smell a rose. Have you experienced them all? I doubt it.

People tend to put on the "I already know" to avoid overwhelm. There are so many things going on, we sometimes just shut-down Awareness. The more blunted Awareness becomes, the more stimulus is required to feel anything at all. Then a piece of art, a good movie or book, falling in love or bearing children, winning a game or seeing the stars at night won't amount to much. The ego-self is desensitized to any of that. But it's not the world that is boring, it's the observer.

When I watch the news and see all the atrocities committed in the world, I realize that I too am somewhat blunted. That is, I don't feel much. Everyday there is some new atrocity, and if you see it over, and over, and over again (and add to that thousands of Hollywood movies that show the same thing), you don't really feel that much. The full horror and gravity of the situation can then only be experienced by being in the middle of the scenes, and in the countries where they take place. This jaded blunting of emotion works both ways, until neither positive nor negative events have much of any effect. This is actually why I don't watch much news. I don't want to become the person who sits there watching war on a screen, while in the comfort of my couch, holding a can of soda and munching on popcorn. I'd rather be the person who contributes something positive to the world through action. Not to mention that giving psychopaths Attention and airtime energizes their cause. Have you ever wondered why good people who teach, heal, transform, and improve are given almost no airtime on the news, while those who pillage, rape and murder get the most TV-time? You can't just blame it on the media, as most people parrot the news-media on their blogs, Facebook, discussion forums and whatnot. it's important to know what's going, on, but it's of no help to replay the atrocities over and over again, as if those committing them were some kind of superheroes. Turning off the screen and focusing on the reality at-hand, in your daily life, increases aliveness.

If you want to feel more of life, let go of the purely conceptual and informational, and lean towards the experiential. If you want to learn something new, let go of "I already know," and open up. Look at life as if seeing it for the first time. Walk around with eyes wide-open. Life is full of surprises. Surprises can happen any minute, if you allow them to. Put your loads of information and knowledge aside for a day, and see what happens when you go for joy instead.

When you get a new job, move to a new place, fall in love or go on an unexpected trip, you get that feeling of excitement and aliveness.

But what about the rest of the time?

For the rest of the time, some pretend to feel alive when actually they feel hardly anything. If you get promoted in a job and everyone congratulates you, and you are feeling high, then after three weeks, the novelty wears off, and you have to pretend to still be high about it... Sound familiar? When you are in your tenth year of marriage, and suddenly notice that the intensity of the first weeks of the relationship is lost... Sound familiar? You feel high now and then, but...

What about the rest of the time?

The in-between times are what you call "normal life" where you are working towards the next wave of high. However, there is a way to become less dependent on these waves, on these peak-experiences that only show up once in awhile. And that is to simply go from concept to experience and to **feel.** Becoming familiar with your inner nature is directly related to how much happiness you have. Everything people do or purchase is somehow related to feeling more. But if you learn how to allow that aliveness from within, you will become independent of outside substitutes. Not that there is anything wrong with them as such. You will even enjoy them more than before. But life is not about how you feel sometimes, it is about how you feel day-to-day, in normal life. Even a professional athlete who feels an enormous high from winning a gold medal, only has a few minutes of that moment in time. What about the rest of the year before that and the rest of the year after? Your typical 3-act Hollywood movie does reality a disservice by making it look like life takes place in that short span of time. Real life is neither triumph nor tragedy, it's a whole lot more in-between.

Put time aside to experience your inner self. Don't wait until an emergency happens before you direct your Attention to your inner or higher nature. All illnesses, all addictions, all depression, all compulsions and all disorders arise because feelings were ignored and pushed away for too long. You can dissolve problems many years before they happen by tending to this kind of energy work.

All impatience, all anger, all fear and all denial comes from dissociating from feeling and fully experiencing. And by feeling life I don't mean sitting around crying all the time, or looking for some problem to dissolve. Feeling life can also mean taking time to smell the flowers, to look at children play, to listen to the rustle of leaves or to ponder one's week. Experience the physical sensations in your body. Experience the objects around you. Look at your computer. Put your Attention and Awareness inside of your computer and feel it. That's how to experience the computer.

People who suppress their emotions more deeply develop strange obsessions, compulsions, muscle-twitching and ticks. One can get rid of all compulsion through emotional clearing processes. These things cover-up deeper hidden pains that want to be processed, so you experience them, you invite them up. Also fully experience your deepest desires and the hidden emotions behind them. Fully experience your impulses and moods. You can also experience and feel spaces. When you enter a room, fully experience that room. That room has a history. That room has a vibratory frequency, an energy-pattern. That room can tell you everything that happened in it. Stop conceptualizing about it and actually **experience** it.

Feelings are energies. Energies want to be integrated. You integrate energies by fully feeling them without wanting to hold on or get rid of them. "Feel them to the end." Every energy is limited in space or time. Even the greatest fear runs itself out if you allow it to. There are a lot of people walking around that should have integrated their feelings decades ago. Overweight is an indicator that you have unintegrated feelings. Constantly looking for the next big rush of excitement is an indicator of unintegrated feelings. Frequent bouts of rage are unintegrated feelings. Continually spouting conspiracy-theories and regularly engaging in heated political debate are unintegrated feelings. Unintegrated feelings equals disempowerment. Integration equals empowerment. The way feelings and energies feel is not determined by events but by our thoughts-about-events, our labels, judgments and beliefs.

On the journey of emotional integration, more and more feelings that want to be processed, come up. Feelings from the past, from childhood, from other lives, from mass-consciousness, from the planet, from parallel-selves, etc. And with every integration of energy you get a gain of energy. So the more you integrate, the more energy you start having. People always ask me why I have so much energy. I have a dozen unpublished books on my computer, and I am still writing. Why are they unpublished? Because it would look weird to be publishing a book every week. How was I able to perform such a feat? It's because I am constantly overflowing with energy.

When you integrate an energy it goes from form back to formlessness. That's how it works. That's how all of reality is de-created. What they call "enlightenment" in the far east is nothing more than the return back to formlessness. As more and more is integrated, you become more creative, intuitive and energetic.

Feeling life is not to be mistaken with catharsis or overidentificiation with feelings or "being emotional", much less with being hypersensitive and whiny, but simply accepting, allowing and welcoming whatever is there. You don't ignore, avoid, medicate, repress, tense, distract from, talk about or daydream-away your feelings, neither do you try to hold on to or get lost in them. "Getting lost" in your feelings means you cannot see a separation between you and what you feel; you become the effect of it instead of its witness. Resist your feelings, and they become worse or turn into problems, dramas and tragedies. Integrate your feelings, and they turn into pure energy and many different types of flow.

You can **feel it** anywhere and at any time. In fact, I recommend you practice **actively feeling** in different situations because we tend to be able to feel in certain contexts and shut-off feeling in others. Also, most of our feeling is passive and reactive, as an auto-response to what is going on. But that has nothing to do with active feeling. You may be easily able to fully experience life sitting on a park bench. But you may not be able to do so when your grandfather or boss is nearby. The best time to practice feeling it or going from concept to experience is when it seems you can't; when you have gone unconscious or into the conceptual world. There is nothing wrong with the conceptual world by the way. But when you spend too much time in it, you tend to lose your aliveness because you are then living in thoughts about the world instead of being-with the world itself. That's like thinking about love all the time, instead of being in love. It's like pondering skydiving instead of doing it. It's like reading about Juicy Fruit instead of chewing it. It's like looking at pictures of a country instead of going there. Would you rather study life or experience life?

Breathing will help you feel the world. If a person walks by you, you can actually experience more of that person if you "breathe with" him/her. That is, your Attention is with him/her and you "breathe him/her in". If you feel a contraction in your chest, that's because energy is stuck. You can dissolve that energy by "breathing with it". When you feel it, you should also know that there is no such thing as "no feeling" or "not feeling anything". If you think that's what's going on, then you actually are feeling something, namely numbness, dullness, tightness or dissociation. Those are also feelings, even if they are not as obvious.

Emotional Integration

We are used to categorizing our feelings such as anger, sadness and fear, but when integrating those energies you do not have to label them that way. If you allow yourself to simply experience them as energy, label them as energy or as feeling (or not to label them at all), they more easily integrate. Another way to transform them is to label them *differently*. That is an alternative method to integrating energies. You would, for example, label fear as "excitement", and try to experience more of it, and more of it and more of it, pretending that you really wish to experience that. You'd be surprised at how rapidly fear dissolves. Just a moment ago you were really scared, then you are completely free of the thing called "fear".

Sometimes it can be good to consciously say "hello" to your feelings or welcome them with gratitude. They are performing a fantastic service to you. You don't want to get rid of your navigation system that is providing such valuable feedback. There are various ways to "converse" with emotions. You could ask: "Where are you from?" And see if your Attention does not trace the feeling back to a past experience. You could ask: "What would I have to be thinking to feel this way?" And trace it back to some belief. You could ask: "What do you want?" You could ask what the value of a particular feeling is or what its pay-off is. Sincerity is key. I know some people who actually manage to use my emotional clearing audios not to explore and integrate feelings, but to suppress them even more. It's about the sincerity with which you use those audios. Do not use them to "get rid of that stuff quickly" but to explore and integrate.

A trick to deepen emotional integration and releasing is to not only welcome the feeling, but also welcome the part of you that is trying to "handle" or "get rid of" the feeling and the back-story to it, the part of you that is wanting to change it, the part of you that is judging it and the part of you that intends to overcome it. Check whether you have unconsciously attached labels to the feeling and breathe/peel those labels off.

Can you intensify the feeling you have? Can you de-intensify it? On a scale from 1 to 10, can you move it up and down that scale in intensity? Can you determine its color, weight and exact location? If it is in the chest, how many inches behind the surface of your chest's skin is it? Can you see where it is and where it is not? Can you allow the energy to flow to another part of your body, then back to where it was? Could you generate the opposite feeling, then shift back-and-forth between the original feeling and its opposite? Is there an underlying deeper feeling than the one you are experiencing? Some things are not immediately visible.

What happens when you go to its center? When you accomplish doing that, you will notice that behind the feeling there is....nothing. You have made it disappear. It is then replaced by an even deeper feeling.

What causes you to stop or go out of fully experiencing your nature? What are the blocks to processing your emotions? The main block is resistance. But that resistance can manifest in many ways. Some who attempt to go deeper encounter new types of blocks...they lose control, lose consciousness, get confused and/or get distracted by something happening in their surroundings. I can't tell you how often I have started a Coaching-Process with someone, only for him/her to suddenly get distracted by something big happening in his/her life, a lot of work suddenly coming in, suddenly meeting the woman/man of his/her dreams etc. Even positive events can be a distraction to fully experiencing."Yeah, I was just starting the process of feeling-life, as you recommended to me, but then, a few days ago I met the woman of my dreams and kind of forgot about practicing." There are millions of reasons not to start the process of feeling life. These reasons are subconsciously created to keep yourself from becoming **lighter**. Why are you preventing yourself from that? Because it messes with the amnesia you came to earth with intentionally.

Remember that you are never overwhelmed by a feeling, but by your resistance towards it. It's your own pushing that is feeling intense, not the feeling itself. Try to raise your threshold of overwhelm so that you can take more, and so you can say "yes" to more. Once you can say "yes" to anything that comes up, and take it inside you to integrate it, there will no longer be a need for you to reincarnate to the earthly plane. What follows are examples of things humanity has yet to emotionally integrate; traumas, wounds and upsets you can emotionally clear:

War
Crime
Abuse
Rape
Loss
Accidents
Injury
Sudden Death
Failure/Loser
School Failure
Love Loss
Betrayal
Shock
Embarrassment
Humiliation
Deprivation
Abandonment
Being Cheated
Abuse of Trust
Feeling Shame
Rejection
Isolation/Alienation
Dissociation/Numbness
Confusion
Feeling Untalented
Feeling Insane

Afraid of Being Normal
Afraid of Being Different
Vulnerability
Needing to Control
Resisting Being Controlled
Avoiding Contact With Others
Wanting Closeness/Togetherness
Obsessed With Pleasing Others
Sadistic
Masochistic
Addicted to Work
Addicted to Information
Loneliness
Feeling of Entitlement
Feeling of Superiority
Feeling of Inferiority
Needing Approval
Seeking Answers
Complaint
Perfectionism
Lack of Discipline
Obsessive Sexual Fantasy
Craving
Unfulfilled Desire
Pain
Avoiding Feedback
Having to Perform

Avoiding Crowds

Avoiding Contact

Positive Past Memories (preventing us from the here now)

Concerned About Self-Image

Negative Self-Image

Concerned About Looking Good

Pains From Others

Dissociation Derived from Alcoholism

Dissociation Derived from Drugs

Escapism (very popular in the self-improvement/New Age scene)

and many more.

All feelings are stored in the body or in the energy-field surrounding the body. Once something is integrated, you will experience relief or gain in energy. A good chunk of your emotions are stuck in the muscles, which is why sports tends to release stuck emotions and traumatic incidents. If you have an aversion towards sports, you might want to rethink your stance.

To increase feeling something you might want to place your palm there. The reason we lay our hands on people when healing them is to help them integrate the energy. Placing your palm on your forehead, the back of your head or on your heart can also intensify your sense of feeling yourself. Pressing two fingers in the notch below the nose is another way you can activate feeling. Yet another way is to ask: "What if I experience this forever?" Or: "What if I never again experience this?" Absolute statements tend to bring up subconscious pockets of emotion. Many feelings are connected to memories. Therefore, an emotional clearing session may bring up things you have not remembered in a long time.

Most pockets of stuck energy are in the torso, and there, in the various chakras, especially the stomach, solar-plexus and chest. But they do not have to be there. An energy can be under your armpit, forehead, foot, slightly outside of your face or back, or wherever else in your energy field. Get a felt sense of where the energy or stuckness is. Experience it fully. Return to serenity, love and power.

On Being Spontaneous

There exists a high meditative state that is near thought-less. This thoughtlessness does not translate into stupidity but spontaneity. If you have never experienced this level of consciousness before, you can nevertheless mimic it by being a little more spontaneous yourself. For example, you do not always have to use notes when giving lectures, speeches or presentations. I quit preparing for my lectures and courses years ago, so I could allow the present moment and my higher-self to take charge of the unfolding of reality from moment-to-moment. I don't recommend this if you feel insecure. If you feel insecure, I recommend you plan every minute detail. But in high energy, no preparation is needed. The right words and actions present themselves from moment to moment. They do not come from the ego-self, that part of you that is usually inhibited, but from a higher-self more humorous. This spontaneous-self is allowed to come through when you feel at ease and confident and do not need to micro-manage your day. If you macro-manage your day, meaning you see to it that your own state-of-being is relaxed, your overall intentions are clear, and your demeanor is loving and kind, then the micros of the day will take care of themselves – spontaneously. The idea of living spontaneously is that you do what you do when you are doing it, and you don't do what you are not doing when you are not doing it. The ego-self is filled with "What ifs…". What if this happens? What if that happens? What do we do if that comes to pass? How would we deal with it if this occurs? If there is one thing I can assure you of then it's that most of these "what ifs" are useless. They are an attempt to control what cannot be controlled. Cross the bridge when you come to it. You do not know what is going to be tomorrow. Check in yourself and others how many of your actions are undertaken in the assumption that you know what is going to happen tomorrow. And by pre-paving everything mentally, tomorrow holds no surprises. If you are constantly going to pre-pave tomorrow, then at least do it with positive thoughts. Prepare for the best. But on an even higher level, you don't concern yourself with "What ifs" at all. You deal with what spontaneously comes up. Don't prepare for the bridge crossing today. Never prepare for any negative event at all. There might not even be a bridge when you get there. There might be a rocket.

The Power of Restraint

Too much of something desensitizes you toward its pleasures. When you lose touch with your inner-energy, you increasingly make joy and happiness dependent on outside circumstances. Using your willpower to practice restraint can bring back the joy of certain things. Examples:

* If you watch movies all the time, you'll become desensitized. Try being **without** them for a few weeks or months, and **then** see how excited you get over them.
* If you smoke every day, then you no longer feel any effects of the nicotine. Try not smoking for a day, and on the next day smoke one cigarette. You will feel **high as a kite**,
* If you drink coffee every day, take a one week break. Then notice how **delicious** coffee is again.
* If you are addicted to reading books, take a break for a few months, then notice how **special** and sacred reading one book feels.
* If you do Instagram, Facebook, Twitter, Tumblr, etc. every day, cut it off for a month, then see how much fun it is to discover it anew.
* If you eat every day, take one day break from eating. And then notice how **good** food tastes.

Overload desensitizes you and de-values the thing you are wanting to get pleasure from. This is why the Internet is not always a good thing. Too much information de-values a singular pieces of information. Everything being "available for free" on the Internet tends to breed dissatisfaction, not enjoyment. Less is more.

Accessing Higher Frequencies

This is an exercise to access the soul. The mind can only access information it has recorded throughout this lifetime. Everything the mind knows, only refers to this lifetime. The mind does not have access to past lives, future lives, other lives or other dimensions. A simple way to access the soul is to therefore think of or look at things you have never thought of or looked at before.

Such behavior takes Attention beyond the narrow confines of the recording device called "mind" because you have no past examples of that new thought or object of Attention.

You have probably never been stranded on a lonely island before. But if you were, you would quickly access your soul because you need a new sort of knowledge to deal with the unfamiliar situation. This is why the unfamiliar is empowering. How to deal with a brand new situation? The mind doesn't know. It has never done it before. The soul does know. Intuition knows. This is why strong CEOs sometimes employ types of people they are unfamiliar with or even people opposed to them. This is why a vacation should not be entirely safe at all times. This is why you should not only be reading books in your area of expertise or books that confirm your own belief-system.

Can you think a thought you have never thought before? If so, you did not get that thought from the mind. You got it from other planes of reality.

Exercise: See if you can put your Attention on 5 things this week that you have never before put your Attention on, and learn something new. Notice how it feels.

A 1000 Types of Happiness

There is not only either "happy or not happy", but like a spectrum or staircase, thousands of nuances and levels of well-being. This you discover as you keep ascending in life. There is…

contentment

pleasure

enjoyment

optimism

gladness

glee

buoyancy

sunniness

elation

cheerfulness

merriment

joviality

mirth

delight

peace of mind

joy

felicity

serenity

exuberance

jubilation

effervescence

ebullience

lightheartedness

exhilaration

beatitude

ecstasy

hilarity

euphoria

enchantment

bliss

and thousands of other types of happiness. Simply re-reading this list slowly and thinking about each item should uplift you while reading.

In higher-realms than that of planet earth, such states are commonplace. Experiencing these emotions therefore, is the quickest way to touch upon higher worlds and bring some of their qualities down to earth.

I've done seminars in which I've had people look up these words in dictionaries, and collect sample pictures to each expression of happiness. Why? Well, if you don't know what you are aiming for, you won't get there.

...en·chant·ment:
noun \in-'chant-mənt, en-\: a feeling of being attracted by something interesting, pretty, etc. : the state of being enchanted
: a quality that attracts and holds your Attention by being interesting, pretty, etc.
the enchantment of a snowy field bathed in moonlight...

Once during a taxi ride with one of my seminar translators by focusing on these words and reading examples of how they are used, our own mood actually shifted upwards. By the time our destination was reached, I felt absolutely happy and ecstatic. By having to **remember examples** of ecstasy and elation from my life and explaining them to my translator, I had to get myself into those states. And that's how I had the happiest taxi ride of my life.

The lesson learned here is that our normal daily states are only habitual. It's just a habit to be riding in a taxi in a normal state. The reason we do not experience higher states habitually is because we are not aware of them, do not think of them and are not used to them. Not only do we rarely use vocabulary such as "mirth", "merriment", "joviality", "hilarity", "euphoria", "lighthearted", etc, we rarely think about what they mean and how they might be experienced. Just the act of looking up, defining and using high-energy vocabulary is a great state-changer.

Paradise Is a State of Mind

Paradise could be seen as a place that you go to. And it's certainly easier to feel better in beautiful and peaceful environments than in others. But as you grow in consciousness, you realize that paradise is *more a time than a place*. It's about the good times you have had at any particular place.

I once returned to a beautiful island north of the Netherlands because I remembered the last time I was there, it was paradise. We had played guitar and sang at sunset, played tag in the dunes and let the waves of the sea wash us. But when I returned there was something missing: The group of people I was with. So while the island was still nice, I could not quite recapture the times I had back then at this place. Walking along that beach alone was different than with that group of people from back then.

As you grow even more, you realize that **paradise is neither a place nor a time, but a state of being.** After visiting that island, I arranged a get together, a sort of reunion, with that group of people. But only 5 years later many of them had strongly changed. Sitting together in that particular restaurant was interesting, but the atmosphere we had back then could not be copied. As you grow in consciousness, you stop trying to recapture past paradises and instead make the best of the here-and-now. That may include good memories in the now or future visions in the now, but you no longer create a split between the supposed "better times" and today. New paradises can unfold today.

At this **level** of consciousness, paradise can be had almost anywhere and at almost any time. You can aid this state by your Attention to the present moment and with thoughts of the uniqueness and mystery of the present. There is a part of you that is untouched by all past experience and undisturbed by anything that has happened before. This observer-self is closer to the true you and can appreciate the present moment differently than the part of you that is preoccupied.

Joy Is Contagious

Joy – a sense of lightness and exuberance that is often sparked by sound health, fresh discovery or new achievement. Children are generally more joyful because they more often discover new things and attain new abilities.

Joy is an inner quality that can also arise when there is no external cause for it. Becoming too dependent on external cues before joy can be felt is one of humankinds foremost limitations.

Joy can also be defined by what it is not, as the absence of heaviness, tightness, seriousness, cynicism, despair, complaint and regret.

Experiencing joy provides fuel for your daily activities. Being energy channeled from higher domains, it positively effects your health and clarifies perception.

So how does joy arise, and is there anything you can do or be to allow for more of it to flow?

Joy may arise in a state of meditative calm or during a moment of insight or learning. It can show-up through your own acts of care and kindness, as giving produces a unique "natural high". Joy can come by directing your Attention to specific memories in which joy was felt. Everyone has memories of peace and laughter. Joy can be reclaimed by wishing others joy and happiness. When I walk around town, I sometimes target random individuals and telepathically say: "May you find joy."

One of the easiest ways to experience joy is by contagion. Joy is contagious if you allow it. Of course, you can sit at a table full of happy people and not allow their happiness to effect you. If you focus differently than them, you can stay grumpy. Vice-versa, you could also be at a table full of grumpy people and remain joyful. Ultimately your mood is directed internally. Nonetheless, by observing people who are joyful and empathizing with them, you are allowing their mood to touch you and this will bring up your own particles of joy. Joy therefore is often shared joy, as in the joy that develops when two people are doing something together.

Genuine spontaneous joy can often be observed in very old and very young people because it is they who filter their joy the least. So if you know anyone who is overflowing with joy, spend time with him/her or even think of him/her right now. Appreciate who he/she is and how his/her heart is generous and open. There is more to learn from someone who is joyful than from another who appears to know everything, but emanates no joy. Indeed, if I happen to visit a lecture or seminar where there is much knowledge but no joy, I soon leave.

Life being a balance of darkness and light, it is also beneficial not to suppress its opposite – sadness – but to allow that emotion to pass through when it arises. It is not at all necessary to constantly try to live up to the happy grinning faces staring at you from billboard-ads. Paradoxically, allowing and giving space to your lower emotions will facilitate your ability to experience higher emotions.

Here is an experiment: The next time you try to distract yourself with your phone or computer, instead put those aside and simply feel what you are feeling. Allow whatever feeling is there to just be there and "run itself out". Then, once you are in a fairly calm state, say: "I feel joy," and take a deep and most gentle breath. Repeat that a few times and notice how you have just shifted your state internally, independent of the external situation.

Passion, Desire and Eagerness

If you remove the *lacking* part of **Desire,** it becomes **Eagerness** and **Passion,** which are amongst the strongest creative forces on earth. The dictionary defines the word "eager" as: "of a person wanting to do or have something very much," and "characterized by keen expectancy or interest". Some of the synonyms listed for "eager":

Keen
Avid
Ardent
Zealous
Desirous
Fervent
Impatient
Anxious
Solicitous
Enthusiastic
Greedy

When Eagerness or Desire are mixed with lack-consciousness (The belief that you really want something but can't have it), they become destructive, as in greed, impatience, entitlement-syndrome, craving, addiction, egocentricity, nervousness and anxiousness, and desperation. But if there is the underlying feeling that you are **able to be, do or have whatever you Desire,** then it becomes a potent force of power, concentration and movement of energy. Lack of Desire can make you a boring person whose life is without movement. Strong Desire will get things rolling for you. Belief coupled with Desire will get things to manifesting for you. People who teach that you should have no Desires or can overcome your Desires are either deluded, or they are speaking from a level of consciousness that does not apply to 99.9% of humanity. The result of turning a Desire into a belief in your ability to be, do or have something results in a sense of empowerment, and sets you on a journey of achievement. You achieve it and what follows is great **relief,** and you realize the journey was even more significant than the goal. So then you choose another, and another, expanding your consciousness more, and more, and more, because there is no limit upwards...

Want to Feel More Alive? Reduce Your Screen Time

Cutting down your screen time (time spent in front of screens of computers, Internet, smartphones, televisions) will help you feel more alive. A metaphysical rule of the thumb is: **Whatever you give your Attention to is what you start feeling like.** If you give a lot of Attention to a flat screen, don't be surprised if you start feeling kind of flat. I may sound like a hypocrite saying this, but the Internet is overrated. It is only loads of information, nothing more. Information is not experience. Information is not transformation. Information is not higher states of consciousness. Information is just...a bunch of words. Words are useful pointers and guides for instruction, but having more words than experience is like having tons of encyclopedias about food but not getting anything to eat. If information is not applied and used, it is not really information, it's often a self-indulgent waste of time. You don't really need to know all the latest news, to watch every episode of the latest show or to keep abreast of what everyone is doing on Facebook.

Here's the idea that has worked very well for me: If you are going to spend a lot of time in front of a screen, it would be better you do so **as a creator, not as a consumer**. So, why not check how much time you spend in consuming-mode vs. creation-mode? And if you are going to relax and be a consumer for awhile, why not be more picky and choosy as to what you allow your eyes to see, your ears to hear and your mind to touch? Everything you allow your field of consciousness to enter has an effect on you, even if that effect is small at first. The correlation is often missed. For instance, you can't be spending more than an hour a day reading news sites rife with fear and anger, then expect to go about your day in tranquil harmony. Such would be much more likely if you had spent that same time taking a walk in the park.

Quality over Quantity

There are many ways in which **intensity** is more important than **duration**, and quality is more important than quantity. What is rare is more valued. Those who prize quantity over quality are coming from a place of mental or physical starvation. Just a few examples to remind you of this point:

* With more nutritious food, less quantities are needed to fill you up and provide energy.

* Those who workout know that intensity is more important than extent or time spent in training.

* In a relationship, you can be spending a lot of time together and not really *be* together. Clearly the *amount* of time spent is less significant than the **quality of Attention**. When with your child, it's clearly more important whether the time was enjoyed than how many hours were spent. Of course, the amount of time spent is not irrelevant, but it takes second place to the quality of that time. One hour of good playtime with a child or one hour of quality with your partner is worth more than 10 hours of living alongside a person but not really perceiving them.

* In my twenties I taught English. It puzzled me why students *primarily* wanted to know how many *hours* they were booking and what those hours cost. I delivered a basic English course that took 6 days. People complained that it was expensive because "It's *only* 6 days." But I did not count in days, I counted in number of vocabulary learned. "You learn 1000 new words and phrases in six days. On the sixth day I will test you on all thousand words, and you will know them and more. That's more than you will learn anywhere else in the same time." Something easily forgotten is that saving time is a way of saving money. So while it may have been *only* 6 days, it was not *only* 1000 words.

* Five minutes of being present or 5 minutes of conscious thought can achieve more than 3 hours of work. Three hours of passionate work can achieve more than 1 week of scattered or dull work. Conventional ways of working are inefficient. When I employ someone, I never give him/her daily work times or tell him/her how he/she they should work. I instead say, "This project should be completed by…. Can you do it?" It's up to them to determine his/her daily work time.

* "Some of your books are too short!" someone recently complained. The idea seems to be that the thicker a book is, the better. It's never about the amount of knowledge, but its intensity and quality. The more quick-witted a person is, the less I need to tell him/her for him/her to understand something. Sometimes – with very intelligent people – I only just start a sentence, and they already understand the entire concept of what I am talking about before I've even finished. Some only read the title of a newspaper item and already comprehend the entire article. Quick-wit and intelligence are obviously connected to energy-state and Awareness. When someone is tired, more talk is needed for he/she to understand.

* Most people who run a business think that "the more customers, the better!" I beg to differ. In my world, one pleasant customer is worth more than one hundred mediocre customers.

* One day of deep and full relaxation has a much stronger effect than three weeks of a "vacation" full of pressure and expectation.

Quality of life increases when you can selflessly dedicate yourself to the present moment with increased Attention, rather than being egoically preoccupied with past/future events, or trying to "get something" out of someone. You can heighten the quality of everything you do by attending to it more fully. Whether you are taking a shower, washing your car or holding a speech on TV, there is always a higher and a mediocre version of experiencing that.

The Joy of Surprise

Surprise is one of the spices of life. It occurs when you hold a set of assumptions about what is going to happen and something entirely different happens. It occurs when you have a fixed set of rules and routines, and open that fixation a little to let in something new. You have the capacity to experience more positive surprise, wonderment and amazement. One of the doors to this is by providing positive surprise to others. As you positively surprise others, you become the source of surprise and open the floodgates to the Universe surprising you. How could you be the giver of pleasant surprise to someone else today?

Another way to let in more positive surprise is by allowing yourself to perceive more and be surprised by things you normally dismiss as normal. If you look carefully, there is more happening than meets the habitual eye. As a practical exercise, look at something supposedly mundane and pretend for a moment that its actually amazing. As if you were surprised, raise your eyebrows, wrinkle your forehead, open your jaws and widen your eyes. This is the body language of surprise, and it will produce a certain state and perception. You will notice that as you mimic certain states physiologically, your emotions will follow.

With such an expression on your face, check whether previously mundane things such as a parking lot, a grocery cart, people walking on the streets or the buildings around you look slightly brighter and more interesting. You'll notice that as you generate more willingness-to-amazement within yourself, you become more present. You can live life as if nothing were a miracle, or as if everything were a miracle. I have found the latter to be more enjoyable.

The Science of Happiness

These are a few random scientific statistics on Happiness that I have picked up on the Internet:

- Serotonin, which is commonly found in foods such as turkey and bananas, tends to increase one's mood, help in learning, increase ones sexuality and improve one's sleep.
- 20 minutes in good weather (clear skies and sunshine) tends to increase ones mood.
- Married people are on average 10% happier than unmarried people.
- Too much consumerism is one of the main causes of unhappiness
- The ideal temperature for a good mood is apparently 14 degrees Celsius (57 Fahrenheit).
- Healthy and athletic people are on average 20% happier.
- Getting plenty of sleep is the basis of energy and happiness.
- Children's most important source of happiness are close friends and family.
- People who are part of a community, a religion or follow a specific life purpose tend to be happier.

- People with a higher monetary income say they are happier.

Humor as a Higher Level of Consciousness

Humor can sway crowds. Humor is the best aphrodisiac. Humor closes big deals. Laughter eases pain. Humor makes things move along smoothly. In my book *Levels of Energy*, humor is described as an actual energy-form, with a tangible relative strength and effect, as compared to other states and emotions. It is described as one of the strongest forces available to humankind. It's so much more than a nice distraction.

I am not implying you should become a clown. But I am saying that the you can feel and transmit this energy – even without making jokes or acting up – just non-verbally, and it will bring a smile to people's faces. If you are radiating this vibe and ask someone, "Why so serious?" They will crack up.

The presence or absence of humor becomes a measuring stick by which you can tell the consciousness-level of any group, activity, seminar, relationship, etc. Being a self-improvement coach, I used to visit a lot of seminars, workshops, retreats…and always got a good laugh at how grim and serious so many of those "teachers" were. If you see a teacher without humor, or find yourself at some meeting without the slightest smile, my advice is to run…run far away.

If any of you have had difficulty finding a partner, herein lies the key. If you can't get a man/woman to laugh, you hardly stand a chance…unless you are comfortable with getting together with other extremely serious minds. Laughter is a very powerful aphrodisiac. That's why the Casanovas of this world have used humor as their primary weapon of seduction. That's why laughter wins the hearts of reluctant men/women.

If you cultivate humor as an actual energetic-skill; as something you radiate outwards, you can non-verbally influence any situation with it, even while you are keeping a straight face. If there are a group of people having a fight or argument, and you stand there radiating gentle waves of humor, you can dispel their fight by the power of your energy. THAT is how powerful it is.

There are three basic levels of consciousness:

1. Animalistic

2. Intellectual/Robotic

3. Spiritual

Love and humor are what differentiate you from animal and robot-consciousness, elevating you to spiritual consciousness. I'd argue that a comedian potentially has more healing-power than most actual healers out there.

Asking someone in a somber state of mind: "Why are you so serious?" immediately interrupts their mind/ego-spiel and opens them up. Too much seriousness acts like a glue that keeps problems stuck in their place. Humor on the other hand, acts like a dissolvent that evaporates energies of hardness.

"Why so serious?" is a question you can also ask yourself throughout the day. If you knew the nature of the Universe, you would not be as serious as you are because you would know that the world is a stage, an epic theater-play in which we are the actors of many roles. "Humor" in this sense, does not mean to mock tragedies or make fun of suffering. But it *does* mean not to take the world as the only and most important thing there is. It *does* mean not to take yourself and the events that happen quite as seriously as someone who is too identified with the movie-of-life. **Angels can fly because they take themselves lightly.**

Lack of humor is rife in the fields of spirituality, psychology and religion, and the main symptom of the decay of various movements/groups. From the perspective of Infinite Consciousness, the world and its little dramas and stage-plays are hilarious, a joke: a comedy. Humor cuts through the BS of the world-self (ego) that constantly takes himself, his opinions, his goals and problems much too seriously. Exaggerated seriousness is an indicator of a belief in a problem or that life is problematic. Lack of humor is also indicative that a person has something to hide. As hidden agendas cost a lot of suppression, repression and energy, there is not much left for lightness and humor. So do not trust anyone who never has a sense of humor, never laughs or is continuously uptight and grim.

In the field of spiritual coaching, lack of humor indicates that someone is fixed in narrow positionalities and rigid rules/formulas, rather than connected with the spontaneity of reality in the here and now.

Humor allows the aspirant to handle life's issues and resistances with more ease and clarity, rather than assigning overblown importance and fear to them. Humor is the lubricant that keeps the engines of the body and mind flowing smoothly. Watching comedy is a spiritual activity. Laughter releases vital energies and chemicals for your health and emotional well-being. Humor comes about when confronted with the paradoxical and with deviations from the norm. Evidence that there is such a thing as a universal standard or norm is that we laugh when that standard is broken, when people and nature behave differently than how they are "supposed to". Failed comedy (comedy that does not make us laugh) is when too many deviations from the norm occur, so that the deviation becomes commonplace. That is, if you tell too many jokes, it becomes boring. If everything is crazy, crazy becomes the new norm. Humor then, only works in contrast to the norm.

Also, what I find funny is not necessarily what others think is funny. When I have tried to watch my favorite comedies with others, they've often solicited nothing other than a slight chuckle, while I was rolling with laughter. What does this tell me? It tells me that we live in vastly different frames-of-reference and what is hilarious for one may not be for another. Something is only funny when it deviates from what *you* are personally used to. And it's the same with all other things in life. One person's frustration is another person's sport, one person's romance is another's boredom.

Do yourself a favor and find a good series to laugh about. If it does not make you laugh, discard it and find something else. Once you have found a comedy-maker that is on your wavelength, watch all of that person's works. You will become lighter and more free.

Top 7 Ways to Regain Your Sense of Humor

Folks who lack a sense of humor have a lot of bottled-up emotions and social insecurities, much of which they aren't even aware about. Life is very amusing if you look closely, but I often find myself being the only one laughing at its various scenes. It seems as though people, through hardship, become subdued. They then walk around and actually believe and feel that life is serious.. But seen in a larger, more universal context, life is not serious at all.

Sometimes, when I meet someone who shows not even the slightest sense of humor, I suspect he/she has something to hide, and I suspect he/she is a fraud. Why else would he/she be so tense? Here are top ten ways to regain your sense of humor in case it has gone lost:

1. Get a series of intense massages to loosen up.
It may come as a surprise to some, but one thing you can do to regain your sense of humor is to relax deeply. Unwind and go get a massage or something. Some massages release so much tension that you feel light and in a smiling mood for hours thereafter

2. Get into conversation flow with a circle of friends.

Sometimes you meet up with a circle of friends and not much seems to be happening. Then there are those days where you are sitting together at the table, and your whole table is having one laugh after another, making other tables look over to yours in wonderment. Everyone feels giddy and "in the flow" with the group. This usually happens when people have given-up their own self-importance, have given up trying to look good and are just chiming in and going with the flow, going wherever the conversation happens to be going. The group talk then becomes like some kind of comedic brainstorming in which all participants feel elated and high while being together and afterwards.

3. Watch good comedy.

It can take awhile before you find comedy that really suits your character and the overall mood of your life phase. But once you find the comedian, stand-up-act or TV-series that will make you laugh, you have a certain way to regain your hearty laughter.

4. Process suppressed emotions.

One of the best ways to regain a long-term sense of humor (which does not always express itself as laughter, but can also simply be a warm-hearted or light-hearted mood) is with emotional processing. Get all the emotional processing tools you can get your hands on, and release those fixed traumas, shocks and resignations. (see "The Bliss Course").

5. Change your physiology.

The way you move your legs, arms, body and facial muscles can make a difference between a low state and a high state. Deliberately smiling, even if you don't feel like it, will positively effect your state. Try it. Smile. And smile some more, until you actually feel the positive change. Now quit slumping your shoulders. Take in a straight position, put out your chest a little. You will feel better now. Now try to move funnily or awkwardly, and you will feel some of that humor-vibe arise.

6. Break routine.

Break your thinking, speaking and acting routines. If your spouse is used to you getting up and taking a shower, instead get up and make them breakfast. If you are used to talking about how great and important you are, talk about the most embarrassing moments of your life. (This will create a lot of humor!) Breaking routines frees you from fixed and rigid emotions, freeing you up for **the unexpected, the surprising and the spontaneous**...all of which facilitate humor. Humor cannot be faked because it is spontaneous. It's **real**.

7. See life through a funny filter.
Intend to go about your daily life with a funny filter, by looking for funny things, trying to see mundane things through an amused point of view, asking people what funny things occurred or happened to them today, and by observing people and their behavior in a little more detached sort of way.

*"Never stay up on the barren heights of cleverness, but come down into the green valleys of silliness." -
Ludwig Wittgenstein*

5
Concentration Training

Attention is focused Awareness. Concentration is focused Attention. The word "concentration" describes the most intense form of focus. Concentration however, should not be mistaken with the previously described "rigid Attention". It is a total focus on something without being strained.

Concentrating Yourself into Flow

All learning, ability, personal magnetism and knowledge you acquire are a matter of concentration. The effort you invest into creating a new reality must be higher than the momentum of the old reality. The power of Concentration is not a natural default, it must be developed as if developing a higher mind. Without concentration, your emotions, impulses, habits, physical needs, whims, aversions and attachments run your life. The only faculty that can overcome the "animal-self" is Concentration directed by will.

I recently worked with someone who wanted to become a painter. Like so many others, he was intent on painting "as soon as he felt like it". And like I have with so many others, I told him to paint whether he felt like it or not. "You don't begin with Flow," I taught. "Flow is something you get into while Concentrating." He had been wanting to paint for a decade, but had not started yet because he "didn't feel like it". In this way, his emotions controlled his actions, instead of him becoming bigger than his emotions. So he learned to just start painting, no matter the mood. And soon, while painting and concentrating, "not feeling like it" turned into zest and passion for painting. Such is the power of Concentration.

One of the most powerful exercises of my audio-program "Reality Creation Supercourse", is where I take a boring, random text and energize it through the power of concentration, instead of allowing the circumstance (the "boring" text) to dictate my mood. That exercise clearly demonstrates that the energy-state you have is determined by nothing other than your concentrated intention.

Concentration Leads to Well-Being

Concentration means you are no longer swayed by numerous appetites, obsessions and restless behavior. You slow down. You are poised. You know what you want, why you want it and you focus. Since most people's concentration is untrained, developing it will make it appear as if they have magical abilities compared to others. But it's not really magic, it's just Concentration. Concentration implies that you choose something to concentrate on. Being too broad and general as in, "Well, doing either X, Y or Z – it's all good," will not necessarily help. Concentration requires you to be specific. And as you concentrate on one task, energy begins to accumulate until you enter a state of "flow". A concentrated person cannot experience any troubles, any anger, fear or frustration. Since he/she is dedicated to the task at hand, in the here-and-now, all other considerations recede into the background and are not remembered or felt. A concentrated person does not walk to the refrigerator every 30 minutes to get some food, the very food that can, in turn, stimulate emotions that distract concentration.

A negative state is not the result of Concentration. That is a misconception. A negative state of mind and emotion is the result of a lack of concentration. As a rule, concentration is usually uplifting, mind-clearing, energizing and even relaxing. Contrary to popular opinion, effort and work are relaxing when done without resistance. If you are weak-minded you will not be able to focus on any particular subject, skill, thought or action, and your overall state will deteriorate. Soon your health and life circumstances will reflect your weakness. Because concentration is undeveloped, it will seem difficult to remove your mind from the undesirable and re-direct it to what is good for you.

Scattering your Attention to too much entertainment and news media weakens your Concentration. If your mind is roaming here and there all the time, no energy is accumulated, and nothing is accomplished. One way to strengthen your ability to concentrate is to stop scattering Attention and start prioritizing. Priority-lists are a helpful success tool. Another way to strengthen your concentration is to slow-down. Don't act, work, walk or look in too much of a hurry. Slow-down your eyes for example. Shifty eyes can only come from an unconcentrated mind. Concentration slows the eyes down. Slowing-down the eyes improves concentration. The same goes for walking. Awkward, hurried and nervous walking creates a state of scattered tension, and a state of scattered tension creates awkward, hurried and nervous walking. Slow-down and walk with more poise and Awareness. When you are talking to someone, don't allow that person to completely distract you from your poise. Keep your own intentions in mind. You can appreciate the other person, but you don't have to let their words and actions remove you from your own intentions.

Breathing and Time

Some self-regulation is a prerequisite for Concentration. While it may be nearly impossible to control one's thoughts much of the time, it is possible to control some of your Attention, speech and body movements. If you observe any person you consider charismatic or very successful, you will notice that they control their movements and physical body posture. You will also notice that they rarely participate in activities that stir-up emotions – noisy locations, drugs and lurid movies for example. This is because stirring-up emotions tends to be a distraction to steadiness and cause erratic energy-patterns. One of the secrets of concentration is: "Do what you are doing when you are doing it, and to not do what you are not doing when you are not doing it." That means, when you make love, be fully present. When you work, be fully with the work. When you wash the dishes, be fully with washing the dishes. When you play, be fully with playing". This not only expands your sense of time, it also builds your concentration and your well-being. Being on vacation and thinking of work is just as mind-weakening as being at work while thinking of vacation. The same goes for playing while thinking of work and working while thinking of play. Or being in a relationship while yearning to be alone, and being alone while yearning to be in a relationship. Such tendencies need to be overcome if you want to live a really fantastic life. When you go out and take a walk, see if you can be fully with the walk you are taking. Look at your surroundings. Look at the trees, birds, cars and buildings. Do not go elsewhere or try to be elsewhere. When you are meeting someone you deem "unpleasant", try to maintain your focus on him/her and the conversation or task at hand anyway. Centralize your mind on what is happening right now, and you develop the powers of the mind.

Since concentration is connected to the nervous system and the muscles, doing sports and workouts benefits your concentration, as well as taking in nutrition that is fairly wholesome. Without being a health-food fanatic, you can reduce eating too many sugars and carbs for example.

Slowing-down your breathing and sometimes breathing deliberately will improve concentration. If you are in a situation you deem important – a flirt encounter, a business negotiation, a job interview, a lecture you are holding, an argument you are having with someone – watch your breathing and exercise some control of it. If you can control any one thing, you have more control over the present reality. And it does not even have to be your breathing, it can also be controlling the movement of your fingers, hands, feet or legs. Any form of self-control will increase your concentration and also your power over the situation. That's why, when in conversation, I let others do most of the talking. I save my energy and only talk when I have something kind or interesting to say. This allows me to keep my concentration instead of dispersing.

Presence and Success

Your power of concentration will allow you to succeed in almost anything. Really, almost anything. To further develop your concentration, quit spending too much time with or associating with people who are fearful, dogmatic, nervous or angry – unless your powers are developed to a point where these no longer bother you. If you feel yourself getting scattered, nervous, self-conscious, shy or weak and unconcentrated, assume an upright body-posture and slow-down your breathing. Slow-down your eyes and look at something or someone for longer than 20 seconds. It takes about 20 seconds to regain concentration.

Let go of wishful thinking, magical thinking, desire, yearning, longing and ideas of entitlement. That is, instead of having the childish mind cry, "I want, I want, I want," have it say, "I can, I can, I can, I can!" or, "I will!" Or, "I have!" If there is some reality you want to manifest, hold the thought of it already being true. And then concentrate on that thought again, and again, and again and again. If you concentrated on a thought yesterday, see if you can do it again today, tomorrow, also next week and next month. You concentrate until it manifests. You can repeat the thought in your mind or visualize its representation. Allow your words and actions to be aligned with that thought.

Your actions reveal what you really believe. If you say, "I don't mind him not calling me," the action of staring at the phone every few minutes reveals your true beliefs. If you say, "I really believe I am successful" but find yourself grovelling at every offer of success, you know you don't really believe you are all that. It is easier to see what someone believes by looking at his actions and the fruits of his actions, than by what they are saying or wishing. So let your words and actions be congruent with your thoughts. This super-charges your concentration for the manifestation of new realities. Every day offers opportunities to develop focus. Let's say you are shopping and looking for an item. The shop you are in does not offer the item. So you go to another shop. They don't offer that either. So you go to another shop. They don't have it. So you ask the manager how to get it. He does not know. So you go to another shop. They don't have it. You again ask the manager. He doesn't know. You ask him to look it up in the catalogue. He tells you where you can get it. It's in another town. So you drive there. They are out of the product but tell you how you can order it. So you go order it. How many people would have given up long before? Most people, unfortunately. The person who went through all this is a person of concentration and power. He/she has a zest for life, he/she embraces challenge and a, "No!" turns on their determination even more.

Concentration, Decisiveness and Willpower

You can also exercise concentration by making rapid decisions. The higher your concentration is, the more quickly you will tend to make decisions, whereas when you are of weak state you will tend to procrastinate and put decisions off. Since not-acting usually requires less effort, choosing and action develops your inner-muscle. I really do believe that it is better to make a "bad" decision than no decision at all because the act of exercising choice and will is primary, and what decision is made, secondary. Even no-decision is a decision; it is a decision for nothing in particular.

Write down three things that have been waiting for a decision:

*

*

*

Decide on them quickly, right now. Don't worry about a decision being "wrong". Just go with what you intuitively sense is alright. Then, notice how the mere act of deciding gets energy going and moving. A life that was at a standstill has received another fresh injection of life.

Next, list 5 things you could do ahead of time:

*

*

*

*

*

Examples:

* I could get up one hour earlier the next 3 days.
* I could shop for food before I am asked to.
* I could take care of all the stuff on my to-do list today instead of this week.
* I could immediately stop procrastinating regarding some forms I have to fill out

What makes things "difficult" to do is not doing them. The power-to-do is determined by concentration. Once you tackle something, it is no longer bigger than you. You become bigger than it, and it becomes easy.

"Little things well done opens the door for bigger things."

Concentration and Intentions

Having a strong intention is a matter of concentration. Making a mental demand concentrates your life energies to a specific outcome. Such an intention effects your perception (you see opportunities others don't). Your facial expressions direct your behavior and actions, and give your life a new context from which to operate. A strong intention is one you can hold in-mind without other thoughts distracting you. For example, on a bike ride recently, I chanted a certain idea over and over again for several hours. I sang it in different melodies and tones, I changed the wording or added words here and there, but the basic idea was held on to for hours. The subsequent relief from such high effort put me into a state of high, not to mention that the thought I held is now in effect in my life. When you concentrate strongly and with full willingness, there is not much you can't achieve.

It's alright not to be fully satisfied with life. That little edge of dissatisfaction is what drives you to more strongly concentrate. When you are dissatisfied but at the same time believe you can achieve more, that's the perfect place from which to launch new intentions.

Retrieving Concentration

Learning to Concentrate should also involve learning to retrieve Concentration. You need not be fixed so strongly on something that you can't retrieve Attention when needed. For example, you may have been concentrating on getting into romance with a certain person, but then, when he/she is gone, have difficulty getting your mind off of him/her. Or you may have been concentrated on your business to such an extent that you can no longer enjoy meeting friends or family, or reading a book at the lake because your Attention drifts back to work. So you learn to concentrate, but do not become a slave to what you concentrate on. You don't become so absorbed in anything that you can't release it. You maintain the ability to let go of anything, at least temporarily. Scattered Attention is the cause of all kinds of fatigue, focused Attention the cause of all kinds of success.

Concentration and Memory

If you walk around a city and nothing in particular attracts your Attention, you will later not really remember what you saw. You will have a general idea of the city but hardly remember specifics long term. The things you remember the best are the things that attracted your Attention. You only perceive and remember what you put your Attention on. You only put Attention on what you think is important or interesting. Once you stop putting your Attention on something in front of you or something in memory, the item or event begins to recede until it finally disappears from your Awareness. When you concentrate on one thing, you are absorbed by it, and it becomes your reality.

Concentration and Persuasion

You cannot convince anyone of anything you do not yourself feel. You can only have others feel what you yourself feel. If you want to be a comedian, you must be one who laughs a lot. If you want to be a politician, you have to feel a whole array of emotions yourself, if you ever want to push the buttons of the audience. You can change your reactions and your state in an instant by mere concentration of intention. Once you change your own state, less "persuasion" of others is required because you transfer your state.

Simplicity and Concentration

Simplicity heightens your concentration. Complexity scatters Attention (unless you are well trained). When you simplify your work, your life, the questions you ask, the answers you give, energy is saved and focused. Your communication is improved. Complexity tends to obfuscate the truth, simplicity tends to bring out the truth. If you get lost in complexity, relax and back-up to distill your situation to its essence.

Concentration and Habit

You are responsible for effort, not result, for action, not outcome. Life is easier if you concentrate on living and being your potential to its fullest instead of trying to achieve results. In this way you concentrate on what is and under your control, and leave the rest up to "the Universe".

Effort and concentration can be trained to a point where nothing bothers or distracts you anymore. I seek to do something difficult every day because it is difficult. And I do that "difficult" thing until it is no longer difficult, but fun. The "fun" is not inherent in any object or situation, it is created by me, through no longer having resistance to it. Any situation you deem "difficult" is an opportunity to grow. Nothing is really "difficult", only thinking (instead of just doing it) makes it so.

To break a pattern of habit, follow this Concentration-Technique:

1. Define the habit you'd like to release.

2. Define the opposite of that habit or a new habit you'd like to replace it with.
3. Act out the old habit deliberately (you gain control over what you do intentionally).
4. Act out the new habit deliberately.
5. In the next weeks, keep intentionally switching back and forth between doing the old habit and the new habit. After a while, only do the new habit, never doing the old habit again.

Slowing Time

In society, concentration is associated with great effort and tension, but the release of tension (relaxation) is what makes concentration possible. If you can carry out day-to-day actions without feeling rushed, hurried, or under stress and duress, you improve your concentration. You reject the perceived "pressures" of the world and simply do what you are doing more consciously and lovingly.

Feeling victim to the world comes from early childhood in which negative behavior (crying, shouting) seemed to get you what you wanted (food/Attention). Feeling negative to get what you want becomes a conditioned response which then, as an adult, no longer works. Adult life turns everything upside down: Now, to get what you want, it is wiser to feel well and positive. The "pressures" we perceive from the world also come from early childhood. But as an adult those pressures are not really there anymore, and you can allow yourself to have some time. You can slow-down and finish whatever task you are doing in your own time.

An exercise I frequently recommend in this context is to do things in slow-motion. You can walk the stairs in slow motion, fix a lamp in slow-motion, pack a car in slow-motion, cook in a slower motion...all of which will put control over your body back into your hands. As you slow reality down deliberately, you regain control over reality. And this is what turns scattered Attention into poise and concentration.

Choosing Employees and Partners by Their Ability to Concentrate

Of course, you can predict a person's potential and future by their ability to concentrate. If they are unable to do so, you have trouble coming your way if you employ him/her or take him/her as your partner. One of the reasons I write long and elaborate articles is because only people with some concentration will be able to follow or even complete reading them. This way I can make sure that if any of them become my coaching clients, they will be capable of succeeding with the coaching.

Priority-Lists Reduce Stress

At least 80% of all fear is due to lack of concentration. Scattered Attention causes sensory overload or overstimulation. When Attention is scattered too widely and there are too many things and impressions flooding awareness, this first causes (dis)stress and overwhelm. Scattered energy also weakens the immune system. Fear is an early warning that energy is either being wasted or invested into the wrong channels. In most cases, you should feel fear when your energy is being depleted. As you ignore the fear and continue with the not-good-for-you behavior, whatever problem it was warning against becomes bigger.

That is why making priority lists, doing tasks more slowly, creating to-do-lists, breaking-down big tasks into many smaller steps, and focusing on the here-and-now, as well as establishing what is really important and letting go of what is not important, strengthens concentration and lessens fear.

If you can reduce 50 things to focus on to only 10, or if you can shift from what you don't want to what you do want, you will be reducing the possibility for fear. Fear is a contraction of your muscles, reflecting a contraction of your being, and a contraction of your Attention to avoid something you are worried about happening. You can ask yourself: "What thoughts or actions must I be preoccupied with to feel this contraction or resistance?" And: "What positive thing would I like to be focusing on instead?" You will notice that I asked: "What thoughts or actions must I be preoccupied with," and not "must I be focused on". This is because if you were actually focused (even on the negative), you would not be feeling that much fear. Some techniques to overcome fear do focus on the fear itself by asking: "If what you are afraid of happens, then what?", "And if that happens, then what?" and so on, until the mind is calm and focused and has fully confronted what is actually going on.

6
Psychonavigation

Contents of this Chapter:

Intro

In exploring consciousness as the cause of reality, I wanted one single tool, one single technique that would include all aspects of psychological and spiritual development. One that would be empowering and uplifting to anyone, and one that could be applied anytime in an infinite number of variations. A limitless but integral method for exploring perception, Awareness, creation and being. Something that is both practical and mystical. Something all-inclusive. In decades of search and exploration, I have not found this tool, this "instant-enlightenment" magic wand.

So I had to create it myself. I have created it and given it a label: Psychonavigation. This chapter was written to present the news to you. I am not promising sex, money and enlightenment, but I am promising that you will find more of yourself and a certain degree of inner-peace and creativity. And in finding that ocean of silence and the wellspring of creativity that flows from it, you, will need less of the smaller goals of sex, money, and enlightenment (in no longer needing it you will of course suddenly have it chase you, rather than you chasing it, by the way).

Psychonavigation

Before we talk about where this technique comes from and how it is totally comprehensive and fantastically effective in any area of reality, I will describe the tool itself. If you are well-versed in psycho-spiritual topics or simply have some common sense, you will already start understanding its precious value before I've even talked about the background.

"The Art of Psychonavigation" is at first simply the art of guiding, directing, removing, focusing, intensifying and softening your Attention or Awareness. What you put Attention on is where your energy goes. What you put Attention on grows. What you continue to put Attention on becomes more important, perceivable, familiar and ultimately more solid and real. Attention is the prime tool with which you create your reality. What you release Attention on dissolves. Release Attention on everything, and you have a type of meditation that evolves into a blissful ocean of consciousness. We are not primarily talking about what the eye (and the inner-eye) sees, as billions of other books would, but about the eye (and the inner-eye) itself. We are looking at the looker rather than the looked-at. We are putting Attention on Attention. Self is looking at itself.

Psychonavigation can be viewed as a "guided Attention exercise" that combines hundreds of methods into one single action. In its most basic form it involves softly and gently focusing on something for 60 seconds. And then, after that, focusing on something else for 60 seconds, and then, after another 60 seconds, switching to something else (and so forth and so on). In "Basic Psychonavigation", a 60-second-rhythym is kept for about 15 minutes. Once in a while during this period, Attention is rested and put on nothing specific in a 60-second break. Attention can be focused on the inner universe of thoughts, concepts, memories, ideas and fantasies, or on the outer universe of objects, forms, spaces, structures, people, plants and events. It can be focused on the near (immediate surroundings) or on the far (somewhere else).

During practice you alternate Attention in a 60-second-rhythym thereby including the negative, the neutral and the positive. For the sake of simplicity we will identify only these three modes: "negative", meaning something you currently view as unpleasant or problematic, "positive", meaning something you currently view as pleasant or desirable, and "neutral", meaning something you neither desire nor resist. The three modes do not have to be focused on consecutively though. You might for instance have three 60-second-rounds of something you deem positive or any other variation that arises. In the beginning stages, it is more important that you keep a self-determined flow of Attention (energy) for a certain time span, and that you learn to decide what to focus on next. In the later stages it becomes more important what you focus on.

But the main point for the beginner is to even be able to deliberately focus on anything at all. Most people aren't even yet quite aware that they can direct where their Attention goes independent of what is going on around them, and independent of what others tell them to think and do. And if they are aware of it, they rarely make use of it because the untrained ability seems difficult, or they do not know how powerful it is. Most people's Attention jumps around like a nervous ping-pong ball, reacting to environmental stimuli, inner cravings and resistances in a random fashion. Alone, the step of taking conscious control of one's Attention for 15 minutes is a quantum leap in power and realization...before even beginning with "what you can put Attention on" and "how to focus Attention".

The mere act of focusing on something, anything at all, will calm the stream of thoughts (clear the mind) and let you regain a sense of willpower and purpose. This is where to begin on your journey

The Negative

Within the framework of Psychonavigation, when you focus on the negative, some problem, misemotion or unwanted issue, you are experiencing something entirely different than either "negative thinking" or denial-of-the-negative. Firstly you are doing it on purpose (this implies and facilitates creative-control over the issue), and secondly you are doing it in a way that is specific to this technique and has the result of de-sensitizing the issue rather than prolonging it. Automatic focus on the negative is "negative thinking", which undermines the quality of your life. Ignoring and suppressing the negative is an even stronger half-aware focus on the negative, which has even stronger detrimental effects on your life. The purposeful and intentional focus on the negative for a Psychonavigation-Session stops this automatism and allows you to regain a handle on it.

When incorporating the negative, difficult and heavy into the exercise, you do this by on the one hand confronting (courageously facing), and on the other hand gradually releasing your own resistance, reactiveness, judgment, fear-of and "wanting to get rid of it". You do not resist; you de-identify. Paradoxically, full acceptance equals de-identification. What you push against, you empower. Trying to get rid of something means giving even more Attention and energy to it, than if you were simply observing it in a relaxed, non-reactive way. It is true that focusing on the negative will initially make the negative grow, and will make it more real. This is why Psychonavigation-Sessions do not involve deliberately looking for negative things to focus on. The negative that is included in the session is the negative that is already there, already created within your field of consciousness. Ignoring it or pushing against it means giving even more Attention to it than if you were simply observing it. The way to focus on it is the same way you would notice clouds in the sky...they are there, they "just are", but they don't have much to do with you. It is in this manner that you can gain an emotional and psychological handle over any problem whatsoever.

In the case of an especially charged or emotional issue, Psychonavigation is used in the following manner: You alternate back and forth between the uncomfortable subject and the neutral and positive. An example (in 60 second intervals):

Problem X
Neutral Object

Problem X
Neutral Object
Problem X
Positive Thought
Problem X
Neutral Memory
Problem X
Nice object
Problem X
Neutral object
Etc.

This sort of back and forth movement, this way of turning a problem on and off deliberately, de-charges the emotion surrounding an issue, initiates new insights, and eventually allows you to regain total creative control of your Attention and emotions towards it. Focusing on it deliberately presupposes you are no longer afraid to look at it. Switching presupposes that you can do that, and directs your Awareness to things you would prefer to be focusing on.

In general, the negative or problematic is not included into the session on purpose, but only in cases in which things arise in your daily life or during the exercise, that you want to handle. You do not force bad things to come up just because you want to see how you handle them. Nevertheless, we will later talk about the usefulness of so-called "negative" issues, and in which ways you can utilize "bad vibes" to your growth benefit. Sometimes swimming upstream can make you stronger. But the beginner definitely ought to learn swimming first, and this is best done downstream: with the positive.

The Neutral
When deliberately focusing on the neutral, you do this to relax. Something that is neither charged negatively nor positively has a most relaxing effect on body and mind. In this way, the neutral is a gateway to allow dissolving the negative or immersing yourself in the positive, to be easier. The neutral is also focused on when it seems difficult to make the immediate transition from the negative to the positive. In this case, the middle "stepping stone" of something neutral is taken. The neutral is also used to collect and center oneself or to even "get into the exercise". Focusing on neutral or on only mildly interesting or boring objects in your surroundings seems the easiest for most practitioners. and is a good way of starting a Psychonavigation-Session before using this stable platform to dive into the darkness or fly up to the light.

The Positive

When deliberately focusing on the positive, you do so to come into energetic (emotional and psychological) alignment with things you would like to experience as reality. Rather than being a non-reactive observer looking at something from the outside (as you would do for the negative), you are here allowed to become more identified, "go into the creation", enjoy it and feel pleasure about it. This usually happens by itself, and you don't have to put extra effort into enjoying things you like anyway. If it takes too much effort to feel joyful emotion when focusing on the positive, then this means it is not something you currently really enjoy, or it is something that is currently too far out of your reach (experientially).

In Psychonavigation, there is this slight difference in your behavior between focusing on the negative and focusing on the positive. While on the negative you relax more and breathe softer. While on the positive you become a bit more interested or involved. One is "releasing-resistance", the other is "letting in". But from a higher vantage point "letting in" is the same thing as releasing-resistance. You might be surprised to read that many people not only resist the negative but also the positive, subconsciously. In advanced stages of Psychonavigation, you will find out that the ultimate purpose of the exercise is to gently guide your Attention towards more and more beautiful, joyful and positive thought forms and feelings, and in this way become accustomed to higher levels of energy and consciousness.

The Audio Tool

A helpful tool that could support your practice would be an audio-recording that provides a tone-signal every 60 seconds. I've used such self-made recordings in the past as they are useful for beginners who are easily distracted. The mere ritual of putting on headphones, hearing the sound and the 60-second-signal can discipline you.

Of course you *don't need* such a tool for practice. You can switch by your intuitive "inner clock", you can use breathing-rhythms to pace your time, walking-rhythms, stop-watches or whatever else you wish. After your beginning stages, you don't even have to necessarily use a 60-second pace anymore but can try 20 seconds, or 3 minutes or whatever other rhythm seems interesting to you. Sixty seconds was chosen and is recommended for beginners because it is the approximate time your mind needs to properly identify with something, feel something and "come into energetic alignment" with it. What Psychonavigation definitely is about is that you do define a pace and a time. Failing to do so is not Psychonavigation. The reason for this is that the mind tends to drift, be distracted, lose track, wander off, get stuck on something and fall back into non-self-determined Attention. Keeping a pace strengthens your "muscles" of self-determination, centeredness, your ability to make decisions (of where Attention goes next) and ultimately your sense of inner power.

Unlimited Use

The wonderful thing about Psychonavigation is that there are no limits to the variations in which it can be used. You can vary the pacing, you can include other techniques and exercises into this one, and you can learn to extend your field of thought and Attention outside of habitually programmed patterns. An example of including other techniques into Psychonavigation:

60 seconds of eye-training
60 seconds of breathwork
60 seconds of chakra-energizing
60 seconds of an affirmations
60 seconds of pranayama-breathing
60 seconds of push-ups
60 seconds of no-mind-meditation
60 seconds of muscle-tensing and relaxing
60 seconds of visualizing
60 seconds of…whatever you want

Once you get a regularity going in your practice, perhaps starting out as a daily session of 15 minutes, you can re-utilize any psychological, spiritual or body-technique you have ever learned, including the ones you might have failed to follow up on. Or you can choose to dedicate a whole session to a specific topic. Topical Examples:

15 Minutes of "Beautiful Visions" (60-second-pace)
15 Minutes of "Gratitude" (60-second pace of different things to be grateful for)
15 Minutes of "Remembering My Childhood" (different memory every 60 seconds)

15 Minutes of "This Painful Issue" (noticing various aspects of it every 60 seconds)

It is the all-inclusive nature of Psychonavigation that makes it to my personal no. 1 tool.

What makes it enormously powerful is that during practice time the world and its ever changing waves of circumstance, babble, noise, confusion and urgency are no longer sources of your reality, but you are. If you do not consciously determine where your Attention ought to go and what is really important to you, the world will. Guiding your own Attention – no matter to what – is an already potent source of power. It means you have stopped the world for some minutes and taken charge of what goes on in your mind and feelings. You stop the bombardment of overwhelming input from the world, and start guiding your Attention...which is a prerequisite to guiding your thoughts, words, deeds and ultimately your reality. There are many things to be learned by guiding your Attention on a regular basis. One of them is, that what you put the most Attention on, will eventually grow, start attracting similar thoughts and feelings and finally manifest as reality in your everyday life. Attention is accumulative. Put it on something, and watch it grow. Stay with it repeatedly and watch it manifest in your life. The reason you are experiencing something similar everyday is because you focus your Attention in a similar way and on similar things from day to day, filtering out the trillions of other options of things you could be focusing on (thinking about, looking at, remembering, hearing, listening to, smelling, feeling, touching, tasting and perceiving).

Expansion of Awareness means to perceive things you haven't perceived before, or have only peripherally perceived before.

Basic Session Examples

This chapter is to give you examples of the amazing bandwidth of this one simple technique. I will put some of sessions with myself and others into written form. As you will notice, there is absolutely no limit to where Attention can go. As your life and experience change, include it all into your regular session. Daily, bi-daily or weekly, the choice is yours. In parenthesis I will note the purpose of some of the specific Attention switches. These notes were not part of the sessions, but I add them for the reader who will want to use Psychonavigation for self-therapeutic purposes, or in order to achieve altered states of being.

Session: Myself, 40 Minutes
Intention: Feeling overwhelmed by the day, intending to regain calm
Pacing: 60 seconds each
Pacing-Tool: Audio-recording "60 second pulse"
Location: Lying in bed

Lamp in front of my bed

Spot on the wall

My right foot + breathing

My left foot + breathing

Back to the lamp

Back to my body

Back to the lamp

Back to my body

(Note: Were I to repeat this body-object alteration, it could induce a phenomenon called an "out of body experience".)

To a tree outside

To a memory of another tree

To my favorite actress

To me going to bed with my favorite actress

My favorite actress nude from behind

To my work

Again to my work

Overview of my work

To Melbourne, Australia

To a shopping mall in Melbourne

To a pair of socks in that shopping mall

To the lamp in front of my bed

To a hotel in New York City

To my body

Again to my favorite actress

(Note: When looking away from something and back to it again later, acuity is increased.)

To nothing in specific (relaxing Attention)

To no-mind (stopping thoughts as they start to arise, as in "This cat is….")

To that beautiful sports car

To my breathing

To breath-counting

To a person I appreciate

To a daydream

To the wall of my room

Through the wall of my room

(Note: If Attention is relaxed, this could lead to extrasensory-perception of what is behind the wall.) Softly to a problem I have (causes rush-through-body as energy is discharged)

To a point in the air

To the planet Mars

Exploring the surface of that planet

Back to my left foot

Back to my right foot

To breathing

Result: A sense of complete peace and freshness

Session: Myself, 20 Minutes
Intention: Wanting to Intensify my focus on a desired car
Pacing: 60 seconds each
Pacing-Tool: Audio-Recording "60 second pulse"
Location: Sitting in a hard-back chair (increases focus)

Breathe-Hold-Pace-Technique

Breathe-Hold-Pace-Technique

(Note: Near the end of the first 60 seconds, I decided to continue with the breathe-holding-technique for another cycle. This is permitted in Psychonavigation as long as it is deliberately decided.)

Breathe-Hold-Pace Technique (I decided for another 60 seconds of it.)

Spot on the wall

Beautiful shiny sports car

Driving that car

Driving that car in a beautiful landscape

Driving that car with people I love in a beautiful landscape

Notebook on my desk

Purchasing that car

Seeing people impressed by that car

Spot on the wall

Breathing

No specific focus (break)

No specific focus (thinking about what to focus on next)

Selling the car later

Driving the car, feeling and smelling the leather of the seats

Silence, observing, meditation

Silence, observing, meditation

Silence, observing, meditation

Important Note: When "visualizing" for the purpose of "manifesting desires by mind alone", as it is known, there are three major rules to be aware of:

1) You do this without expectation-pressure that the thing you are visualizing "must" manifest in reality. In fact, forget about it after your session by doing other things. Visualize only in a light-hearted and playful way, without any neediness whatsoever.

2) You don't visualize so that it happens "later, in the future" and "out there in reality". You visualize so that it happens right now, "in here" In other words, you can feel the joy of it as-if-it-has-already-happened. Do not fragment your inner reality between now and future or between "inside" and "outside". This knowledge will help you use Psychonavigation to work some "magic".

3) Gradually move towards not only visualizing a two-dimensional picture in front of your forehead or in your brain, but embodying, feeling, being, moving-as and in a three-dimensional, touchable, joyful reality. Do not continue to visualize something you do not feel or you are not happy about. Make your visualization a whole-body event. It is the energy-frequency that effects physical reality. It

is belief/intention, not desire. Closing the gap between desire and belief means no longer looking at something from an outside viewpoint and "desiring" it, but merging with it, becoming it and being it.

Result: I actually forgot about this session. Years later I found this session and realized I am driving the exact car I had visualized back then.

Session: Myself, 5-10 Minutes
Intention: A refresher or separator between work and private-life
Pacing: 30 footsteps each
Pacing-Tool: Taking a walk; footsteps
Location: Outside, after work, before going home

Footsteps (starting out by counting 30 footsteps)

A building in the distance

A building close-up

The window of another building

A person walking towards me (without staring). Attention can also be focused without the eyes!)

Footsteps (I restart the exercise because I got distracted and forgot about pacing. But rather than berating myself for it I simply restarted!)

The concrete I am walking on

Thinking about what I am going to do tonight

Rethinking what I intend for tonight

Intending a great evening (vocally spoken)

The clouds in the sky

Wide focus (focusing on everything in my view, nothing specific but general).

Result: My mind is off work-time and on to play-time. So much so, that I have even forgotten what the problem was at work today.

A Basic Course

If I were to teach Psychonavigation in a seven hour, seven day or seven week course in a step-by step fashion, this is what it would look like from easy to challenging:

Week 1: Outside & Neutral

You start with neutral objects in your immediate surroundings. These are the easiest for most people. This is also the mode I use when someone is too distracted or overwhelmed to apply any other variation of Psychnonavigation. Look at that lamp. Look at that spot on the wall. Look at that picture. Look at that floor. Look at that spot on the floor. Look at that vase, and so on. If someone is totally fresh to focusing, meditation or energy-work, I would start in a pace of 20 seconds and not 60. Twenty or 30 seconds is also the pace I personally often use when taking a walk (using Psychonavigation while moving the body).

Week 2: Inside & Easy

Here you focus solely on thoughts, inner impressions, images, memories or fantasies. In week one you focused on the "immediate surroundings" in the physical world, and here you focus on the "immediate surroundings" of the inner world. What would that mean? It would mean that you choose thoughts that are "easy to think", "easily activated" or "easily remembered". Thoughts that are not too far away from your "inner surroundings". The thoughts that are the most easy to think tell you a lot about your current condition or state of being, by the way. Finding out what type of thinking comes to you easily, allows you to define where you stand (energetically) and thus improve your state. But for now, simply alternate Attention between different thoughts. For men, thoughts of sex might come most easily, or memories of what just happened yesterday. Do not yet reach for "too positive" thoughts, this would cause a strain between current situation and desire. If you don't know what to think about or focus on then use objects in your immediate surroundings by copying them, thinking of them or seeing them in front of your mind's eye. "Not knowing what to focus on" is the main obstacle when it comes to living a fulfilled life. If you can't decide what to focus on, others will decide for you. Psychonavigation eventually solves this problem. Visualization is helpful to keep focus, but you don't have to be an expert in visualizing in order to focus on the inner world. It can also be a vague impression, a feeling, a "sense of something" or a memory. Inner Psychonavigation is preferably done with eyes closed.

Week 3: Inside and Outside

Here you start alternating between outer objects and inner "objects" (thoughts). In relation to other variations this is still quite simple. When you alternate between an object in your immediate surroundings and a thought or imaginary image, you will probably notice a difference. But when you alternate between a thought and something "outside" that is not in your immediate surroundings, you might come to the point where you realize: There is no difference between "inside" and "outside"! Here's an example:

Put your Attention on the wall in front of you. Now put it through the wall, to the other side of the wall. If you don't know what is on the other side of it, speculate about it. Now put your Attention even further "outside" to the Empire State Building in New York City. Alright, now put your Attention "inside", and think about what is behind that wall. And now think about or imagine the Empire State Building. What is the difference? Is the Empire State Building "out there" or "in your head", or neither nor? I'll leave that up to you to figure out for now. Just understand and realize one very important thing: Your consciousness is not limited to your brain or to an area around your forehead. Don't have everything happening in that tiny space. You are welcome to extend your Attention all the way to the actual Empire State Building and "touch it" with your Attention's-fingers. Awareness is not limited to your body or mind, it is limitless and can travel anywhere. Later on we will figure out the difference between imagination and perception in order to use Psychonavigation for extrasensory or remote viewing.

Week 4: Neutral and Positive

By now it doesn't matter if your Attention is inside or outside, and in the context of Psychonavigation, you are welcome not even to differentiate too much anymore. Rigid separation between "imagination and reality" is one of the main things that keeps you from fulfilling your dreams! In this sense, focusing on a thought of a car, seeing the car on TV, seeing a picture of it and seeing the "real car", have the same overall effect on consciousness. The differentiation and separation is only made by you. Focus on the neutral and the positive. By positive, I mean things you feel good about, that interest you, things you like and enjoy, things and people you love, places you are fascinated by and so on. See if you can find things that actually spark an emotion within you. The ultimate purpose of Psychonavigation is emotion, as emotion is the energy that gets things moving in your life. Your perception, actions, what you notice and do not notice, your intentions and vibes...it is all directed by emotion.

Week 5: Neutral and Negative

By alternating between the negative and the neutral you give yourself a rest for a little rejuvenation before you dive back into the unpleasant. The more emotionally charged or problematic an issue is, the more important it is to pace your time, because Attention easily gets either distracted from the process (resistance) or gets lost in the negative. Being able to switch back out of it on purpose will give you a good handle…and being able to switch back into it on purpose, an even better handle over it. With unpleasant issues you will find that you might need a longer time frame than 60 seconds to "get into it". In this case you can pre-define something like 3 minutes, or you can decide to repeat 60-second-cycles. Of course the neutral should then be focused on for a similar length of time. I repeat what is important when processing the negative: Relax, breathe and release resistance. Alternate between the issue and something else. Don't be shy to face what is really bothering you…several times. Shying away from it will not solve it.

Important Note on Losing Track

What to do if you do get distracted? What to do if you find you have forgotten the time-cycle? What to do if you have gone over time or under time? This is no problem at all. Do not berate yourself for it, otherwise you heighten the probability that it happens again. Don't be too strict with yourself. The purpose of pre-defining a pace before you start is so you can re-instate it when you lose track. Losing track is a typical symptom of "modern life". So when it happens in your session, merely acknowledge that it happened and use the event as an opportunity to re-start the pacing. You will sometimes lose track within a session. This does not make the session invalid. Just like in "real life", when you lose track of your goal, you can either use that knowledge to get back on track or to forsake yourself. Do not put yourself down just because you have a break in concentration. Praise yourself for even having started a session with the best intentions.

If you frequently lose track during sessions then experiment with changing the pacing (e.g. 20 seconds), or restart with the easy mode of neutral and outside. Another very helpful trick to get back on track in a session is to devote an entire cycle to conscious breathing. I might notice myself having drifted off and think: "Alright. Let's get back to the session. Sixty seconds of breathing."

Week 6: Negative-Neutral-Positive

Now you involve all three modes, with eyes open for the "outer world" and eyes closed for the "inner world". You don't have to do that in the succession of negative-neutral-positive, but it is interesting if you do so. If no more negativity pops up automatically or offers itself to you in your field of Awareness, then don't include it. In this case you only run neutral and positive. Some practitioners will have deeply seated traumatic incidences to handle, while others will only notice mild disturbances in their daily life. All of this can be included into Psychonavigation. In fact, anything and everyone can be included and any aspect of this "anything". In the advanced section of the book, we will talk about how to handle the more problematic issues.

Week 7: Reaching Out Further

Finally you reach out further. By habituation we keep putting Attention on the same things. As we keep putting Attention on the same things, we keep invoking similar types of energy. In invoking similar types of energy, we keep experiencing the same things or variations thereof. If you want to experience something new in life, you will have to learn to gently guide your Attention towards other realities and higher octaves of joy. Have you ever put your Attention to the other side of the world? Ever put it to Antarctica, and flown over its icy surface? That would be an example of stretching Attention beyond your habituated focus in a relatively neutral mode (though that might be somewhat enjoyable). In the positive mode you would be reaching for higher, lighter and better thoughts (without straining yourself). So if that sports car has been your focus in many sessions, you might up the level one notch by putting your Attention not only on the sports car but actually driving it yourself. At one notch higher you might put your Attention on driving several different types of sports cars. And even one level higher you might ask yourself why you want a sports car, find out that it's a feeling of joy that you actually want and focus upon that joy, bringing what you really want into the here and now. One notch higher you might focus on flying a designer-spaceship rather than only a car. "Reaching Out Further" is the highest level of basic Psychonavigation and a stepping stone to the advanced levels. Staying on this level of sessioning for the rest of your life would teach you to gently and gradually climb to higher and higher levels of intelligence, creativity and happiness. You begin to understand that consciousness does not differentiate between "reality" and "imagination", and the two begin to blend as you walk through the day feeling high. This is where Psychonavigation is heading.

Priority Management

Psychonavigation means that you are directing your energy (mental, emotional and spiritual) to places and things that are good-for-you, right-for-you and appropriate-for-you. In this context let me advise the most serious consideration of what has been called "Priority-Management", "Attention-Management" or "Selective Sifting".

As a participant in this society you are most probably living in a state of constant overwhelm. This is due to the constant bombardment of information and Attention-grabbing offers coming from all around you, most especially from television, the Internet, the press, mobile phones and colleagues, employers and friends who have been influenced by such media. When you do not define what is important to you, on a near daily basis, what happens is that you, without wanting to, allow in any random type of information (vibration). You are then focused on the immediate rather than the important. And because of the intense forms of multi-media, the "immediate" has become everything and anything that is happening in the world. Bombarded by too much information, choice and offers, you close-down, the mind shuts-off, becomes hypnotized, you become numb and lose your ability to feel. Occasionally some offer might come along that awakens your senses a bit, that seems interesting or inspiring, but because you are on overload, you rarely have the energy necessary to pursue it.

It is not an exaggeration to say that this numbing-down and dumbing-down of people by information-overload has already reached way beyond the advanced-stages with a majority of people. To such a degree has the overload progressed, that the personal will doesn't go beyond saying, "Ok, just tell me what to think and do, and I will do it."

What you give your Attention to will grow, but when you give your Attention to too many things, your energy field is a muddled mix of randomness out of which nothing specific will grow. The way out of this situation in which you most probably find yourself to some extent (as a participant of society) is to become a "selective sifter", an "options-manager", and a "priority-hound", making decisions on what is important on a daily basis...or even segment by segment. The sad alternative is: The world directing Attention for you and making decisions for you.

One of the most major distractions to this type of life is the authority you have given others. Having become lazy in thinking for yourself (because of overload), you prefer the creative thoughts of others, rather than your own. This is how the minority of the world influences the majority.

By allowing yourself to define your Importances on a weekly, daily or even segmental basis, and letting this become the same type of effortless habit that the hypno-trance you once called "life" was, you reverse your state from confusion, overwhelm, "feeling nothing", and exhaustion, to freshness, eagerness, loving-to-act, and eventually regain complete creative control of your life. May this writing serve to re-emphasize that a lot of actual magic can be regained by simple priority-management, rather than what many associate with the term "magic".

Some teachers defined 4 Zones in which your time can be spent:

ZONE 1: unimportant and non-urgent
ZONE 2: unimportant and urgent
ZONE 3: important and urgent
ZONE 4: important not urgent

Examples:
ZONE 1: Watching TV for 12 hours in a row
ZONE 2: Doing tax-statements (unimportant to you, urgent for outside sources)
ZONE 3: Doing your job
ZONE 4: Having a massage, going windsurfing

I have labeled spending too much time in any one of these zones as follows:

ZONE 1: Zone of Stupidity
ZONE 2: Zone of Slavery
ZONE 3: Zone of Success
ZONE 4: Zone of Happiness

The approach is to spend hardly any time in Zone 1, as little time as possible in Zone 2, some of your time in Zone 3 and even more time in Zone 4.In order to achieve anything, energy is required, and energy is available from Zone 3 activities and even more from Zone 4 activities.

There are many ways to go about defragmenting Attention, managing time and priority, but the following "Weekly Awareness Page" is a good example of how it can be done.

Weekly Awareness Page

What my Attention has been on:

*

*

*

*

*

*

*

*

*

*

Rate each item by which zone it is in, and define if you wish to finish (F), delegate (D) or abandon (A) the item.

Things I want the Universe to take care of for me this week:

*

*

*

*

*

Things I want to do myself this week:

*

*

*

*

*

Who I want to be this week (write about states of emotion or "I am's" here)

*

*

*

Wouldn't it be nice if the following things happened this week (use joyful imagination without any expectation-pressure that it must happen. The purpose is to direct your Attention and intention higher, not necessarily that these things "must" manifest. Some of them will, some of them won't).

*

*

*

*

*

Things I appreciate (the purpose of gratitude and appreciation lists are, again, to direct your Attention to higher energy levels).

*

*

*

*

*

Some will understand that the "Weekly Awareness Page" in and of itself would suffice to maintain almost full creative control of your life.

Contextual Definitions

What now follows are some definitions that the prospective Psychonavigator might be interested in. In the frame of the Psychonavigation concept, there are some things you want to know before we proceed to the advanced levels.

Free Attention
The state of having no unfinished business, unclear issues, urgencies, outside pressure, time-pressure, unfulfilled cravings or fears or any overwhelm whatsoever. Attention is fixed on nothing in specific and therefore free to be directed on any reality of your choice. Free Attention is mostly accompanied by feelings of inner peace, joy without reason, elation, and curiosity. Freeing Attention without having interests leads to boredom. Ways to free Attention: "Guiding Attention Exercise", "Priority Management", Releasing Fixed Attention and Neutralizing Attention, Taking a Walk, Opening Attention, Clearing Clutter, Humor/Laughter and high quality entertainment (movies, writings, music).

Fixed & Charged Attention

Resistance (fear, aversion, rage) or unfulfilled desire (craving, neediness, wanting but not being up-to-speed with what is wanted) - fix your Attention so that you either keep having to think about something and keep using compensation-actions to make up for mis-creation.

Intensifying Attention
Examine something closely. The longer you examine it, the more you find out about it. Unknowns are converted into knowns. This is the basis of learning. The more free Attention you have, the more you can invest into what you are examining. Continue to focus on that subject/object, and you begin to lose yourself in it, forgetting everything else, including your surroundings, time and space. Your energy-frequency starts vibrating in-sync with it as you gain familiarity with it, immerse yourself into it and become it. This is the basis of reality creation.

Imagination
Imagination is something Attention can intensify on as a substitute for it not being in your immediate surroundings. If you have something you would like to create or experience as reality, intensify your Attention on it regularly. If the reality is not at hand, use your imagination. From an energetic standpoint there is hardly any difference between focusing on a real car, a car you see in a picture, a remembered car or an imagined car. They are all the same concept and will produce the same sort of energy within your being, and therefore create the same sort of energy-interaction with the Universe.

Physical Emulation

An even more intense form of magical "visualizing" is to copy what you imagined into real life objects, events, places, behaviors and actions. You are imagining in a physical way, or "acting-as-if" or embodying a certain reality.

Out-of-Body-Experience

Put Attention on three places on or in the body. Then put Attention on three places outside of the body (near or distant). Continue this while your body falls asleep and your mind stays awake. If you sense "falling sensations", "astral noise", "temporary body paralysis", or "rapid heartbeat", these needn't distract you from the exercise as they are pre-pavers of the so called "out-of-body-experience" in which a copy of your energy body projects into a standpoint outside of your body. "Falling asleep while staying awake" is the key to this.

Remote Viewing

Put your Attention anywhere you want, beyond what your five senses can perceive. While residing there you will begin with imagination, but then allow your Attention to soften and neutralize while you become more "receptive" than "creative". This is the key to extrasensory perception. If afterwards you can test your perceptions (see if what you perceived is what was really there) you will soon be able to discern between imagination and ESP).

Resting Attention

In guided Attention Exercises it is suggested to occasionally "take a break" or "let Attention run on idle". This however, is also a form of Attention. In fact, there is never any time you do not practice some sort of Awareness (even during sleep). "Resting Attention" during practice will allow you to see what topics come-up without you deliberately focusing on them, give you ideas for what to focus on next or allow you 60 seconds to think about realizations you have had during the exercise up to then.

The Observer Mode
De-identified, peaceful, closer to source, neutral
Attention does not create or identify-with, only observes what-is.

The Experiencer Mode
Does not look *at* an experience, but *as* it, dives into, feels and thereby creates.

Spaces and Spaces within Spaces

Everything other than the infinity of pure Awareness is defined as a space. Any reality is a space. A space can be entered and left. Everything you can perceive is a space that has size, weight, texture, structure, borders and limits. Infinite Awareness has incarnated to this planet by entering a space, and within that space another space, and within that space another space, millions of times. Putting Attention on something means to open a space. Keeping Attention on it means entering that space. Observing something without reaction until it discharges, transporting Awareness to an outside viewpoint, is akin to leaving a certain space.

Belief

A belief is a thought-form (inner object) that has been repeatedly given so much Attention (in the form of looking at, talking about, thinking about, agreeing with, and especially giving-reasons-for) that it develops a life of its own. It is a thought you have identified with to an extent that you can no longer view it from outside, but view through it or as it. You are not seeing the sunglasses, you are seeing through the sunglasses. It is no longer seen as a mere thought, but as a fact. It is taken for granted. This type of mega-thought that you are not entirely aware of as a belief, controls your Attention, emotions and actions and therefore your entire reality. It will filter out anything that does not match it, and emphasize anything that does match it.

Advanced Psychonavigation

You can easily come-up with your own variations and extensions of Psychonavigation, and I encourage you to do so. This chapter is merely to give you a few hints of what is possible with this amazing tool. The basic tool is based on a few simple principles:

a)   What you put Attention on, you create (unless you neutralize it with putting Attention on something which contradicts that). If you want something in life, continue to put Attention on
it and watch it grow. It will start as something small, but as you continue to focus on it, it will emerge more and more and more…first as feelings and other equivalent and similar thoughts, then as intentions,
plans and actions (which follow naturally and effortlessly from your focus), and then with certain events, coincidences, night dreams and people "popping up", which uncannily match that exact
focus, that exact emotion you were practicing.

b)   It therefore follows that it is more fulfilling and effective to put Attention on what you want rather than putting it on what you don't want. Being "against war" will produce more war, as the
Attention remains on war. Being "for peace" will produce more peace. Understanding and learning this does need some practice, as we have forcefully been conditioned to believe that putting
Attention on problems will solve problems. This will never work. Putting Attention on solutions, on what is wanted instead, on the good, will create more good.

c)   We therefore do not use Psychonavigation to focus on the negative just for the sake of focusing on the negative. The negative that is focused on is only the negative that is already there,

already created. Because of your past focus you have created something unwanted. With lots of willpower you can uncreate it by focusing solely on the positive. But there is an easier way: The

negative that you create intentionally (rather than having it pop up automatically), you can assume creatorhood over; you become cause of. And as cause of it, you can easily let it go. You can let go of

something that you have. If that negative is only a slight disturbance, it is advised that you do switch to the neutral, the positive or both. If however it is deep seated or a bit more persistent (meaning it

keeps coming back no matter how much you switch Attention), then start focusing on it deliberately, creating it deliberately, in alternation with something else. This on and off switching will

make it much easier for you to then, in the end, remain with the positive.

Advanced Psychonavigation involves the very same things as Basic Psychonavigation, except that you are adding other forms of Attention to the process. Attention is not only looking at something with the eyes. It can be hearing something. That would be audio-Psychonavigation. Do you hear the birds whistling outside? Your Attention is there. It can be smelling or tasting something. It can be sensing something. Have you ever sensed someone behind you staring it you? That is "sensing", another ability you have not been told about in school. But you know about it. You can put your Attention on that person behind you without actually turning around and looking at him. Try this right now: Put your Attention on the wall behind you without turning your head. Verbal Psychonavigation would be to talk about something or write about something. When processing negative issues this can be somewhat more effective than purely mental Attention, because talking and writing are more intense forms of focusing. Write about the problem. Write about something else. Write about the problem, write about something else. After awhile the whole thing will dissolve in the light of your Awareness and understanding. Or dialogue and talk as the person you want to be. Then dialogue and talk as the person you normally are. Switch back and forth between these two roles until your body and consciousness learn the difference in "life scripts" and can actually enter the new self easily. This is a form of very advanced Psychonavigation. In courses I have used this exercise for many hours with phenomenal results. Collecting a bunch of beautiful pictures in a box or computer file is a form of advanced positive Psychonavigation. Giving your eyes something good to focus on, and it will grow...not only in that box or file, but in real life.

Extra-sensory perception involves putting your Attention someplace else, releasing imagination and waiting for "what comes up". It's really that simple. Imagination is the anchor to get you there, but once you're there, simply receive and perceive, without adding any of your own flavor. In this way you train your ability to perceive things that you can't see in your immediate surroundings. It would be helpful if you then actually go to check if what you perceived there is really over there. It may take some time until you get some "hits", but it can be fun and worth the while.

In advanced Psychonavigation we are no longer as strict with the time pacing. We only return to time pacing when your energy level or life circumstances have dropped. The pendulum of life has its ups and downs, and time pacing can be returned to when we want to regain that sense of control, clarity and Awareness. If you are in a high state of energy and Awareness, you don't need to pace your time rigidly. Just see where your Attention wants to go and take it there. Remain there for as long as feels interesting. Then remove it to somewhere else. As long as you are consciously directing your Attention without getting totally lost in something or drifting off, you are practicing Psychonavigation.Very advanced Psychonavigation applies this tool to conduct healing sessions, induce lucid dreams, quickly shift events and create realities, or explore other dimensions and planes of existence. The next book section will give you an idea of all this.

Advanced Session Examples

This chapter will contain side-notes with lots of new information for Psychonavigators or facilitators using the tool to help others. These side-notes were not part of the session (not part of what Attention was focused on) but are for learning more about the background of some steps implemented.

Disclaimer-Note: I can and will not make claims that Psychonavigation is a substitute for contemporary medicine and doctors. Not only would this denigrate the healing ability of doctors and medicine and create a false "good guy bad guy" duality often found in new age circles, but would also put too much pressure on the Art of Psychonavigation. Although I have healed a number of issues with it, it is better to be seen as an add-on to contemporary medicine, rather than a substitute.

Session: Student with Allergy

Intention: After having tried dozens of approaches from contemporary medicine to alternative medicine, she still has allergic reactions to chocolate, nuts, apples and a few other foods. The reactions range from itching to dark red rashes, and in extreme cases heart- and circulation problems and fainting. She would like to improve her situation a bit.

Method: I am using Psychonavigation without her knowledge, in that I am directing her Attention to and away from the issue repeatedly, inserting several different types of approaches and methods in-between. It is the seeming professionality, diversity and interesting approaches that heighten her belief in the idea that "something significant is happening". In my opinion, the belief in the process may be more vital than the process itself when it comes to healing. For this reason, it is sometimes very helpful when the client is not totally aware of everything that is going on. Were she aware, the questioning and doubting mind might arise. Some things remain a "coach's secret". This does not mean that trickery or manipulation is applied (as you will see in the sessions), but that the healing power of belief is best nurtured if there's a little bit of naivety or awe in the client.

Pacing: Freestyle. Estimated Session Time: 3 hours
Location: Sitting and lying on a couch

Although warned by her doctor not to touch these foods anymore, I ask her to bring a bag of cashew nuts, a chocolate bar and an apple to the session.
Conversation about the issue, asking her when it started, when it's worst, etc. (3 minutes).
Asking her to describe her life before the issue started (2 minutes). Note: Already directing her Attention to the absence of the issue.
Asking her how she will react when the issue is gone (who she will tell, how she will feel, etc.) (2 minutes). Note: Again directing her Attention to the absence of the issue.

Meditation/guided imagery to a sunshine beach "for relaxation" (10 minutes). Note: I tell her this is for relaxation, but what it actually is, is guiding Attention to something else, something uncharged and unrelated to the negative-positive talk we were having.

Asking her why she thinks she can't get rid of it (1 minute). Note: This is a deep dive back into the negative, to uncover some of her beliefs about the issue. It is here she gets tears in her eyes.

Asking her what foods she can have and has no reaction to (1 minute). Note: This guides her out of her current low state.

Asking her what all she has tried to heal it (1 minute). Note: Guiding her back into the other side of the pendulum. Tears well up again.

Asking her to focus on a neutral object (3 minutes). This is where Psychonavigation begins with her knowledge. Before that she wasn't quite aware of what I was doing.

Asking her to close her eyes and mentally focus on the issue that wants to be healed. On her skin. On memory of rashes, fainting, problems, etc. (5 minutes). Note: The way I guide this is that she does this not in resistance or self-hatred, but in curiosity and a sense of exploration.

Meditation/Visualization on imagined-medicine color (mint green) flowing through the sensitive areas (1 minute). Note: This is very pleasant, back to the positive side.

Meditation on her ideal healthy self (3 minutes). Note: Even more positive processing. This gives consciousness/body an example of how she wants to be instead. Her Attention has been fixed on how she "is", rather than how she wants to be.

More conversation and smalltalk (1 minute).

I tell her to take a break and go for a walk. Note: While she is thinking of this as a break or as in "maybe he has to make a phone call or something", this is of course returning to the neutral, to a discharge (15 minutes).

Meditation: I ask her to re-visualize her "ideal self" who never had, doesn't have and never will have the issue. I ask her to "enter it", looking from that person's viewpoint rather than looking at the person (5 minutes).

A short break

I ask her what the symptoms and reactions were when eating chocolate (1/2 minute). Note: I am saying "were" and not "are".

I ask her to eat a tiny piece of chocolate, so tiny it shouldn't make a difference. I tell her that we will eat tiny pieces of the stuff, and then wait for the symptoms to come-up "because we can work best on them when they are actually there" (5 minutes of waiting for the symptoms). Note: While it is true that you can best process and heal an issue that is currently active, this is not the reason we are doing it. We are doing it because it's difficult to believe that such a tiny piece will cause anything. And once she experiences that, this upgrades her belief that it might be healed all the way.

After the waiting period I ask her, "So, where are the symptoms?" She laughs and shrugs it off with an, "I don't know." I ask her to eat another small piece, just slightly bigger. And then I ask her to watch out for symptoms (10 Minutes of waiting and conversing casually). Note: Again nothing happens as she sits there slightly puzzled by nothing happening.

I ask her to take a slightly larger piece of chocolate and start talking to it in a friendly, loving, appreciative way. At first she finds this silly but then follows through with it (5 minutes). Note: Something you fully appreciate is unlikely to harm you.

I ask her to eat the whole piece, which is obviously larger, and really enjoy it, fully taste it. And then we again sit and wait for symptoms...which is already starting to get silly in her eyes. She says, "You know what? I think it was purely mental. I think I'm over it." – "Yeah, but we just wanna make sure, so let's go on with this," (15 minutes of waiting. This time a longer wait just to "make sure"). Note: Nothing happens.

We have a conversation about why it might be that there are no adverse reactions whatsoever, although her last doctor had warned her that she could die (!) from eating chocolate. She does not know, but she is in a very good mood (5 minutes).

I ask her to eat the whole apple (3 minutes). Note: Now we are going for the big stuff.

She says she thinks she feels very slight symptoms in her body. I ask her to close her eyes and flow with them. Soon she opens her eyes and says, "No, actually it was nothing," (1 minute). Note: There might or might not have been an adverse reaction arising. If it had, I would process it like anything else and continue with the program. The belief-barrier however, has already been broken by now, so the rest of the session would have gone more easily (should she have needed it).

Afterwards she starts eating up everything on the table. She does not get rashes from it or faint, but instead gets a bit full.

Result: In a check-up a week later and another one after a few months, she reported that she never had the issue again. Her allergy had been healed. Unfortunately, she went around praising me as a "healer", until I explained to her what we had done and that she did all of it herself. This session was a good example of combining Psychonavigation with "using every trick in the book".

Session: Myself
Intention: Attract new business
Method: Attention Magic and Affirmation-Combos
Pacing: While walking I define objects in the distance where I will shift Attention. Reaching them, I first define the next object and then shift my Attention.
Estimated Time: Undefined
Location: Taking a walk

Note: Each line represents my activity until the next object is reached.

Voicing reasons I want more business

Voicing reasons I can have more business

Voicing examples of past businesses I am grateful for

On the in-breath, I focus on something distant, on the outbreath. I focus on something near (Note: This improves, among other things, spatial perception and the idea of bringing "things far away" closer).

Visualizing emails with orders for my services and products

Visualizing conducting my services for large companies

Beginning every sentence with: "Wouldn't it be nice if..." (Note: This type of speculative and playful talking without the pressure of expectation is a great vibe-increaser).

Result: About 4 days later (I had already forgotten about the whole intention and was busy with other things), I got one of the largest orders in my personal business history.

Session: Myself
Intention: Attract even more new business
Method: Massive focused action
Pacing: None
Location: Computer desktop

Take care of all unpaid bills (owed to me and owed by me)

Book several avenues of Internet advertisement

Email special offer to a hundred especially selected people

Get rid of excess clutter by selling it all on eBay or throwing it away (Note: Letting go of things creates a vacuum in which new things may fall into).

Calling 5 different former customers just for fun (without expectation of them ordering anything)

Result: This type of action-focus gets its magic from the mass of things done in succession. Any type of discouragement or disbelief is taken care of and a momentum is built in which techniques like the previous one (Attention magic) work even better. The result was that from the momentum I had already gained with the result of the previous session, I added even more boost and ultimately tripled my income that month.

Session: Student

Intention: She wants to stop her employment as a secretary and become successfully self-employed as a massagist.

Method: Physical emulation (Role-playing, acting-as-if, vibratory alignment)

Pacing: 1 minute per role

Location: Seminar room

Note: Acting-as-if or "becoming the role" is a magical technique that is, for certain purposes, even more powerful than the "acting in order to" shown in the previous session. Each of the following lines represents a one minute cycle.

Demonstrate your old (employed and fearful) self with your body, posture and style of walking.

Demonstrate your new (self-employed and joyful) self with your body, posture and style of walking.

Imagine the old self and enter it (switching viewpoints, not looking at but as).

Imagine the new self and enter it (switching viewpoints, not looking at but as).

Talk like your old self talks, intentionally.

Talk like your new self talks, intentionally.

Do something your old self would do.

Do something your new self would do.

React to a problem as your old self.

React to a problem as your new self.

React to financial shortcomings as your fearful self.

React to financial shortcomings as your joyful and confident self.

Be someone with financial shortcomings in mimics, gesture, posture, talk and emotion.

Be someone with financial abundance in mimics, gesture, posture, talk and emotion.

Be the old self.

Be the new self.

Be the new self that embraces the old self.

Be the new and the old self, be strong enough to be the entire self.

Being the whole self, talk about your doubts in this new life.

Being the whole self, talk about why this new life is important to you.

Being the whole self, talk about why you believe you can do it.

Be the old self wishing it were the new self (verbally and emotionally).

Be the new self remembering the old self (verbally and emotionally).

Be the new self not wishing anything (verbally and emotionally).

Be the old self knowing it is already the new self.
Be the new self.
Be the new self even more.
Feel the new self.
Talk like the new self.
Write an email as the new self.
Make a list of typical things the new self does on a regular basis.
Do one of those things right now.
Make a list of places the new self likes to go.
Make a list of typical objects the new self owns or will purchase.
Close your eyes and feel the joy of being the new self already.

Result: We repeated this session and variations of it a few times in the course of a week. The transformation that occurred was remarkable. She had been wanting to take this step for years but hadn't out of fear. Within 2 months she was not only long gone from her company but also running a successful massage business. "Coincidences" from all over the place kept coming up. One of them involved getting a massage room for free (in conjunction with a seminar house that offered various other things). Another one involved being able to afford a massage bed and advertising because of a lucky "unexpected income" that had arisen. Today she runs a very successful business and can't even remember what her "old self" was like.

Session: Myself

Intention: I want to find out what is on the planet Mars.
Method: Attention travel
Pacing: None
Location: Bed, before falling asleep

Note 1: The day before the session I had bought an "Atlas of Mars" which show pictures of the planet. In bed, I am flipping through the book in order to focus my mind on the sessions issue. This is an initial anchor for my session.

Note 2: There are several realities and parallel universes my perception could be attracted to. But in this session, I want to know what is on Mars in the context of this current state of earth society and this specific timeline. I intend this, make this clear to my consciousness with a brief conversation. Otherwise, all kinds of bizarre images will interfere. Also, there is the problem that I have been indoctrinated by certain books, TV shows and lectures as to what is allegedly on Mars. According to scientists it is a red, rocky desert with no signs of life, and according to others there are artificial structures such as the "face" on Mars, and even an ancient pyramid city called Cydonia, which is apparently a duplicate of the Egyptian Pyramids. I will have to release any opinion on any of these stances in order to perceive what is really there. This is easy to do. One puts Attention on Mars in neutral mode, neither for nor against perceiving something. Anything not coming from neutral mode is dismissed. Once something is discovered though, excitement may arise. This is something different than going into the session with an excitement or resistance based on pre-conceived notions or in order to "prove" something.

Note 3: Sometimes, when practicing remote viewing sessions such as this, there are apparent "barriers" to what you can access and perceive. These barriers can be acknowledged or effort can be invested to break them (ultimately there is no limit to where Attention can go). These barriers or black screens are either put there by a hidden aspect-of-yourself (what some call "higher self") that doesn't want you to see something at this stage in your life, or by someone else that wishes to conceal or hide something. It is a rare occasion (at least when the intention of your sessions are sincere and integral), but when it does happen it is either experienced as a black screen, fog, blur, a sudden onrush of sleepiness, slight nausea, or the inability to concentrate (if you were able to concentrate a moment before).

Note 4: Each of the following lines represents an Attention switch. Some took a few seconds while others were explored for several minutes. As I did not record the time I will not give any estimates here. These are only examples. You will come up with your own timing, your own style and your own method.

Orbiting Mars, seeing it from the distance and slowly zooming in. (Using the memory of a picture I saw in a book.)

Improving the reality of it: Adding more color and three-dimensionality to the sphere. Rather than only seeing a small ball in front of my forehead, I relocate my viewpoint to the orbit around Mars. So now it's my small body floating and hovering in front of the sphere. (Note: This step creates a jolt in my body and heightens my emotions. This is something that often happens when you shift from a vague two-dimensional image in front of your forehead, to a huge, "real-scale" 3-D reality).

Floating around the planet, examining and studying it. Releasing expectation as to what it is and what is on it. (Note: The moment I release expectations and opinions about it, the color of the planet automatically darkens slightly.)

Still floating around the planet, releasing science-fiction fantasies that occasionally pop up.

Feeling it. By now I have been focusing on the planet for a few minutes and really get the vibration; the "feel" of the planet. It does have a certain vibe that is different from anything I know on earth.

Before even having landed on the planet, two things are obvious in the context and frame of this earthly timeline and reality: The feeling that this planet is most definitely not inhabited with intelligent life (now), and the feeling that this planet most definitely has been inhabited by intelligent life (long ago). This information comes up in the form of feeling, after having rested there with neutral Attention for several minutes. As strange as it may sound to readers of this time and age: neutral, undistorted Attention followed by a feeling is the most reliable type of information in the universe.

I move up closer. The sphere becomes a landscape I fly over. It is indeed similar to the pictures taken by NASA, but what these pictures fail to capture is the mood; the energy-field; the feeling of the place. This gives me an impression of Mars that is quite different from what I thought it was. There is a lot of historical significance in the air, but I cannot yet quite grasp what it is.

My Attention starts blurring after several more minutes, and I adjourn the session.

Result: I can later return to Mars for deeper exploration, finding out even more (I.e. Are there artificial structures on it?). But for now I am quite happy with the information I obtained.

Session: Myself
Intention: Increasing my state of energy
Method: Psychonavigation, higher and higher
Pacing: 60 seconds, using audio tool
Location: Couch, sitting upright.

I will not outline the exact types of focus I had here as they are private. Instead, this is the process: After each 60-second-gong I ask myself: "What is an even higher thought than that?" and then proceed to spend the next 60 seconds with that. In this way my focus goes to higher, higher and higher levels of fascination and bliss.

Result: Being in a state of joy or ecstasy, even only for a few minutes, does have real-life effects. When you change the energy you emanate, the occurrences and realities of your life are shifted...what you magnetically attract is shifted. You don't necessarily attract what you visualized, but moreover what you feel.

States of Bliss

States of bliss can either be experienced by Psychonavigating yourself towards higher and higher thoughtforms or by practicing neutral Attention. Neutral Attention does not mean neutrality or a neutral attitude or point of view. It is a word that expresses a state of mental relaxation, in some ways the opposite of "focusing Attention". Rather than focusing or identifying with something, you be still and observe. "Be still and observe" is the purest form of meditation and is taught in any meditation school that knows what it is talking about. "Be still and observe" is the only command needed to understand how it is done. Still I will elaborate on synonyms for it to make sure every reader gets the point. Falling back on, relaxing into zero-point, pure Awareness, non-reaction, pure being-ness...without falling asleep, are other ways to describe what is going on. You should be well-rested or have had a good sleep the night before when practicing eyes-closed silence. Otherwise you will just fall asleep. You are observing what-is without analyzing, reacting, labeling, judging, agreeing, disagreeing, pushing away or pulling toward you. You are observing your stream of thoughts without wanting, needing, intending, not-wanting, having to, shoulds, do's, don'ts and so forth. But this doesn't mean that you are just drifting away or letting yourself become immersed in senseless thinking. You do remain aware, clear and observing. When practicing this, what happens is that first surface thoughts drift by. Not reacting to them, they soon disperse and open a gateway to deeper, more intelligent and creative thought. Once the surface layer disperses, you'll be surprised at the depth of well-being and creativity at a deeper level. Should you find yourself reacting, judging, drifting away, etc. then observe this. Make it part of the process. You needn't react to reaction. You needn't resist resistance. You needn't intend not to intend. These things happen, these thoughts come and go. By getting impatient or angry that you are not in "neutral Attention mode", you go even further away from that mode-of-consciousness.

I practice "silence" at least 15 minutes a day, sometimes longer and will continue to do so because I understand the benefits. For example, many talk about "creating reality by the power of focusing one's thoughts", but how do they suppose one will focus one's thoughts when one has 100,000 random thoughts racing through one's mind each day? Before something is created it can be beneficial to experience nothing, and then place that something into that nothing. Otherwise you will just be piling up thoughts upon thoughts upon thoughts, and nothing will be "created". Another benefit of "be still and observe": You begin to see through the flimsy nature of the thoughts that appear to be bothering you in your daily life. And soon, not much of anything will bother you anymore. A sense of calm and peace will be carried over through the day, and you will find yourself staying present and confident even in situations that you once found "challenging".

For our purposes these words suffice. If you wish to find out more about meditation, there are plenty of books out there (also see my book *Parallel Universes of Self* for more on the topic). As the years of your life pass, you will find a deeper and deeper self. And when you think you have reached the deepest level of consciousness, and find yourself in a vast ocean of silence, this is only the beginning...it gets even deeper, it gets even higher. There are states of being to be experienced in meditation that no drug in the world can emulate.

Reality Creation Procedure

Background and method of the Reality Creation Procedure are detailed in my book *Parallel Universes*. Here I will only give a short summary of "how it's done".

Preparatory Exercise: "Viewpointing"

Look at any object without expectation, in a relaxed, receptive manner for a few seconds or more. Next, look *as* the object. You are no longer looking at the object, but as it. This means you identify with it, be it, get a real body sense or feeling of being it, and view your surroundings from this new viewpoint. From this new viewpoint, look at the next object. Then look as that object. From the new object, look at your surroundings and choose the next object to look at. And then merge with it and look as it. Continue this until you experience an obvious shift of energy, feeling, and consciousness to the better, until you can clearly discern between "looking at" and "looking as", and have the impression that you can effortlessly and easily take on any viewpoint or identity.

Preparatory Notes

While "wanting to manifest a desire" is required as a first step to this technique, it is, paradoxically, also a obstruction to actually creating the reality desired. Why? Because desire implies separation between the "I" that is desiring and the object of desire. Desire implies lack. Contrary to most new age teachings, you cannot "have everything you desire". You can have what you believe you already have. Reality Creation therefore means closing the gap between what you believe and what you desire. Furthermore, "reality creation" is not about creating circumstances, conditions or physical evidence. Why? Because the circumstances you experience are a reflection of your belief. Reality corresponds to whatever identity or viewpoint you are looking at the world from. This specific and very powerful technique involves no longer looking at what you desire, but looking as the person for whom the desire is already fulfilled. This is how belief is created...a belief with which physical reality then corresponds. But you do not "make anything happen" in physical reality, you simply take on the viewpoint/identity of someone for whom it has already happened, rest in the fulfillment,, and reality takes care of the rest. The supreme universal intelligence which creates hearts, bodies, planets and galaxies effortlessly will have no difficulty in creating the things you identify with. Once you truly identify with something you no longer desire it, try to get it, try to make it happen, work for it, go for it, achieve it, look for it, wait for it, demand evidence of it, or ask how, where and when it will happen. You also no longer visualize or affirm it. You wouldn't be doing any of these things if you were resting in the viewpoint of the person for whom it has already happened. Furthermore: In this technique, "imagination" is no longer viewed as mere imagination or "opening to possibilities", but as already existing, already real parallel-reality versions-of-yourself that do exist here and now. Physical reality and its circumstances are viewed as irrelevant when you are truly identified with who you want to be. In this technique, you are not trying to have more, but be more. You will not get the mirror of physical reality to smile before you smile. Before anything can show up "out there", something has to change "in here". But you are not looking for any "evidence" "out there" because there really is no such thing as an "out there" that is independent from the observer or consciousness. Consciousness is all there is, and it comes in two modes: Observing and Identified. In an Identified mode, it starts attracting everything that is like it. In a neutral Observer mode, it attracts nothing.

The Technique
Before beginning this exercise, define which reality you would like to experience.

1. Relax into Zero-Point (Be silent.)

Before receiving a new somethingness, we return to nothingness. Call a time-out, sit or lie down, close our eyes and become very silent and relaxed. Retrieve Attention from any issues and problems of the "outside world" for now. Gently and gradually release any wants, needs, have to's, shoulds, coulds and woulds, and breathe gently. Gradually release any judgments, labels and concepts, knowledge, opinions, definitions and reactions about anything and everything. How to do this? You don't do it. Instead you stop doing anything. You stop doing anything but observing/noticing. But observing and noticing is not even something you have to "keep" or "hold"…it's always present anyway. Behind the clouds of the mind lie a clear sky of Awareness, ever present, ever silent. This does not have to be created. It happens naturally when you become silent, open and receptive. Once an ocean of silence is experienced (and this may take from a few minutes to many minutes, depending on your willingness to release resistance to the here and now), enjoy it. You are in neutral observer mode, neither desiring nor resisting. Nothing is being created, nothing is being discreated. Thoughts may come and go, but they are irrelevant, like clouds passing in the sky. Do not advance to step two before you feel at ease. Wellbeing is not the goal of Reality Creation, but it's prerequisite.

2. Allow yourself to look at the new version-of-yourself.

Once silent, allow an image to appear that represents the Version-of-Yourself that is already experiencing the reality you want to experience. This is not so much a "visualization" in the sense of creating something with effort or concentrating on something, it is more of a relaxed receiving of something. You are not merely "imagining" something or "opening to possibility", but perceiving a version-of-yourself that already and really exists in a parallel reality. You are becoming aware of someone who is already there. (Analogy: Maybe you're familiar with the "Magic Eye" books where you first look at a picture and notice nothing coherent. Defocus your eyes or change your viewpoint, and suddenly a picture comes up that was there all along.)

3. Enter the New Viewpoint
Rather than continuing to look at that version-of-yourself as a separate observer, as someone "desiring" it, enter the viewpoint (energy field) of this person (who is already experiencing the fulfillment of the reality), and look as the person as the person who is living in the fulfilled reality. Immerse yourself into it, enjoy it with natural ease, gratitude and happiness. You may have a smile come to your face. Rest in it for a few minutes, before releasing it and ending the closed-eyes part of the exercise.

4. Rest in the Viewpoint

In the hours, days and weeks after the exercise you "rest in the viewpoint" of the fulfilled reality. This means you don't try to "make it happen" because it's already real. You don't affirm, visualize, repeat or wait for it. You don't hope for it in some future. Instead you simply do "what's before you to do", which are the usual and normal activities of your daily life (example: washing the dishes). Your daily life continues in a natural manner without any hint of neediness or lack. Once in awhile you may want to re-activate the body-sense or feeling of your new viewpoint, but most times not even that is necessary. Furthermore, you also will not be "acting-as-if" the desired reality is fulfilled. For "acting-as-if" still presupposes that it is not already so. You will cease to do anything that presupposes that the reality you formerly desired is not already so. There are only two willful things you are allowed to do when using this procedure: 1) Refuse to ascribe any relevance to events that seem to contradict your newly chosen reality, and 2) You can turn any "expectation" concerning the reality into a "memory". Notice the felt difference between expecting something to happen in the future and remembering something happening. Because you are resting in a new reality, you "remember" that reality. Rather than thinking, "So be it," you are thinking, "So was it." The corresponding physical manifestation will appear when you stop looking for it and are truly identified with it. It is not done by you, but by universal consciousness that has more effective (but sometimes mysterious) ways of bringing about reality.

Have fun!

Exciting Experiences

I have already described many of my personal experiences in magic in many other books. This habit gives my readers examples of what is actually possible in this life, and at the same time reminds me of how beautiful and truly magical life can be, as I too sometimes forget. All of these events happened to me personally just the way I described them. Experiencing magic or something previously considered impossible ups your self-confidence and lowers your need for "proof", or the need of legitimation from others or "authorities". I will focus on events that happened from 2005-2007.

Pre-Cognitive Dream

It was while I was writing this book that I dreamed of two women that I had never seen. One was a red-haired woman, who appeared first in the dream, the other was a black-haired woman, who appeared second and seemed to be observing me and the red-haired woman. Both were somehow admiring something about me in the dream, but I couldn't tell what. Upon awakening they were still vividly in my Awareness, and I went to take a shower wondering who they were and what the dream could possibly mean. That day I was scheduled to do a coaching for a group in a building in town. I was renting a room from another company. At around 10 o'clock the red-haired woman entered the rooms. She was not there for my coaching, but visiting the owner of that company. I stood in the "coffee room" stunned. She must have noticed the awkward look on my face because she smiled at me. This was not a woman that was "a bit similar" to the one I dreamed of the night before, but the exact same one. I didn't tell her I had dreamed of her lest she misunderstand it as an attempt to flirt. She was Spanish and hardly spoke any English, but we exchanged smalltalk the best we could. And then she was off into another room. I stood there considering what had happened. Pre-cognitive dreaming had happened to me many times before, but just like many times before, I had forgotten all about it, and it took me by surprise all over again. The linear mind is a curious thing. It will sometimes easily forget, trivialize or ignore the most lucid states of Awareness. Standing there, I understood that the second black-haired woman would probably be showing up too. And some hours later she did. I went back to the coffee room in the afternoon, and she was sitting there talking to the owner of the rooms. She too smiled when she saw me, almost as if in recognition. Had I been in her nightdream like she had been in mine? Quite possibly. We seem to meet different kinds of people in dreamscape, some of which we don't even know in our waking life. We too exchanged a brief chat about this and that, and when I returned to my room I was beaming with fascination from the occurrence. I tried to explain what had happened to the group, but they did not find it as entertaining as I did. Maybe it reminded them that they had not experienced a pre-cognitive dream recently. Maybe they thought I was making it up. In any case, maybe I ought to stop being surprised about it and just take it for granted by examining my dreams more closely. In this way it may occur more often. What did the dream mean? It doesn't matter what it meant. No need to do a "dream interpretation". As far as things developed, it didn't mean anything because I never saw the women again after that...neither in my dreams nor in waking-life. What *does* matter though is the fact that time is so much more fluid and non-linear than we believe. And that is exciting.

Synchronicities That "Built" up on Each Other

This story is not spectacular but it is rather funny because it shows what intense focus of Attention can lead to. In October 2006 I was conducting a "business English Course" for a company that does civil engineering, construction and building planning. During the three weeks, I was conducting courses in which I was immensely focused on vocabulary and concepts that concern construction, building and engineering. I became aware of procedures and words I had never heard of before (having to learn the words I was supposed to teach my students, myself first). In the November and December weeks after these lengthy courses, I had several registrations for single-sessions of my Reality Creation coaching. This was nothing new. What was new though, were the professions that these people had. Without having any relation to the construction planning company I had worked for, they all related to buildings, building, real estate or architecture! No, not some of them, but for the remainder of 2006, all of them. There was a house builder from Germany, another building planner from Austria, an architect from Seattle, a real estate agent from Sydney, Australia, another home builder from Nottingham, England and another architect from Toronto, Canada. There were a few more related to buildings and building. Some might think that this is due to satisfied customers referring others, but I have established that none of these clients had anything to do with each other. I asked them if they knew person x or company y, but they didn't. They found out about me either from my books, my website or from speeches I had held. This was an excellent example of "coincidences", referring to the same or a similar topic (building) stacking up on each other. The more you focus on something, the more of something you get. The more of something you get, the even more of something you get. Energy is accumulative. This was by no means the only occurrence of that kind that year, but it was one of the most massive and obvious, as if the Universe wanted to drive the message home by exaggerating the events.

7
Presence Training

Contents of this Chapter:

24. Seeing with the Eyes of a Child

Reality Is Not Only Fact-Driven, It's Perception-Driven

It is a fact that flying in airplanes is many times safer than riding on a train or a bus. And yet the post-9/11 security measures at airports are many times higher than on trains or buses. Last time I took a train cross-continent, there was no security at all. Airports security measures are a nuisance to millions of people every day. Every time I fly from Europe to the U.S. I am asked for my passport at least 8 times on the trip. And even though I have an American Passport, I am quizzed, questioned and my snack is split open to see if there are any bombs in it. It's a fact that there are thousands of ways a terrorist could bring down a building, and preventing him from flying will not stop him. And it's also interesting to note that security measures for airport staff – from the stewardess to the luggage handler – appear to be surprisingly lax in comparison. Did the airplane-cleaners go through all these numerous security checks before they entered the plane? Somehow, I doubt it. I'd wager there are numerous people who could easily plant a bomb on a plane if they really wanted to.

The point is that the reality of super-tight, paranoid and costly airport security is not based on facts, it is based on the perception of facts. Authorities perceive and believe that there is a threat, and that these measures will prevent that threat. Passengers accept being strip searched because they perceive that it's necessary. But the fact is that a lot of time, money and emotional energy are being wasted without all of these measures actually "preventing" terrorism. Thus, to create reality for millions of people, no facts are required.

I am not saying that there should be no security at all, and that anybody should just walk onto a plane right off the street (although that's the way it will be on an enlightened planet). It's the paranoid exaggeration of security – the hassling of billions of innocent people out of fear of a few that is somewhat problematic. At many flights to the U.S. I go through two baggage checks, even though one would be enough. What exactly are they hoping to find that was not found at the first baggage check? The amount of money this is costing on a daily basis is enormous. This loss is created by perception, not facts. The loss of the money is a fact, but it is generated by delusion. If the security and police forces were trained in intuition and face-reading, they could smell and spot a suspicious person from miles away, without having to empty granny's suitcase.

Go to Google and type in: "What you perceive a burger to be and what it really is." You will see pictures of what a hamburger actually looks like vs. what advertisement boards for hamburgers make you think it looks like. A real burger looks nothing like the one in the ads.

Reality being created by beliefs rather than facts happens all the time. For a recent private coaching, I visited a town where it rarely snows. A few snowflakes were falling that day, and my host showed me how people were stocking up on food as if the end of the world had arrived. They also all started driving really carefully. And all that just because of a couple of flakes of snow that melted once they hit the ground! Stocking up on food and driving incredibly slowly was not necessary. These actions were not driven by facts, they were driven by perception and interpretation of the facts. Because the townspeople were not used to snow, they envisioned something different than me. Where I live, snow falls frequently and thickly, and we still drive around in it even if it's piling up to body-height on the side of the road.

This applies to positive things too, of course. People's perception that it is Christmas time, and that this time is all about giving and coziness, creates precisely that reality. So when someone comes along and says, "But the fact is, the whole nativity scene of Jesus took place in January," we ignore that person because his facts are a disturbance to our positive feeling.

So what can you take away from this that is useful for your life? Well, in short: You can create positive emotions and real experiences by positively distorting your perception, and you can de-create negative realities by strictly sticking to the facts. So when a coachee tells me a negative story, I often say, "Stick only to the facts of what is really there, of what is really happening here-and-now, please." If one sticks only to the facts of the here-and-now, it is difficult to maintain negativity because negativity is often based on perception and past or future events, not on here-now facts. And when a coachee tells me a positive story, I often say, "Yes, go on, tell me more please," because I know that even if the story is not fully accurate or factual, it will create a positive factual reality.

I know quite a few men who go to the gym and feel as if they were Mike Tyson or Cristiano Ronaldo, when they actually look nothing like them. Their perception of what is going on is vastly different than the reality. But who am I to tell them they don't look like that? Their perception of being "like" these people will give them a positive feeling that will motivate them to keep going to the gym for more self-improvement.

Most mothers believe that is absolutely wonderful and lovely to have babies. For this, they censor all the trouble they have to go through, including changing dirty diapers, being kicked in the head at night and having to put up with constant shouting. They envision their baby as the most lovable and cute creature in the universe. If they stopped being in denial about reality, they'd be horrified. In this case it is better to let them believe that it's all a very blissful experience.

One coachee recently told me that he thinks a certain woman likes him. I could see that clearly she wasn't interested in him. But instead of telling him the facts immediately, I went along with the story for a little because it brightened his whole mood and outlook, it made him optimistic about the day. I could have said, "You are kidding yourself." But who am I to burst his bubble? Bubble-bursting would only become necessary if his delusion started producing negative results/facts. It then turned out that he was so convinced that she liked him, the woman actually started changing her views of him. And now, they have started going out together! The lesson learned here is that sometimes it's better to let someone believe something if their belief is strong and produces positive results. Cynics and skeptics are only needed for negative realities.

Reality is more perception-driven than fact-driven; driven by beliefs and emotions, not by what's really there. There are so many applications and usages of this knowledge I could write several books about it. From your choice of partner, to what you purchase at a store, to why you choose one life path over another...none of this is primarily fact-driven but emotion-belief-perception driven. That's why I teach changing emotions and beliefs because when those are changed, your perception changes. And when your perception changes, your factual reality changes. What you believe will come true, if your belief is not too far away from your factual experience.

Expanded Attention

Being too concerned about yourself is a limitation. If you release your concern about your reputation, how you look toward others, whether you will succeed or what others think about your work, you gain creative freedom. Why? Because your Attention is no longer stuck on a small sphere around your own head, no longer stuck on worry. No longer strongly identified with "I" and "me, me, me", your sphere of influence expands to things "outside of yourself". "Paradoxically" the more concerned you are about yourself and your influence, the less you have. Here are a few small exercises that will expand your sphere-of-influence and perception, and help you get out of identifying with that tiny body and head you call "me":

* While taking a walk, notice when you are preoccupied with thinking. Release that tendency and instead, shift your Awareness to your surroundings, the objects, plants and people in your surroundings. Become interested in the world. Every time you have a relapse into thinking, return to extroverting your Attention again.
* Anonymously make someone a gift or an act of secret charity.
* Genuinely forgive and then publicly praise someone you held a grudge against.
* Spontaneously give up trying to solve something you've been thinking about for a long time, and just forget about it.

Enjoy the Expansion.

Attention Capacity and Success

To succeed at anything, you need to put Attention there. If your Attention is already occupied by many other things, you won't have the capacity to put it on something new. Sometimes old things must be shed, especially those that do not serve you. The Attention you invest in something, gives you a return-on-investment. But Attention must be given to the "end result" that is wanted, not to the lack of what is wanted.

The Here-Now Technique

The following is one of the best here-now techniques I know. It will help you gain a sense of being fully alive, fully present and fully aware of reality. It's really one of the best ways to achieve "witness/observer consciousness" as taught in so many schools of meditation. The technique is not that easy, so it is suitable mostly for serious practitioners of consciousness techniques. This present moment is your "place of power", the state from which all ability, clarity and well-being spring. The mind tends to get caught up in thought-stories of the past and future – which are the origin of all worry and fear. Teaching a person to be fully "here-now" is therefore teaching him/her to lose fear and burden. If you examine life closely you will notice that most "problems" a person has are not really present here-and-now, but rather constructs of past and future events made in the mind. In the exceedingly rare moments there really is a problem in the here-now, we don't think about it, we deal with it. Here-Now Awareness has been taught by mystics for thousands of years in order to promote a more peaceful and loving version of humanity. It is only the constant replaying of past upsets and issues without forgiveness that allows conflicts to go on.

In general, the mind keeps replaying past events (or more precisely, its own perceived version of past events) until it becomes present. In my videos on "Attention and Reality", I give the example of someone who is heartbroken and ask: "How heartbroken would he be if a bomb exploded nearby?" This extreme example shows that the external event of a bomb would jolt him into the here-now immediately, whereby he would start looking for shelter and forget all about his broken heart instantly. But such extreme measures as bomb-throwing are of course not necessary to awaken you. Not even an external event is necessary to awaken. You can become more present from within, independent of external factors. The mind also tends to replay positive events until something better comes along. So if someone is addicted to watching movies, he will keep doing so until something more interesting happens in his life. If he falls in love, he will rapidly cease watching movies, and instead, spend all his time with his new love. It is only after a few months have passed that he will tend to fall back into his subconscious programming, and then perhaps begin watching too many movies again, this time perhaps with his loved one.

With the following technique, all of this replaying of past events subsides, eventually leading to a more silent mind. The technique is repeated over and over, hundreds or even thousands of times, as a meditative discipline, until the mind is still-enough, the world looks much brighter, and you feel more energetic. A session should never be interrupted until you feel fully at peace. You can only do one session at a time, ; doing the following session on another day, or you can do all sessions in succession. Each session represents a different level of practicing here-now-consciousness, so you might want to stick to session 1 for awhile before proceeding. Those of you acquainted with meditation techniques can do any session according to preference.

Session 1 of the Here-Now-Technique

1. Remember a scene from the past.
2. Locate a specific object in that past scene.
3. Locate a similar object in the here-now.
4. Note similarities between the past object and the present object.
5. Note differences between the past object and the present object.

Session 2 of the Here-Now-Technique

1. Imagine a scene.
2. Locate a specific object in that scene.
3. Locate a similar object in the here-now.
4. Note the similarities between the imagined object and the present object.

5. Note the differences between the imagined object and the present object.

Session 3 of the Here-Now-Technique

1. Notice an object, event, situation, space, thing or person in the here-now.
2. Ask: "What does it remind me of?"
3. Note the similarities between the past and the present scene.
4. Note the differences between the past ,and present scene.

Session 4 of the Here-Now-Technique

1. Look at a thought or memory in the mind.
2. Look at an object in the present.
3. Go back and forth between the two several times until you feel relief. End with the object in the present.

What follows are examples. These are just examples, there are millions of different ways this could go:

Example of Session 1

1. The scene I remember from the past is being bullied at school.
2. I look out of the window and see a group of teenagers who look like those bullies.
3. The similarities are the clothing and the aggressive voices.

4. The differences are the language and that these boys aren't bothering anyone.

At this point, consciousness lets go of the past and feels a relief, realizing it was only projecting past fears onto the present moment, which usually has less in common with the past than assumed.

Another Example of Session 1

1. The scene I remember from the past is my grandma making cake for me.
2. I see a cake on my kitchen table.
3. The similarities are that they are both cake.
4. The differences are that one was cheesecake and this is an apple cake. One was made by grandma, this one wasn't. The other was not tasty, this one I like. Back then I was a little boy, now I am an
   experienced adult.

Example of Session 2

1. I imagine a romantic future scene in the city of Venice, Italy where I appear to have rented an apartment.
2. I notice my current house.
3. The similarities are that in both places I feel confident and well-off.
4. The differences are that there is no romantic situation here-now, and I am not in Venice.

Another Example of Session 2

1. I worry that I will remain lazy, and procrastinate important business in the future
2. I notice my body posture and office right now.
3. The similarities are that I am lying on the couch instead of sitting at my desk.
4. The differences are that I know exactly what I am going to do now to take care of important business.

Example of Session 3

1. I notice a nice car parked in front of my house.
2. It reminds me of the fact that I always wanted such a nice car but can't afford one.
3. The similarities to the past scene are that I feel exactly the same after all these years. I still feel lack.
4. The differences to the past scene are that back then I wanted a Ferrari, and today I'd prefer a BMW. Back then I felt completely desperate, today I think I might actually be able to afford at least a used one.

Back then I took this feeling of lack for granted. and today I can change my emotions regarding nice cars.

Another Example of Session 3

1. I notice Jim. I don't like him.
2. He reminds me of my former boss who fired me.
3. They both look similar and have bad breath.
4. Jim is not my boss, in fact he is unemployed. Jim needs help, my former boss didn't.

Example of Session 4

1. I remember an embarrassing event at a party last week. I should have acted differently.
2. I notice the lamp on the ceiling.
3. I move my Attention back-and-forth between the two, dwelling on each for about 20 seconds. After several repetitions, I begin feeling release. I have let go of that event and returned to the here-now.

Another Example of Session 4

1. I remember my last vacation. Those were nicer days.
2. I notice the trees outside the window.
4. I move my Attention back-and-forth between the two, until I feel relief and more Awareness of the here-now.

You can see that all four techniques are essentially comparisons of past/future to the here-now. The effect of practicing this is that all past/future events tend to fade or crumble under the stronger impressions of the here-now. The long-term result of such practice is that you are no longer easily "triggered". What do I mean by "triggered"? Well, when you walk around in daily life, the impressions of the external world tend to "trigger" the mind, and make automatic comparisons and assumptions based on past experiences. This blocks clear perception of the here-now, and forces you to live a delusion or projection. So you see something happening, and automatically assume that it's similar to something that has previously happened, then re-create the same emotional reaction of the past. Students of mine who have practiced this technique (which I have been teaching in private sessions for the last 20 years), are less triggered and less compulsively react to external circumstances of the present. "The past does not equal the present or the future." The mind tends to project what things "mean" based upon past experiences. But in the here-now things do not mean anything until you ascribe a meaning. And once you ascribe a meaning to something, you are creating certain emotions and behaviors. And if those meanings are negative, the outcome will be negative.

A recent example of this is my recent trip to Kuwait. Because I only had a temporary "emergency passport" that was good for a year, I called the embassy to check whether I could travel. I received the (false) information that "Kuwait does not accept temporary passports. You cannot travel to Kuwait until you get a regular passport." But getting a regular passport would have taken many weeks, and I'd have missed the trip. Because the statement, "You cannot travel to Kuwait," did not trigger me, (I fully believed that I could travel to Kuwait anyway, and had absolutely no worry or emotional reaction to the statement), I traveled there anyway. I thought, "I'll figure it out once I arrive." It turned out that the information was false, and there were no problems at all upon entering Kuwait. This carefree attitude however, comes from many years of practice of staying in the here-now. I neither called upon past similar events ("Oh no, it's happening again!") nor future worries ("What if I arrive there and they don't let me in?"). Staying purely in the here-now, there was no problem. The energy-field that says, "There is no problem," tends to magnetically attract un-problematic events. But that is not to say that I can ignore this issue or bury my head in the sand. Despite my carefree state, I recognize the issue and immediately upon returning from Kuwait, sent for a new regular passport so that the question never arises again. Hence, here-now consciousness does not ignore problems or cover them up. The difference is, problems do not trigger a whole array of low states and heaviness.

The Step of Remembering a Past Scene usually brings up emotion. The purpose of this step is to allow the emotion to release on its own. The purpose of noticing the differences between the past and present scene is to realize that the present situation is not the same thing, and you are bigger than it. Noticing similarities equals a deliberate association, noticing differences equals a deliberate dissociation. Up to now, all of these processes were running automatically in the mind. With this technique, you go through each step deliberately. The technique feels good because you are converting subconscious programs into consciously and deliberately done programs, so they lose their power over you.

The alternative to this is to keep recreating the same memories, emotions, patterns and behaviors over-and-over again, instead of defining the here-now anew. You are not a product of the past, you can create a new reality in the here-now by making new decisions in the here-now.

There Is Nothing to Wait For

Are you tired of waiting for the next episode of your favorite show? Of waiting for "Mr. Right" to show up in knight's armor on a white horse? Tired of waiting for a breakthrough? Have you ever found yourself impatiently waiting for a phone-call or message from someone? For people who live as conscious reality-creators, the rule of thumb is: If you're tuned in and in the flow, you don't wait for anything. "Waiting" is not a creative state, it's a reactive state. When I find myself waiting on something, I feel that sense of waiting in my stomach or chest, and release it on the out-breathe. Then, instead of waiting, I go-on creating. "Waiting" assumes that there is something preferable or better in the future, and takes you out of the enjoyment of the present.

Too much waiting leads to emotional pain. Why? Emotional pain comes from believing things that are unreal. The more unreal something is, the more emotional pain. Unreal and contrasting thoughts should be painful to show you that they are unreal and extremely contrasting. So when you feel hate or fear, grief or frustration, that is because whatever you are holding in mind is not true. A common saying is that, "Truth hurts," but what actually hurts is falsehood. Instead of "Truth hurts," the saying should be, "realizing that you have not been thinking the truth hurts". Too much waiting is untruth because you are saying that something external needs to happen before you can feel complete internally. And that's not the truth.

The same applies to society. A wise saying I recently read was, "A society grows great when old men plant trees, whose shade they know they shall never sit in." What is the old man doing? He is not waiting for the future to accommodate him, but planting the seeds of the future in the here-now.

The Power of Presence

Attractiveness and influence are not only determined by looks and status but by one's state of consciousness. Heads turn when you enter a room or walk the streets not because of fame and beauty, but because of your energy-field. Even if you are not blessed with good looks, a slim body or fame, you can develop the kind of aura where people say, "I just don't know what it is…there is something about her." Such magnetism is a spiritual quality that can help you gain command of business situations, score a flirt, hold lectures and entertain dinner gatherings.

To experience Presence, be in touch with what is going on here-now. Your mind is not wandering around in some story about the past or future but with what is going on in your current surroundings. When you are sitting in a meeting and you catch your mind wandering off, that's alright, but if you want to be appear more present to others, you have to bring your Attention back to the room you are in. Instead of wanting to be elsewhere, your Attention is fully dedicated to the people around you. Attention is extroverted and highly interested. The body is not tense, the mind is not worried, you are completely at ease. That's a good starting point for that special aura called "presence". People then realize you are completely and totally here…with all your parts. You fill the room with presence.

In various social situations, tension prevents people from being present. They are more concerned with what others think about them or how they look than with the present moment. Letting go of such considerations and relaxing your muscles on the outbreath will help you ease tension and become more present. Exaggerating the importance of a situation can also lead to unnatural tension. If you happen to strike up a conversation with Scarlett Johansson or George Clooney on a plane, the mind tends to project more meaning into that, than if you had met some "normal" stranger. Then the ego with all its desires and resistances comes in, you tense up, and presence is lost. So while taking your meetings with other people seriously and importantly, it is not necessary to inject too much importance and seriousness. When talking to celebrities, in order to reduce the tension, I simply downgrade their importance in my mind by imagining their normal-human sides, not the Hollywood-projected side. Instantly, I am able to relate to them and talk to them as if talking to an old friend.

Notice how easily your Attention goes internal, to mind-stories and away from the external. That is natural, not something you have to control or overcome. However, for purposes of Presence, you can learn to extrovert Attention when needed. When you talk to someone and go internal or become preoccupied, it's as if you have cut the connection, and others can sense that. Rather than internally calculating possible advantages or disadvantages of the encounter, just be present with the other person.

For the purpose of Presence, let go of any expectations. This includes projected expectations. A "projected Expectation" is an expectation you think someone else has of you. The truth is that you don't really know what – if any – expectations others have of you. It's only the mind creating all kinds of suspicions and scenarios. Let go of it all, and become Present. Let go of everything you think you know, and just be-with-what-is.

Move less, slower and more deliberately. Cease all fidgeting, foot shaking, scratching yourself and making nervous gestures. Stop shifting back and forth in your seat. Stop constantly walking back and forth or pretending to be busy doing something. Stop playing with objects on the table. Not in general, but for the times you wish to increase your presence. Being unmoving or less moving indicates that you have conscious control over yourself – which implies conscious control over your reality. As a teenager I tried this in disco/club settings several times. I would either dance or stand there unmoving but open. Friends of mine would walk back-and-forth, reacting to every impulse. Stability is magnetic, that's why sooner or later people started gathering around me, trying to strike up conversations. There is a big difference between not moving because you are shy, and not moving out a state of Presence. The latter radiates power. There is also a difference between moving because you are nervous or moving deliberately. And between being silent because you are afraid and being silent out of calm. One repels, the other attracts.

If you're on a date, the way you use your hands is indicative of the way you will treat him or her. Pay some Attention to the way you touch and handle objects such as the table, your coat, a glass, a knife and fork, the door, etc. Seventy percent of communication is non-verbal.

In being present, you simply accept what-is, as-it-is. There is no concern with what might happen, what might not happen, what must happen and what must not happen. There is no attempt to try to get rid of something, heal something, solve something or change something. All of those things take you away from Presence. Neither are you looking for "the right thing to do or say" because what "the right thing to do or say" is reveals itself naturally from moment-to-moment, and that could be something entirely different than what was the right thing to do or say yesterday.

Finally, your presence grows even more when you radiate states such as:

Interest
Respect
Appreciation
Gratitude
Amazement
Reverence
Love

You can either find things to appreciate or simply intend more appreciation for something you are beholding. That will increase your energy-field.

Presence never needs preparation. It can hold speeches without any notes. It does not need rules because it is naturally harmless. It does not need protection. Presence is Awareness. And Awareness is the invisible substance of which all things throughout infinity are made of.

Silent Radiance Makes People Laugh
What follows is a very-high-energy exercise that will leave you feeling fundamentally transformed for the better. Go to a park or a cafe, planning to sit there and watch people for hours. It should be a place where you can see hundreds of people an hour, some passing by, some standing, some sitting. Intend to sit there for several hours, with infinite patience. If you are sitting in a cafe, you may want to switch cafes or switch over to a bench after an hour or two, as not to arouse the suspicion of waiters.

Begin this meditation by externalizing your Attention and having keen interest in the people walking by. Put and keep your Attention on them exclusively, with very little Attention on yourself or your concerns. In the next hours you are not important, you are not interesting, you are not the center of the world. Other people are. Look at their faces, their clothes, their mannerisms, listen closely to their voices and words, and study their behaviors. Be more interested in the world out there than ever before in your life. But remain relaxed about it. There is no effort, expectation or hard concentration involved. You will notice that any sort of expectation you develop (for example wanting a certain nice looking person to return your gaze), interrupts the flow of appreciation. So view people without pressure, without desire and without resistance...completely open, completely free. You will notice some resistance to certain people. If that is so, you can either shift your Attention to someone else, or release your resistance, and focus more closely on that person. Reduce preferential looking to some extent. There will always be natural preferences for one person compared to another, but you are trying to reduce labeling somewhat, so as not to get sidetracked from the meditation.

Do not worry about people thinking you are strange for holding your gaze on them this long. You will learn that most people are not even aware of it. Especially in busy cities or towns (where you should be doing this exercise), they will just pass without noticing you. Some people who are aware of other things than themselves (which is rare!) will notice that you are looking at them, but they will keep moving. And then there are some people that will return with a smile or give back the appreciation. You might find that these are often older people who are no longer stuck in the prison of the ego, but indeed interested in what is going on around them.

At the onset of your meditation, you may or may not feel appreciation toward the people passing by. Do not force this. Appreciation will arise of its own after some time. You simply maintain keen interest in all people walking by. You do not get fixated on one person, but maintain free Attention. Once in awhile you examine the people sitting or standing near you. Some people you examine for a few minutes, most you examine for a few seconds. As your patience and relaxation increase, your love will increase, and you will notice a shift in your state that gets stronger by the hour. You are now seeing people as your soul sees them. As you continue keen interest in the world and its people, you will not only learn everything there is to learn about humans, you will also start radiating on a higher frequency. And then people will start noticing you differently. You will begin feeling a sense of laughter and humor. Don't be surprised if you start laughing for no apparent reason, and the people around you start looking at you in a strange way. You will see the comedic hilarity of life and the human condition.

The last time I did this, I was sitting in a street-side sushi bar on North Michigan Avenue in Chicago. After about two hours of sitting, people who passed the sushi bar and noticed my state, began smiling and laughing themselves. I saw that some entered the restaurant just to sit close by. The waiter had gotten impatient at my sitting, came over to me and asked, "Will you have anything else, sir?" I looked at him, and he immediately drew a smile that was suppressing laughter. I looked over to another table and immediately drew smiles from there. People recognize higher states of consciousness, and when you are "in state", your mere gaze can make people laugh.

You will notice that after completing the exercise your state may return back to normal...but it will not return quite as low as it was before. And you can go out "sitting and gazing" again any time, and get into the field again, any time. The smile that arises from this exercise is not a forced or fake smile. It does not even require your face to go along with it. It is an inner-radiance and glow that makes anyone who sees it laugh.

Augmented Presence

Isn't it ironic that computer-based products such as "Google Glasses", that will diminish our perception and presence are called "Augmented Reality"? They should rather be called "Decreased Reality". Real "Augmented Reality" is when you become more present, when you wake up to and participate in what is happening right now. A distracted and preoccupied mind does not make for presence. Full presence is very much related to well-being and energy. For instance, if you are truly dedicated to a task here-now, past and future cease to exist – and with that, all worry ends. Being fully present allows you to feel reality as it unfolds, empathize with yourself and others, and truly make use of the day.

Diminished reality/presence is actually more widespread than commonly known. Yesterday I went shopping for groceries and decided to do it in a fully present state of being. I extroverted Attention and let go of all desire or memory of elsewhere. I became fully aware of others, taking note of them with calm interest. When touching goods, I felt their texture and handled them with care. This of course led to reality becoming truly augmented and lighting-up. Colors became more beautiful and the whole supermarket-experience more enjoyable.

Then they played the remade song "American Pie" by Madonna, and that quickly and easily triggered a loss of presence. Well, presence was not entirely lost because I could see what the mind was doing. The song moved me away from the present moment, and threw me back into the year 2000, to a time when the song was released and played everywhere. Memories of what I was doing in 2000 arose, and my mind started wandering around there. At that time, I was conducting fairly boring seminars for the Siemens Company. I did not much enjoy those seminars, so the song triggered some of those emotions (and I didn't like the song either).

Such "loss of presence" happens often. I'd say that we are not fully present most of the time. Sometimes we are taken away from the here-now by external triggers, such as a song. To break the conditioned-response I could decide to stop thinking about those days every time the song played. Or, I could decide to associate it with something else. Memories only replay in the mind if the present moment is believed to be less interesting or intense than the past moment. So if the memories/emotions had been too intense, I would have to look for something more interesting in present-time, something or someone irresistibly beautiful for example. If your loss of presence were very intense, you could splash cold water over your face which would inject instant present-time Awareness, and the troubled emotion subsiding (want to release painful emotions rapidly? Return to present-time!). Or, I could hold a gun barrel at your head, which would wake you up to present-time right away. I'm kidding of course, I would not hold a gun to your head. But I am not kidding about danger-situations calling you to rapid presence. Any situation of great danger or great beauty induces presence. Sometimes our higher-selves send us accidents in order to call us to more presence. It would not have to send us accidents if we were more present to begin with.

Being Present with the Other

There is a state of consciousness I refer to as "unconditional love". One of the typical components of this state is to easily be able to be "present with the other". When you are not in a state of "unconditional love" (and most of us aren't most of the time), you can nonetheless be present-with-others through deliberate will. This involves gently extroverting Attention so as to "be with" the other person. It involves relaxing, slowing down and breathing out judgment and expectation, and instead being awake and aware in the other's presence. As judgment or expectation arises, it is released on the spot. It is normally required to sit in complete silence and eye contact for some amount of time with the other until one feels comfortable, and all tensions and labels are gone. As this is impractical in daily life situations, one can extend this presence while talking. There is however a reduced reaction time while talking. One need not immediately respond or go into knee-jerk mode. From the Attention-connection to the other, empathy arises. If it is someone you don't normally like, then some deliberate intent is required to release all past knowledge of the person and look at them anew, as if viewing them for the very first time.

Attention being the first stage, the second is compassion. It is understood that the human across from you has good times and bad times, just like you. To be able to view a person as having good and bad times, allows compassion to arise. Whatever history you have built up with the person melts away, and he/she is simply viewed by merit of being a human. If compassion does not come easy, one can deliberately allow some empathy to arise by taking note of what one likes about the person. Someone with this kind of presence will be un-hurt-able, never self-conscious or shy and of pleasant charisma.

A third stage of practice is being able to emit, radiate, pulse or transfer waves of love or humor from body-to-body and being-to-being. It is called advanced because it is not normal practice for someone to emit a ray of love or humor, and get a reaction from the other. However, this invisible energy can be so strong that you can change moods, heal tension and evoke laughter.

"Being present with the other" only "normally" arises when two people have just recently fallen in love. They then can stare at each other for hours, until they conflate. This extroverted Attention and appreciation is where the high-feeling of being newly in love come from. You feel yourself floating on cloud nine. This condition however, need not be limited to the few weeks you fall in love. It can be a more general and more permanent state, which will naturally be higher when you are around loved ones, but also radiating when they are not around. In a certain type of seminar I used to give some years ago, participants of the course would easily fall in love with each other because we were practicing this state all day every day. Then, only a few weeks after the seminar ended, those new couples often broke apart wondering just what on earth they were thinking. The basic misunderstanding is that this state and presence is dependent on others, on seminars and on big events. It can also be cultivated outside of any external anchor. Unconditional love then becomes the elixir of life and a constant source of serendipity.

What You Try to Hide Is Amplified

If you are on a date with a potential partner and you try hiding your chubby thighs, you can be sure they will be noticed. If you are giving a presentation to potential investors and are terrified about revealing certain statistics, you can be sure someone will ask about them. If you are on vacation and afraid someone you know will see you in your bathing suit, he/she probably will. If you are at a job interview and try masking your ignorance about something, your ignorance will be detected and made bigger than if you had simply admitted it. If you are worried to death about being rejected, you will be...very often. If you strongly resist being judged, you will be judged harshly. If you are among friends and impose a taboo on mentioning a certain subject, they will keep bringing it up and make fun of it. And if they don't bring it up, they will keep thinking about it nonetheless. If you very much fear looking awkward in front of others, you will. If you want to avoid being boring at all costs, you will appear as someone boring. Whatever you try to hide is amplified.

Many of the coaching requests I receive from people regard overcoming shyness, awkwardness, stiffness in social situations, fear of public speaking or feeling uneasy about job interviews. Many would like to feel less stilted, artificial, tense, embarrassed and self-conscious. The key to transcending awkwardness is to allow yourself to be awkward. The key to transcending your fear of mistakes is to allow yourself to make mistakes. The key to transcending being boring is to allow yourself to be terribly dull. Resistance is what amplifies and attracts that which you resist. Before you have that important meeting or important date, you can first realize that, compared to Infinity, nothing is important. From an Infinite Perspective you can neither possess anything nor get rid of anything because all is part of one Infinite Field. So as you can neither have nor lose anything, there is no need to worry about anything. You see, having or losing, possessing or getting rid of something, imply a limited Universe. If the Universe is unlimited, you can't put anything outside of the Universe, hence you can't get rid of it. Nor can you add anything to the Universe; you can't possess it. Everything is already there, always has been, always will be. This simple metaphysical understanding has the power to liberate you from any problem at all.

If you feel awkward in social situations, it is because you are strongly judging other people. Because you are subconsciously judging them, you think they are judging you. However, most people are too busy or too self-conscious themselves to be judging you. Almost nobody is actually judging you. You are judging them, and that is when you start to feel shy in their presence. So if you want to feel more free and light in the presence of others, feel more of your own Being. Stop judging people and stop assuming what they are thinking of you. Most of them are not thinking of you at all (If you want people to think of you, think of them first.)

As what you resist will persist, let go of seeking approval from others. People do have the right to disapprove of you. If you think people aren't allowed to disapprove of you or criticize you, you are like a little dictator who opposes freedom of thought and freedom of speech. Whatever you try to hide is amplified. So if you try to suppress people's right to criticize you, they will criticize you to your face and behind your back. If you think others should not think badly of you, you are really concerned with censoring their freedom of thought. That's an interesting way to see it, isn't it? So many people are secretly totalitarian dictators without realizing it. Give up resisting, accept that nobody owes you approval, nobody owes you love, and nobody owes you an explanation of their thoughts. When you stop resisting peoples disapproval two interesting things happen: You will experience much, much less disapproval and you will also see that, it's almost never personal. People's judgment of you has more to do with who they are than who you are.

So if you are afraid of being boring, then be boring deliberately. Tell the person you are having conversation with: "I am a rather boring conversation partner." They will probably laugh! If you are afraid of stuttering, stutter deliberately and on purpose several times. If you are afraid of your secret affair being discovered and find yourself unable to release the fear, then disclose and expose your secret. Does that sound difficult? It is. It's a temporary pain for a long-term gain. When there is nothing you need to hide or protect from, nothing to suppress or resist and nothing to avoid or run away from, your light shines very brightly because no more energy is wasted on suppression.

10 Ways to Become Fully Present

Presence is a stable platform from which all else is more easily explored. A place of calm and poise, of self-control and Awareness, of relief and truth. Where there is presence, there is no worry about past, future or elsewhere. There is only crystal clarity. With that said, these are five simple ways to become more here-now; more present:

1. Just sit and do nothing for a few minutes.

The easiest thing in the world...to just sit and do nothing for a few minutes, is actually very difficult for modern people. They are always driven, always thinking, always planning the next step and always doing. So just sitting there and doing nothing feels quite empowering because one is no longer at the effect of inner and outer expectation and pressure. Release any guilt, time pressure and impatience.. Sit there, breathe; be. You should be fully present within a few minutes.

2. Describe objects in your surroundings.
While you are sitting, standing or walking, describe objects in your surroundings. How would you describe the various things you see? How would you describe them to someone who isn't present, so that he/she can imagine them? How would you describe them to a blind person? One thing that most people will notice is that they sometimes lack the vocabulary to give fully satisfying descriptions. But in doing this, you also become very focused, very present and the world starts looking brighter and more interesting.

3. Walk around and touch objects in your surroundings.
If you are overwhelmed, stressed out, have a headache, feel exhausted or any other form of non-presence, you can take a nap. Or, you can go around and deliberately touch various objects, feel their texture, size, temperature, weight and shape. A few minutes of this will make you much more here-now and much less worried or fearful. Presence has a stabilizing effect on your emotional state.

4. Apply the Being-Source exercise.
The "Being Source" exercise is probably the best of these five ways to become fully present. You simply announce or intend every movement you make or action you take before you take it. So you decide-then-do, continually for 5 or 10 minutes or even longer. The key to this is to slow down. As you slow down, you feel more "in control", more deliberate.

5. Look at beauty.
Deliberately looking at something highly aesthetic or beautiful or something new you haven't seen before, helps you become present. It is preferable when these are real objects, buildings, plants, animals and humans, but they could also be pictures of such. You will be fully present within only minutes. Do not look at too many nice things all at once, but linger with your Attention for a little longer (60 seconds +) at one thing.

6. Shower, bathe, swim, or splash water on your face.

Some cultures, such as the Tibetans, do not wash themselves with water (they use other means of cleaning themselves). The reason is, that water washes off many of the energies you picked up throughout the day or night. For us non-meditating westerners, this is good news. By taking a shower we not only wash our physical body and skin, but also some of our non-physical energetic residue. That's why showering, bathing or swimming also feels mentally refreshing. People in a state of panic need only splash cold water over their faces to once again become present. Confused housewives need only take a shower to regain some of their poise. Stressed out business people need only go for a swim to return to calm.

7. Focus on a task.
Choose a task…any task…and intend to focus on it fully and completely, regardless of how you feel initially. Within a few minutes time you start becoming present and feeling better.

8. Feel the emotion behind the thinking.
Too much thinking indicates too little presence. To slow down your thinking (worrying!), feel the emotional state behind the thinking. Gently shift Attention from the thinking to the actual feeling in the body. Breathe with it and relax. Release. You'll feel more present within a short time.

9. Do something courageous you have been putting off.
Taking a courageous step you have been putting off makes you fully present instantly.

10. Observe without expectation.

Sit and observe your thoughts or the world passing by while you reduce expectation, desire and resistance. You'll feel more clear and present within minutes. This sense of presence can be expanded by increasing the time you sit and observe. I sometimes do this for hours. "Taking a walk" is also a method of "observing the world" and always recommended for more presence.

Peace of Mind

Peace of mind is more valuable than all the treasures in the world. The following checklist will help you rapidly regain serenity:

* Make sure you are not trying to solve all issues at once, but moving forward in a calm pace, one step at a time. Instead of scattering Attention, slow down and focus on one thing, one object (literally
   looking at one object for a few minutes), one task, one anything.
* List the criticisms you have been consciously and subconsciously lashing out on others and yourself, and deliberately decide to let go of each point for now. Stop wasting your energy on heavy thoughts.
* If something will not still be important in 100 years, how important is it really? Check what is really important and what you can really control, and focus on that. Let go of things that are not important, and let go

of things you cannot control. If for example you have a big life vision that you cannot do anything immediately about, focus instead on the next-action-step you CAN do something about. The more you focus on

things you CAN do something about, the more in-control and zestful you feel.

* Simplify your life in every way you can. Streamline and automate that which can be automated. Cut your hobbies, cut your costs, cut anything superfluous so that you have more time for what life is essentially

about: Your connection to other human beings, friends and family. Bring simplicity and ease into your business processes, so that you have more free Attention for the essential things.

* Remember that it is alright to feel down sometimes. Do not berate yourself for it. On the other hand, also remember that it is alright to feel happy on a regular basis, for no reason at all.

* Before demanding that the circumstances adapt to you, first accept the circumstances as-they-are. Then, you will (paradoxically) be in a stronger position to shape the circumstances. "Play the cards you were

dealt."

* Check if today you can be of benefit to others. Being of benefit to others increases health, happiness and prosperity. But before going out to be helpful to others, see to it that you are in a good state.

* Restore your integrity in any way possible. Do not verbally say "yes" to things you inwardly say "no" to. Stand up and state your true heart's opinion. Own and take responsibility for what you experience. Keep
 your word.
* Do a good deed without telling anyone.
* Voice words, affirmations, statements, intentions and prayers that are positive and empowering to yourself and others. Ask to think clearly, see clearly, speak clearly and act clearly. Make this a habit.
* Give yourself good and life-affirming material to listen to and/or read.
* Take a (sound and lawful) activity that you think you have to do but resist or have a real problem doing, and try doing it anyway while releasing your resistance and embracing the activity. That is, do not let that
 activity dominate your emotions.
* Write up some intentions and actions for this month. Also take care of things you have been procrastinating. Keep in mind that monthly intention-lists or plans work better than weekly or daily ones, as they
 generalize and release pressure from the process.
* If there is something you have been trying to fix unsuccessfully, monitor it for awhile. For weight loss, for example, monitor (write down) your eating habits. For financial improvement, monitor your
 expenses and income. Monitoring things brings Awareness into them. Awareness is the key to all improvement.
* Sit and do nothing for 10 minutes today. Center yourself before acting and deciding.

* Let go of repetitive thinking. Notice a thought that has been bothering you, breathe it in, and on the out breath, simply let go of it.
* Assess the truth of things by looking at its fruits. What kind of people and culture is produced by any given teaching or philosophy?
* Let go of seeking more information, instead try to experience some of the things you already know.
* Whenever you have lost peace of mind, simply return to this checklist. The solution will be contained in one of its points.

Seeing with the Eyes of a Child
Children feel more energetic and happy than adults because they tend to see the world with:

Awe

Amazement

Astonishment

Admiration

Wonder

Reverence

Marvel

Fascination

Curiosity

Aliveness

Wakefulness

Interest

In adulthood this kind of perception tends to recede...and with it, the joy and excitement. Why? Because we have already learned, seen and experienced it all repeatedly (or so we think), and the world no longer seems new. The first time you see a green landscape you might be overwhelmed with amazement at the beauty. But as you see green landscapes over-and-over again, you become desensitized and no longer regard greenery as unusual. You take it for granted.

As adults, about the only time we get a sense of this fully present state is when we fall in love. It is in those moments we are infinitely patient, our Awareness is fully in the here-now, and we admire our partner. As a result, we feel warm and energetic all the time. This phase is referred to as "wearing rose-colored glasses" because it usually fades after a few months, once we also start seeing the downsides of that partner. But what is actually happening is that we are – in these times – fully present.

The more dulled your senses are, the more entertainment and external stimuli is required to become present. At the lowest level of consciousness, no amount of entertainment will help you feel alive and present. At a mid-level of consciousness, you require movies, travel, new places, new people, beautiful things and beautiful people to become present and feel alive. At a high level of consciousness and energy, you do not need anything to feel alive and present. You could be staring at a white wall all day and would still feel good.

The ideal state of a human being is to have the presence, innocence and aliveness of a child combined with the experience and knowledge of an adult. The key to regaining this state is to quit going around and assuming you "already know", have "already seen" and have "already done" this and that. For example: Even if you have been in your office 10,000 times, and your mind has recorded 10,000 instances of this, it is possible to experience the office as if for the first time. How? By relaxing your Awareness, expanding your sense of time and patience, examining your surroundings more closely, and realizing that there is more to see than meets the eye or your boring expectations of the place. It is only because you expect the office to be the same that it was the last 10,000 times, that nothing new and fresh appears to be happening. Sure, it would be easier to feel that heightened interest in the presence of an amazingly beautiful man/woman. But at a higher level of consciousness, you can see everything more colorfully. The trick is to not see from your mind and its 10,000 recordings of the office, but as if you are seeing it for the first time.

If you have been in a relationship with the same partner for 10 years, it can appear difficult to experience them anew and without all the baggage and information from the past. But if you want to have fun with this partner for another 10 years, you will have to become present with them...and that means to let go of all past that you have with them and be with them as if on the first day. What if it were the very first time you met them? Can you imagine that? And how exciting would that be?

The state I am referring to comes about through a deep relaxation into the NOW, without getting sleepy. It comes about through a full wakefulness without getting tense. Relaxed but awake, pretend you are experiencing things for the first time, and make intentions to experience them more deeply, to breathe with the present moment and to perceive from the heart instead of the mind. There are many aspects of yourself you can "perceive from". You can perceive from your soul, heart and body. You can perceive the general atmosphere of a place or person rather than focus on the same things over-and-over. The "way things are" is not the way things are, it's only the way you focus that determines what you experience. Taking that office or partner as an example: You don't always have to focus on his/her voice, and you don't always have to have the computer screen in the office be the focal point of your Awareness. What are things in the office and about the partner you haven't noticed up to now...even after 10 years? If you were a different-version-of-you, what things would you notice? What might a secret intelligence agent notice about your office? What might a Feng Shui expert notice? What might a boss notice? What might an alien notice? If you can shift your sense of who-you-are, the ways of experiencing the world and learning about it, are endless.

For more, see the author's website: www.realitycreation.org

CPSIA information can be obtained
at www.ICGtesting.com
Printed in the USA
BVHW011727131118
533015BV00021B/60/P